A BLACK MAN'S DREAM:
THE FIRST 100 YEARS

RICHARD HENRY BOYD
AND
THE NATIONAL BAPTIST
PUBLISHING BOARD

Researched and Written by:
Bobby L. Lovett, Ph.D.

"History does not repeat itself, men repeat history."

Bobby Lovett

A BLACK MAN'S DREAM:
THE FIRST ONE HUNDRED YEARS

Library of Congress Catalog Card # 92-063267
ISBN # 1-56742-032 -x

A BLACK MAN'S DREAM:
THE FIRST 100 YEARS

RICHARD HENRY BOYD
AND
THE NATIONAL BAPTIST
PUBLISHING BOARD

TABLE OF CONTENTS

Photographs

Note: All photographs are courtesy of the National Baptist Publishing Board.

Dedication

This book is dedicated to the late Richard Henry Boyd, his wife and family, and the early employees, staff and board members of the National Baptist Publishing Board.

The Reverend Richard Henry Boyd (1843 - 1922) transcended slavery to freedom and gave untiring leadership to the freedman community for a long generation after Emancipation. Loved by many and jealously opposed by some black Baptist religious factions, Boyd became a renaissance man in the twentieth century. He helped to support the development of Negro newspapers, gave leadership to the early twentieth century movement to create black banks, encouraged and supported black writers, pushed land ownership among the blacks, promoted African American racial pride to combat the negative effects of white racism, and expounded on a confident and independent black political economy.

The transformation of the dream of a Negro operated Baptist publishing board into a successful reality became the Reverend Boyd's greatest life achievement. The Reverend Boyd's energy, faith, vision, genius, and hard work transformed the dream about a national publishing house for the African American Baptists into a reality, and his faith in God and trust in man's abilities gave birth to a business enterprise whose success astounded even his detractors. Not only did he create America's largest Baptist publishing house operated by African Americans, Boyd helped to launch a business movement in Nashville that resulted in the creation of a viable local black business sector between 1900 and 1922.

The National Baptist Publishing Board (NBPB) began in early November 1896 through the efforts of Richard H. Boyd and three other black men. A few days later, Boyd established a crude office in Nashville, Tennessee; and in December, 1896, he and a small staff of clerks began sending letters to potential customers. By January, 1897, the board filled its first orders, giving birth to the National Baptist Publishing Board's legacy of good service. Since that time, the National Baptist Publishing Board's message has maintained a resounding effect in the world of religious companies through publishing, printing, and distributing publications and products for every aspect of the church.

Richard H. Boyd built the National Baptist Publishing Board into America's largest religious publishing company owned and operated by blacks. He expanded the National Baptist Publishing Board's operations to include women's auxiliary publications, Baptist young people's publications, manufacture of religious banners and signs, management of the largest Christian education program in black America, and domestic and international missionary work. Like many other contemporary businessmen, Boyd was not a college-trained manager; but he had great intellect, an intuitive vision, a laudable philosophy of life, and an adherence to conservative fiscal management.

The Reverend Boyd became an entrepreneur, a banker, a businessman, a philanthropist, and a born leader. Boyd actively involved himself in the founding of the Nashville chapter of the National Negro Business League, the Nashville Colored Young Men's Christian Association, and the Nashville Negro Board of Trade. Especially, he made a mark in leading the black community's campaign to support America's World War I effort. He helped found Nashville's One-Cent Savings and Trust Company Bank, the Union Transportation Company, and the National Negro Doll Company. In addition, he expanded the board's operations to include book manufacturing, newspaper printing, and church furniture manufacture and sales.

The Reverend Boyd's religious and business activities became inseparable. This principle bothered some of Boyd's detractors and worried certain factions within the National Baptist Convention, but the philosophy that church related agencies should promote businesses and economic development in black America presented no paradox for the Reverend Boyd. He believed that churches and fraternal institutions should be involved actively in promoting Negro business enterprise for the uplifting of the race. He believed that the National Baptist Publishing Board should supply all needs and services to black Baptist churches and give leadership through Christian education and home mission work.

Around 1904, Boyd organized the National Baptist Sunday School Congress to become a "beacon light" of Christian education for churches across America. The annual Sunday School Congress attracted and trained thousands of church workers. The Reverend Boyd extended the board's mission work to the Caribbean where he organized and built several churches and a school building. Boyd and the board assumed publication of the *National Baptist Union* and successfully transformed the newspaper into the *National Baptist Review*, the official paper for the National Baptist Convention and the National Baptist Publishing Board. Boyd organized the Boy Cadets and the Girls Doll Clubs to involve the publishing board and its Christian education program to build character and leadership in black youngsters. He and the publishing board assisted the black Woman's Auxiliary of the National Baptist Convention with its mission work and the white Women's American Baptist Home Mission Society's Fireside School in Nashville with its efforts to import Christian education into black homes. Boyd also initiated cooperative mission work between the black Woman's Auxiliary and the White Women's Home Mission Board of the Southern Baptist Convention.

The Reverend Boyd became influential, and he gave his expertise to local political affairs. He helped lead the local black opposition to the

Republican party's "lily-white" movement to attract more southern white voters and to exclude the black Republicans.

The Reverend Dr. Boyd became such a visionary that he took care to insulate the NBPB from the potentially destructive politics within the black Baptist conventions; and, with an ingenious charter (1898), he insured the survival of the National Baptist Publishing Board both before and long after his death. He involved his children and family members in the large publishing enterprise and his private companies. And through the leadership of his son, grandson, and great-grandson, the National Baptist Publishing Board's operations expanded into two large, modern facilities by 1992.

June 1992

Acknowledgments

Several writers have published books about the black Baptists and included stories about the National Baptist Publishing Board. As early as 1911, the NBPB produced N. A. Pius' *Outline of Baptist History*. This small book attempted to provide a tool to teach black Sunday school students and other Negro Baptists the background of the Baptist faith. Published histories about the black Baptists became more political when the National Baptist Convention divided because of the controversy about control of the National Baptist Publishing Board in 1915.

The first published history of the National Baptist Publishing Board was printed in 1915 when the board of directors authorized the Reverend Richard H. Boyd to write and publish *A Story of the National Baptist Publishing Board*. By that time, it became apparent that the National Baptist Convention had become divided over the control of the publishing board. The directors of the National Baptist Publishing Board resolved in April, 1915 that R. H. Boyd, the secretary - treasurer of the National Baptist Publishing Board, and C. H. Clark, the chairman of the board, should prepare "a brief synopsis of the history of the National Baptist Publishing Board," reflecting on the dispute in the National Baptist Convention about ownership and control of the publishing board. This dispute about the publishing board continued beyond Boyd's death (1922).

In 1924, after the Reverend Boyd's death, *A Story of the National Baptist Publishing Board* was subtitled *The Why, How, When, Where, and By Whom It Was Established*. The Reverend Clark, chairman of the board of directors for the NBPB, and other board members wrote an appendix for the 1924 edition. This appendix provided new materials about the 1915 dispute. Henry Allen Boyd, the new National Baptist Publishing Board Secretary and the late R. H. Boyd's son, directed the compilation of the 1924 edition, a 155-page pocket-size book.

Lewis G. Jordan published *The History of Black Baptists* (1930) through the National Baptist Convention of the United States of America, Incorporated (NBCI). Jordan affiliated with the NBCI under President Elias C. Morris. Jordan and others called the National Baptist Convention of America, Unincorporated, "Boyd's Convention." Jordan's account used as much objectivity as possible to describe the struggle to organize a national convention and to discuss the notorious split of 1915. Because these great men, Morris and Boyd, had been involved in the 1915 controversy and denominational split, both conventions had difficulty writing objective accounts about the black Baptist convention and the NBPB's business history.

Owen O. Pelt and Ralph L. Smith published *The Story of the National Baptists* (1961). This account also focused on the National Baptist Convention of the United States of America, Incorporated. The Pelt and Smith account offered valuable information about the origins and progress of the largest black Baptist convention. Like the Jordan book, but without any real finger - pointing, this story placed the National Baptist Publishing Board and Boyd at the center of the 1915 split.

Leroy Fitts published an objective synopsis, *A History of Black Baptists,* in 1985. By now, much of the bitterness that had surrounded the 1915 division of the National Baptist Convention had faded away.

According to William H. Brackney, *The Baptists* (1988), some recent denominational histories have improved with greater attention given to primary sources and more rigorous scholarly standards. Brackney also concluded that, too frequently, such histories have pursued themes for internal consumption alone.

I agree with Brackney about the need to go beyond parochial interpretations and view Baptist history from the outside. The dynamics of the founding of the publishing board and its role in the Negro Baptist split of 1915 have received little scholarly treatment by any book beyond the rumors, the insinuations, and the bitter accusations of the past. The fact that an important African American business, founded by an ex-slave and his colleagues, has endured nearly one hundred years of turmoil, economic depressions, and religious politics has become lost within decades of controversial legends.

After moving to Nashville in 1973, I became intrigued with the history of the National Baptist Publishing Board and R. H. Boyd. I wanted to know the real relationships between Boyd, the NBPB, and black and white Baptists. Besides, the National Baptist Publishing Board and its four chief executive officers made much history from 1896 until the present. Moreover the source material, records, documents, and photographs seemed rich and untouched by trained historians.

During the spring of 1991, I began exploring sources on Richard H. Boyd, the National Baptist Publishing Board, the National Baptist Convention, U.S.A., the National Baptist Convention of America (Unincorporated), the Southern Baptist Convention, the National Missionary Baptist Convention of America, and the Northern Baptist Convention. I used newspapers, books, journals, biographies, personal papers, official records, census data, city directories, photographs, tax records, court records, and other historical data to bring detail and accuracy to the manuscript. Records and microfilm documents were investigated at the Southern Baptist Convention's Historical Commission, the National Archives and Records Service, the National Baptist Publishing Board, the Tennessee State Library and Archives, the Tennessee State University Library's Special Collections, the Nashville Public Library's Nashville Room collection, and the Fisk University Library's Special Collection.

Some James Marion Frost Papers were preserved at the Southern Baptist Convention's Historical Commission in Nashville; however, I failed to gain access to the J. M. Frost executive papers because the Southern Baptist Convention had undergone recent political changes. Some internal and doctrinal upheaval existed between fundamentalists and moderates. The Frost executive papers probably contained a half dozen letters related to Richard H. Boyd and the publishing board. Yet, the staff graciously furnished microfilm, some manuscripts, many books, and journals and gave valuable help during the several months that I conducted research at the Historical Commission. I located alternative sources on Frost and his relations with Boyd.

I investigated and recorded the following organizations' journals and minutes: National Baptist Convention, 1895 - 1915; National Baptist Convention of America (Unincorporated), 1916 - 1988; National Missionary Baptist Convention of America, 1988 - 1991; National Baptist Convention of the United States of America (Incorporated), 1916 - 1922; Journal of the Northern Baptist Convention, 1908 - 1916; Annual Report of the Southern Baptist Convention, 1890 - 1981; Annual Reports of the National Baptist Publishing Board; Annual Reports of the American Baptist Publication Society; Annual Reports of the American Baptist Home Mission Society. I reviewed and noted the annual reports for the National Baptist Convention's Foreign Mission Board, the Woman's Auxiliary Board, the Home Mission Board, and the Baptist Young People's Union Board as well as the official programs and the annual reports of the Sunday School Congress and Baptist Training Union.

The Southern Baptist Convention's Historical Commission housed hard copies of the journal for the Southern Baptist Convention and the Northern Baptist Convention. Some micofilm copies of the journals for the National Baptist Convention and other black conventions also were available at the Historical Commission. The National Baptist Publishing Board preserved many hard copies of the National Baptist Convention's journals as well as convention programs and programs for the Sunday School Congress.

Newspapers proved quite helpful. Many issues of the *National Baptist Union* and the *National Baptist Review* existed on microfilm at the Southern Baptist Convention's Historical Commission and other libraries. The National Baptist Publishing Board had laminated and preserved huge volumes of original pages of the *National Baptist Union*, the *National Baptist Union-Review*, and the Nashville *Globe*. The NBPB also made available hard copies of most recent issues of the *National Baptist Review* and convention journals. The Tennessee State Library and Archives furnished many microfilm copies of the *National Baptist Voice*, the official organ of the National Baptist Convention, United States of America, Incorporated.

I became familiar with many sources through my membership in the Southern Baptist Historical Society and the American Baptist Historical Society. The NBCI's library in Chicago, the NBCI's Sunday School Publishing Board in Nashville, and the American Baptist Historical Society also preserve copies of important black Baptist newspapers and other documents.

All photographs were furnished through the courtesy of the National Baptist Publishing Board and its publications. Some photographs came from the National Baptist Publishing Board's archives. Luckily for the historian the NBPB's administration preserved these original photographs. The publishing board's publications really contained a pictorial history of the National Baptist Publishing Board, the Boyd family, and national Baptist convention activities. The publishing board's staff, particularly the Reverend Pamela Yates, provided available correspondence and obituaries for Richard Henry Boyd and other staff members.

The works and contributions of Richard Henry Boyd, Charles Henry Clark, and other authors of books, theses, and articles are acknowledged and appreciated for helping to interpret the historical information about Richard Henry Boyd and the National Baptist Publishing Board. Particularly Vallie Pursley, librarian for Special Collections at Tennessee State University, proved helpful in providing master's theses on Richard H. Boyd and microfilm on the Nashville *Globe*. Again, the Reverend Pamela Yates, NBPB staff member, served as host during my extensive search of the publishing board's archives where an effort has been made to preserve the company's valuable historical manuscripts. Mrs. Mable L. Boyd gave a brief interview on her life, some information about her husband, T. B. Boyd, Jr., and some personal photographs.

This project proved to be an extensive study project for me, and I found helpful the works of many other writers who helped to place things in perspective through their books: Cayrand S. Wilmore, *Black Religion and Black Radicalism: An Interpretation of the Religious History of Afro - American People* (1973); James M. Washington, *Frustrated Fellowship: The Black Baptist Quest for Social Power* (1986); William D. Booth, *The Progressive Story: New Baptist Roots* (1981); Carter G. Woodson, *The History of the Negro Church* (1921); Joseph H. Jackson, *A Story of Activism: The History of the National Baptist Convention, U.S.A., Inc.* (1980); E. Franklin Frazier, *The Negro Church in America* (1963); Leroy Fitts, *Lott Carey: First Black Missionary to Africa* (1979); Edward A. Freeman, *The Epoch of Negro Baptists and the Foreign Mission Board* (1953).

Books by William E. B. DuBois, *The Negro in the South: His Economic Progress in Relation to His Moral and Religious Development* (1907) and Walter B. Weare, *Black Business in the New South: A Social History of the North Carolina Mutual Insurance Company* (1973), served as exemplary models of early black business histories. These books, as well as aforementioned studies, helped me to view the NBPB as a business and place the publishing board within the context of which the contemporary religious and political environment the company had to operate.

I researched wills, deeds census data, court records, and city directories at the Tennessee State Library and Archives (TSLA) in Nashville. I used printed and microfilm census data on Texas, through the TSLA. I gained access to some books, bibliography, and city directories at the Nashville Public Library, Nashville Room. These public records proved valuable in the process of corroborating evidence and checking factual data.

The cooperation of the president and the officers of the National Baptist Publishing Board is appreciated. It is not easy to release and allow the publication of sensitive and controversial information about a business enterprise. However, all who have cooperated have been made to understand that simply I intend to give the reader a historically accurate and well - documented history of the publishing board and the story of its founder. It just so happens that many other stories must be told about black and white Baptists to explain the National Baptist Publishing Board's complex history.

Undoubtedly, the story deserves more definition because the National Baptist Publishing has been more than a religious publishing house, and it remains more than a religious publishing house as well as a factor of positive change in America's black community. Moreover the stories about this publishing company and Richard H. Boyd could inspire and motivate young black men and women who struggle to become successful entrepreneurs or business and civic leaders. Histories of successful black businesses, including the National Baptist Publishing Board and ones affiliated with the church, deserve the attention of the public.

Throughout the manuscript, I have used many terms to describe African Americans: Black, Negro, and Colored, for examples. The term "black" predominates through the book. But I often cite the term used by the contemporaries of the period to give better meaning to the particular passage.

Bobby L. Lovett
June 1992

In Memory of Richard Henry Boyd and Family

Foreword

This book attempts to blend the business history of the National Baptist Publishing Board, the biography of Richard Henry Boyd, the history of the National Baptist Convention, and the politics between black and white Baptists. This book includes the relationships of the publishing board and Dr. Boyd to the National Baptist Convention, the Southern Baptist Convention, the Northern Baptist Convention, the American Baptist Home Mission Society, and the American Baptist Publication Society.

The book includes many other issues: the internal politics of the National Baptist Convention and its effects on the National Baptist Publishing Board; the publishing board's successful missionary and Sunday school programs; the human side of the National Baptist Publishing Board including deaths of important family members, annual dinners, picnics, brass bands, and choirs; the Baptist denominational split and the effect of that division on the National Baptist Publishing Board; the involvement of R. H. Boyd and other NBPB employees in local movements; and even the National Baptist Publishing Board's contributions to local cultural and intellectual history.

Although the book focuses on the years 1896-1922, the epilogue includes an overview of the succeeding generations of leaders at the National Baptist Publishing Board including Henry Allen Boyd, who served from 1922 to 1959; Theophilus B. Boyd, Jr., the Secretary-Treasurer from 1959 to 1979; and T. B. Boyd, III, President and Chief Executive Officer, 1979 - present.

For sure, the Reverend Richard H. Boyd's plans to establish a black Baptist publishing board became affected by the politics and the relationships between three groups: the black Baptists, the white southern Baptists, and the northern white Baptists. Factionalism within the National Baptist Convention, division and lingering bitterness in the Texas black Baptist conventions, and rivalry from some black Baptist leaders caused Boyd and the NBPB many painful problems and near destruction. Boyd's success and the phenomenal growth of the NBPB angered the most egotistical of black leaders who gained control of the National Baptist Convention between 1905 and 1915.

This book places the NBPB within the turbulent environment of these black Baptist politics. And this book summarizes the long story about a successful black business when it approached its 100th birthday.

Surely, if the young black people of our cities could read this story and other intriguing stories of black history, they would be bewildered, amazed, provoked to rethink their values, and even inspired to learn from that history.

Bobby L. Lovett

Preface

Preface

This book will highlight the life of a black American man "doing God's Business" through an African American company that operated within a turbulent religious environment.

Richard H. Boyd, a "Race Man," became a leader in the movement to create social and economic independence for the freedmen and particularly to have blacks control their education, including Christian education. The Reverend Boyd dreamed that black people would own and operate their own Baptist publishing board. The NBPB began as part of a general post-Civil War movement to unite black Baptists and decrease their dependency on whites. Organized in 1896, the National Baptist Publishing Board culminated the effort to create a Baptist organization of blacks, by blacks, and for blacks.

Introduction

Boyd's creation of the National Baptist Publishing Board directly related to the historical events that impacted the black Baptists between 1890 and 1915. Since Civil War times, the northern white Baptist agencies, specifically the American Baptist Publication Society (ABPS) and the American Baptist Home Mission Society (ABHMS), had established schools, churches, colleges and spent hundreds of thousands of dollars for the freedmen. The northern white Baptists expected the blacks to remain grateful for that benevolence, and they wanted to maintain a paternalistic relationship with the former slaves and their descendants. Around 1890, Boyd and many other black Americans moved to shake off northern white paternalism. Many black leaders, however, resented black leaders, like Boyd, who seemed ungrateful to the white missionaries.

Moreover during the 1890s, the Southern Baptist Convention (SBC) sought to establish stronger relations with the black Baptists who lived mostly in the South. Many of the southern black Baptist churches had been attached to the Southern Baptist Convention before the Civil War. But the northerners, specifically the ABPS and the ABHMS, approached the southerners about a unified and "cooperative" movement to publish Sunday school materials and sponsor joint missions to the black Baptists. The Southern Baptist Convention rejected the northerners' proposals and pursued their own religious relations with the black Baptists.

Within the National Baptist Convention, the black leaders argued about supporting either the "cooperative" movement, remaining faithful to the northern Baptists, or supporting an alliance with the Southern Baptist Convention. But the NBPB made a decision to form an alliance with the southerners. This decision to work with the conservative white Southern Baptist Convention caused enemies for Boyd and the publishing board and led to political attacks from the National Baptist Convention's pro - ABPS faction. Between 1905 and

1915, a virtual civil war ensued in the black Baptist convention, and Boyd and the NBPB got caught in the middle of the battle. The issues about relations with the white Baptist conventions and the arguments about convention control of the NBPB led to the denominational split of the National Baptist Convention in 1915.

For sure, the Reverend Boyd's plans to establish a black Baptist publishing board would be affected inevitably by the politics and the relationships between three groups: the black Baptists, the white southern Baptists, and the northern white Baptists. Boyd's plans presented a threat to the last stronghold in the South for the northern Baptists and the American Baptist Publication Society. On the other hand, Boyd's plans to establish a black Baptist publishing board met the approval of the southern white Baptists.

Southern Baptist Convention

Boyd mainly received support from the Southern Baptist Convention's Sunday School Board under Secretary James Marion Frost. He had some personal reasons for helping Boyd. Like Boyd, Frost ,too, detested the attitude of the American Baptist Publication Society's officials. And the Southern Baptist Convention needed to develop closer relations with the black Baptists.

In 1896, James Marion Frost succeeded T. P. Bell as corresponding secretary of the Sunday School Board. The Reverend Bell retired and moved to Atlanta to edit his own *Christian Index* newspaper. Frost had founded the Sunday School Board in 1891. But he left the corresponding secretary's position after eighteen months to pastor Nashville's First Baptist Church. Frost returned to the Sunday School Board because it needed leadership and the American Baptist Publication Society had begun to promote the 1894 Fortress Monroe initiative to "unite" the southern and northern Baptists' publishing operations into a cooperative program.[1]

The Reverend J. M. Frost (1848 -1916) was born in Georgetown, Kentucky. He graduated from Georgetown College, got married, and headed several churches in Alabama, Kentucky, Virginia, and Tennessee. When heading a church in Virginia, Frost offered a resolution to the Southern Baptist Convention to establish a Sunday school board to publish literature. At that meeting in Fort Worth, Texas, in 1890, the convention created a Sunday school committee to be housed at Louisville, Kentucky. During the next year, 1891, Frost convinced the Southern Baptist Convention to establish a real Sunday School Board. On July 1, 1891, Frost arrived in Nashville where he started operations at a borrowed desk.[2] However, the creation of the southern Baptist Sunday School Board was not a simple story.

SBC officials endured a difficult struggle to create the southern Baptists' Sunday School Board until 1873 when the *Kind Words* paper began publication. The Home Mission Board adopted the paper and also published a series of Sunday school helps. Then a movement began for the Southern Baptist Convention to make its own literature; but "the opposition became more and more severe as time passed . . ., becoming at times almost a war on the Home Mission Board in every department of its work," said Frost.[3] Frost became involved when the 1890 session of the Southern Baptist Convention included a debate about the creation of a new board to take charge of *Kind Words* and other publications related to Sunday school work.

The American Baptist Publication Society opposed Frost's proposal. Frost said:

The American Baptist Publication Society of Philadelphia, with immense assets and resources was in the field, and had many earnest fields in the South; it was offering creditable periodicals and employing many Southern writers; it had large patronage among our churches, and gathered large harvests in return from its business; it did no little benevolent work among our [southern white Baptist] people, and had come to hold a high and strong place with many. From this vantage ground which can hardly be stated too strongly, the [ABP] Society through its friends and by all the forces at its command, withstood the Home Board movement, even claimed to have preempted the field and challenged the right of the [Southern Baptist] Convention to publish Sunday school periodicals.[4]

Since 1824, the American Baptist Publication Society had supplied Sunday school literature to southern and northern Baptist churches, black and white. This northern agency still had credibility in southern Baptist churches because it did not take part in the split between northern and southern Baptists in 1845. The longtime head of the ABPS, Benjamin H. Griffin, commanded great respect in both black and white Baptist circles. When A. J. Rowland succeeded Griffin in 1895, he pressured black and white Baptist leaders to support the cooperative movement to unite the two white Baptist publishing efforts and jointly administer to the needs of the Negro Baptists.

Frost persuaded the Southern Baptist Convention to refuse the ABPS' offer. Frost said: "I was sympathetic with the [American Baptist] Publication Society and appreciated its work, but not against this new movement of the Southern Baptists."[5] Even though the American Baptist Publication Society had published one book for Frost and planned to publish another one, Frost continued plans to publish the southern Baptists' own literature.

Frost chose Nashville for his operations because it had a good climate, a strategic southern location, and the largest printing center in the region. For the first six months, Frost borrowed a desk and space in *The Baptist and Reflector's* offices. Around January 1892, Frost moved his operations to the Presbyterian Publishing House before locating in the Methodist Publishing House. In 1897, he purchased a two-story building at 167 Fourth Avenue North. This building was sold in 1903 when the Sunday School Board bought a large two - story building at 710 Church Street where it remained until the new four-story building was constructed on Eighth Avenue North in 1913. By 1915, the Southern Baptist Convention's Sunday School Board, under Frost, had net assets of $556,277.20. The Sunday School Board's receipts rose from $19,574.83 in 1892 to $452,729.24 by 1916.[6]

Indubitably, Frost understood Boyd's struggle to establish a publishing board. And Frost easily comprehended the factional battles within Boyd's own National Baptist Convention and the problems with A. J. Rowland and the American Baptist Publication Society that Boyd would have to endure.

Boyd timed perfectly his dealings with the southern white Baptist leaders, and he took advantage of the historical circumstances. Around 1890, the Southern Baptist Convention searched silently for a way to renew the southern white Baptists' relationship with the former slaves, although many of the southern white Baptist churches acted racially conservative and did not desire a highly visible relationship with the blacks. But white radicals had increased racial lynchings which embarrassed white Christians. Partly for this reason, the southern white Baptists welcomed Boyd's overtures at a critical time in the history of the Southern Baptist Convention.

Moreover, southerners generally wanted to decrease the influence of the northern missionaries in the post-war South. For instance, during the 1870s the city council of Nashville, Tennessee, passed an ordinance to restrict public school teaching to residents, a move to diminish the number of northern missionary teachers in the black public schools.

Boyd's decision to use the southern Baptists would cause great opposition within the black National Baptist Convention because the southern Baptists had a vivid history of being racially conservative. The southern Baptists seceded from the American Baptist Association in 1845 and formed the Southern Baptist Convention in opposition to the northern Baptist churches' stand against slavery. From 1845 until the Union army occupied southern territory, the Southern Baptist Convention openly embraced slaveowners and maintained a paternalistic relationship with their Christian slaves. Nashville's First Baptist Church's pastor, an owner of several slaves, held the presidency of the Southern Baptist Convention. The southern Baptist churches organized quasi-independent black congregations (slave missions) under the supervision of white ministers to counter northern criticism about the harshness of slavery. Nashville's First Baptist Church organized the First Baptist Colored Mission in 1848 (Nashville's First Baptist Church Capitol Hill) and another slave mission church in East Nashville in 1861.

Northern Baptists

Boyd and others would encounter difficulty trying to argue that the American Baptist Publication Society and the American Baptist Home Mission

Society were not friends to the Negro. Many of the black ministers remembered that the American Baptist Home Mission Society, the American Baptist Publication Society, and the northern Baptist churches, generally opposed slavery. During the Civil War and Union army occupation, the American Baptist Home Mission Society sent missionaries into the South to organize black Baptist churches and build freedmen schools and colleges. The American Baptist Publication Society distributed supplies, books and literature to black churches, schools, and freedmen colleges. The northern white Baptist association dominated black Baptist education from 1864 through the early twentieth century, spending hundreds of thousands of dollars on the freedmen's behalf. But after dominating religious relations with the black Baptists for a generation since slavery, the northern white Baptists had become overly paternalistic.

The Reverend Boyd desired to use neither the white southern Baptist nor the northern white Baptist church literature, books and materials. He dreamed that black Baptists would ultimately publish their own materials.[7]

Richard Boyd made a political decision to carry his publishing idea beyond the General Missionary Baptist Convention of Texas. He concluded that a publishing house could be supported by the national black Baptist denomination, although his efforts to persuade the older leaders of the National Baptist Convention would become laborious. The publishing Sunday school literature idea had received discussion at the National Baptist Convention as early as 1891.

National Black Baptists

However, factionalism in the National Baptist Convention, division within the Texas conventions, and jealousy from some black Baptist leaders would eventually cause Boyd and his publishing board supporters many painful problems. Factional differences existed about whether a national Baptist convention should be merely an association or a strong, centralized administrative body which controlled its boards. When the National Baptist Convention began in 1895, it was little more than a loose confederation of boards. And for fifty-five years before 1895, the black Baptist conventions represented little more than an association of regional equals.

Indeed the history of the national black Baptists explains the problems of the convention and the problems Boyd and his publishing venture would encounter. The Negro Baptists created an effective national organization quite late and after nearly a half century of efforts. In comparison, the free northern black Methodists had organized the African Methodist Episcopal (AME) Church during the 1790s and had a complex and centralized national structure by the 1860s. But the Negro Baptist churches resulted mostly from slave missions which were organized by the Southern Baptist Convention's white churches between 1820 and 1861, although some black Baptist churches existed in the free North where about five percent of black Americans lived before 1861. Most of the independent Negro Baptist churches originated after the Emancipation. The rural and southern black Baptist churches took pride in their congregational independence and naturally opposed highly authoritative national church bodies. But the growing number of urban black Baptist churches, with their district and city conventions, better understood and appreciated central church associations. The black Baptists had an over-whelming representation of illiterate freedmen until a generation after slavery when the number of literate black Baptists increased dramatically, and college educated preachers took leadership positions in the black Baptist conventions. All of these factors and more caused fifty-five years to pass before the Negro Baptists formed a real national organization.

The American Baptist Missionary Convention became the first black Baptist association. Northern black Baptists founded the organization in 1840 and incorporated it in 1848 in New York. Sampson White, a free Negro, headed this pre-Civil War Baptist convention which consisted mostly of black Baptists in the free states of Pennsylvania, New York, and Massachusetts. The convention publicly denounced slavery in 1853 and opposed membership by slave-owning preachers in 1859. By now, some pastors of slave mission churches, including Nelson G. Merry of Nashville's First Colored Baptist Mission, attended the American Baptist Missionary Convention. Merry and other southern black pastors opposed the 1859 resolution. By 1860, churches in Connecticut, Maryland, Virginia, Washington, D. C. and South Carolina began to participate in the American Baptist Missionary Convention (ABMC).[8]

Another Tennessean and a friend to Merry, Edmund Kelly, became vice president of the American Baptist Missionary Convention and pastor of a church in New Bedford, Massachusetts. He was born a slave in Columbia, Tennessee, where he learned to read and write when working at a boarding school. The Reverend Kelly helped to establish the Mount Lebanon Baptist Church for Negroes in Columbia around 1843. Kelly apparently had gained his freedom and moved to the North. He answered the Reverend Merry's invitation and preached a revival at Nashville's First Colored Baptist Mission during the 1850s. Meanwhile, many of the southern black Baptist churches drifted away from the ABMC, causing its membership to dwindle to a roster of 48 churches by 1865.[9]

A second black Baptist national convention, the Northwestern and Southern Baptist Convention, originated in 1864 at a St. Louis meeting. Some twenty-six churches sent representatives from Illinois, Ohio, Missouri, Indiana, Mississippi, Tennessee, Louisiana, and Arkansas. When the Northwestern and Southern Baptist Convention convened at Nashville's First Colored Baptist

Church in 1866, the Reverend Merry headed a committee to unite with the American Baptist Missionary Convention. Meeting in Richmond, the Northwestern and Southern Baptist Convention and the American Baptist Missionary Convention became the Consolidated American Baptist Missionary Convention (CABMC) in August 1866. The CABMC held its first official session at Nashville's First Colored Baptist Church in August, 1867. The delegates elected Richard DeBaptiste president and Merry vice president.[10]

Nashville's Nelson G. Merry became a key leader in developing a conservative and a cooperationist posture for the CABMC. Baptized and ordained by local Southern Baptist Convention ministers in 1853, Merry became a close and personal friend to Robert B. C. Howell, a former president of the Southern Baptist Convention and pastor of Nashville's First Baptist Church, the mother church of Merry's slave mission congregation (First Colored Baptist Church of Nashville). Merry believed that the black convention should work closely with all white Baptist organizations, including the American Baptist Free Missionary Society, the American Baptist Home Mission Society, and the American Baptist Publication Society. The leaders of the Consolidated American Baptist Missionary Convention (CABMC), however, wrestled with the problem of paternalistic and racial attitudes among the white Baptists. Merry also associated with Daniel W. Phillips, the white ABHMS missionary who founded Nashville's Normal and Theological Institute (Roger Williams University) in 1864. Phillips' freedmen's school operated in the basement of Merry's church for some time, and Merry served on the school's board. Merry, an expert mediator who believed in "doing what is right," served as president for his district and the state Baptist associations in Tennessee. By 1869, Tennessee had three district Baptist associations, 153 Baptist churches, and twenty-five thousand members. Merry served as a missionary for the CABMC, causing him to travel eight hundred miles, organizing four churches, and baptizing thirty-eight converts in 1869 alone.[11] Merry (1824-1884), the "dean of black Baptist preachers in Tennessee" and a slave who won his freedom in 1845, received a private education from white ministers during the late 1840s when he served as sexton at Nashville's white First Baptist Church.

Even though the northern black Baptist churches had more educated preachers, the Southern black Baptist churches inevitably dominated the national black Baptist organizations because nine of ten blacks lived in the South. In 1869, the annual convention for the Consolidated American Baptist Missionary Convention convened in Paducah, Kentucky. By 1871, some Baptist churches in Texas belonged to this convention.

Because the northern churches were accused of mixing politics and religion, in 1873, the conservative southern churches met at Merry's church and formed the Missionary Baptist [General] State Convention of Tennessee, North Alabama, North Mississippi, Eastern Arkansas, and Kentucky. Merry's group also opposed the CABMC's new presbytery-like governance structure and did not want a national body interfering in state and local religious affairs. The following year, August 1874, the northeast black Baptist leaders formed the northeast Baptist Missionary Convention. The black southern Baptist churches countered and formed the Southwestern and Southern Missionary Baptist Convention at Montgomery on May 20, 1875. Four years later, the Consolidated American Baptist Missionary Convention was dissolved by its small membership at Cincinnati although Rufus Lewis Perry continued the CABMC on paper until his death in 1895.[12]

At a December 1880 meeting in Montgomery, the Reverend William W. Colley and other black Baptists founded the Baptist Foreign Mission Convention to promote black missionary work in Africa. A former Virginia slave who devoted his life to African missionary work, the late Lott Carey (Cary), became the spiritual father of the Negro foreign missionary movement. The Reverend William H. McAlpine presided over this convention. McAlpine (1847-1905) was born a slave in Buckingham City, Virginia, in June 1847, and was sold along with his mother and brother to a minister who taught the young slave to read and write. McAlpine became a carpenter, a teacher, college graduate, an organizer and president of the Alabama Baptist State Convention, and president of Selma University. McAlpine presided over the Baptist Foreign Mission Convention for two terms before President W. A. Binkley succeeded him.[13] (The large national Baptist conventions prefer to use 1880 as the date for their origins.) Still, the black Baptists had no unified national convention.

On April 5, 1886, the Reverend William J. Simmons (1849-1890) sent an open letter to Negro Baptist clergy and laymen, asking for a meeting to organize a national Baptist convention to promote piety, sociability, and a better knowledge of each other. The association's objectives included discussion of religious, educational, industrial, and social interests of black people and a forum for the best thinkers and writers. This meeting took place in St. Louis, Missouri on August 25, 1886, at the First Baptist Church. The Reverend Simmons, a citizen of Louisville, Kentucky, and a Negro field secretary for the American Baptist Home Mission Society, received the assistance of the white Society's secretary, Henry Layman Morehouse, in organizing another national Baptist convention, the American National Baptist Convention (ANBC). In 1888, with the support of the ABHMS, Simmons and the ANBC met in Nashville with the Baptist General Association of Western States and Territories and others in a failed attempt to create a truly national black Baptist convention. Simmons died suddenly (1890). The Reverend E. M. Brawley presided over the American National Baptist Convention until 1892. Brawley was followed by President Michael Vann who served until 1894. Reverend Elias Camp Morris was elected in 1894.[14] However, the American National Baptist Convention was controlled by pro-northern black Baptist preachers.

During the 1891 American National Baptist Convention's session, the Reverend M.W. Gilbert, a pastor of Nashville's First Colored Baptist Church, introduced a resolution to establish a Home Mission Society. But the cooperative faction opposed Gilbert's resolution because it clashed with the functions of the American Baptist Home Mission Society which included missionary and educational work among the blacks. Gilbert and Brawley also proposed a Negro Baptist magazine to be published in Nashville.[15] Of course the publishing idea clashed with the function of the American Baptist Publication Society. Nothing came of these suggestions because of "the cooperative movement" between the northern white Baptist organizations and the American National Baptist Convention.[16]

In 1892, the black Baptists formed the Baptist Educational Convention with the Reverend W. Bishop Johnson as president. This group intended to promote black education and establish educational institutions for black Baptists, in spite of the efforts already being made by the white American Baptist Home Mission Society. The Baptist Educational Convention published the *National Baptist* magazine until 1895.

In summary, the black Baptists operated three national organizations:
(1) The Negro Baptist Foreign Mission Convention of
    the United States (founded 1880).
(2) The American National Baptist Convention (founded 1886).
(3) The Baptist Educational Convention (founded 1892).

The three organizations had equal status, and they met annually in the same city but under different leaders. By 1894, these three organizations had agreed to meet jointly in 1895 and attempt a union.

National Baptist Convention

The three national black Baptist groups met at Atlanta and organized the National Baptist Convention on September 28, 1895. Some five hundred delegates and observers attended the sessions. The Reverend E. C. Morris won election as president of the new organization. Incidentally, Atlanta also housed the Cotton States and International Exposition in September 1895 when Booker T. Washington made his famous racial compromise speech, essentially agreeing to accommodate the whites' desires for social segregation in return for giving economic and educational assistance to blacks. The accommodationists promoted the establishment of separate institutions for black Americans.

The National Baptist Convention merely was a national organization on paper. Really, it represented a loose organization of boards. To represent the interests of the former separate Baptist groups, the new National Baptist Convention (1895) created three boards:
(1) Foreign Mission Board to direct missions in Africa.

(2) Home Mission Board to direct home missionary activities.

(3) Educational Board to promote black education and develop Negro seminaries.

The weak structure and the factionalism caused problems for President Morris who struggled to mediate the factions and consolidate presidential power for the next twenty years.

After 1897, the annual sessions of the National Baptist Convention created three additional boards:

(1) National Baptist Young People's Union to organize young persons into religious work and church societies.

(2) The Women's Auxiliary Convention to support religious work and training among black Baptist women.

(3) The Benefits Board to aid destitute and retired Baptist preachers.

In 1896, the publishing board was created as a publication committee by members of the Home Mission Board without initiative by the National Baptist Convention. Similarly, the individual Baptist churches came into existence without permission from any higher, central authority, unlike Methodist, Catholic, Episcopalian, and Presbyterian churches. Not only did the NBC's boards duplicate one another's work, they became incorporated and practically autonomous from the national organization.

So, inherent in the history of the black Baptist convention there existed many factional groups. Boyd and members of the NBPB preferred a less formalized, confederate structure for the National Baptist Convention wherein the boards enjoyed autonomy and became insulated from the politics of the annual convention session. Another group of black Baptists desired to create a strong, federal government for the National Baptist Convention to control the boards and protect against a small group of men gaining control of the boards. The NBC had other factions too, including ones that favored cooperation (the cooperative movement) with the northern white Baptist agencies. Another faction, like Boyd's supporters, wanted to fulfill an alliance with the Southern Baptist Convention's agencies. And a few of the black Baptists maintained loyalty to their state and regional Baptist associations.

Lott Carey Convention

The Lott Carey people became the first factional problem for the National Baptist Convention and President Morris. The newly created Foreign Mission Board (FMB) intended to sponsor religious missions in any foreign lands where blacks lived, and it wanted to move the headquarters to Louisville. But the Lott Carey people argued that the FMB's functions remained the same as those of the former Baptist Foreign Mission Convention, and the headquarters should stay in Richmond.

In 1897 the Virginia Baptists broke away from the National Baptist Convention and formed the Lott Carey Baptist Foreign Mission Convention. Some Lott Carey dissidents formed state Baptist conventions in Virginia and Maryland. The Lott Carey Baptist Foreign Mission Convention resurrected the Baptist Foreign Mission Convention to support the focus of work in Africa, mainly in Liberia where the Reverend Lott Carey, a slave born in Virginia in 1780, had served as the first black missionary. Carey, who served as pastor of Richmond's African Baptist Church, acted as governor of Liberia and died defending the colony against a native raid during the late 1820s. The Richmond African Baptist Mission Society had financed Carey's African venture.[17]

Eventually, the Lott Carey problem impacted the Reverend Boyd's effort to build a Baptist publishing board. The black Baptists and the Lott Carey people in Virginia, Maryland, and North Carolina supported the "cooperative movement" and preferred to use printed literature from the American Baptist Publication Society. The Lott Carey Baptist Foreign Mission Convention supported the American Baptist Home Mission Society's activities among the blacks. The National Baptist Convention's Home Mission Society and the publishing board, both under Boyd by 1897, intended to do home mission activities among black Baptists and publish their Sunday school and church materials. Between 1897 and 1905, President Morris and the National Baptist Convention would form commissions to attempt to settle their differences. The Reverend Boyd served on these peace-making commissions.

All this complex history affected Richard H. Boyd's attempt to establish and maintain a black Baptist publishing board. The ABPS, the ABHMS, the turbulent history of the black Baptist organizations, the Lott Carey controversy, the southern Baptists and the northern Baptists, and the internal politics of the National Baptist Convention help to tell the story about R. H. Boyd and the publishing board.

The Reverend Boyd knew the complexity of the above Baptist history, understood the vicious politics as well as the possibilities of self-destruction within the National Baptist Convention, and comprehended the northern Baptists' fragmented organization, their power and vast resources, and the influence of the American Baptist Publication Society. Boyd quickly learned the real minds and moods of the southern Baptists. He knew that within this complex religious society, this was the "worst of times and the best of times" to create a black Baptist publishing board. Still Boyd forged ahead with his ideas, although all the aforementioned historical factors would come to bear on his plans.

Bobby L. Lovett

Chapter 1

R. H. Boyd, Founder: Years of Struggle, 1843-1896

Chapter 1

Richard Henry Boyd, Founder: The Years of Struggle, 1843-1896

The founder of the National Baptist Publishing Board, Richard Henry Boyd (1843-1922) began his life as a slave on March 15, 1843. Born to a 23 year-old slave woman, Indiana, the child simply was named "Dick,"[1] short for Richard.

White slave masters customarily gave the newborn slave persons a simple nickname for easy identification and sometimes for amusement. Like other slave persons, Dick had no last name except that of the owner who was Master Gray. The child's full identification was Dick Gray. However, the whites did not know that Indiana had chosen the name Dick (Richard) for a good reason.

The former slave persons frequently used either the first name or a derivative of it to connect to relatives back home, a father or mother they had been separated from, and to relate to ancestors, naming a child after a brother, grandmother, uncle, aunt, or father. Sometimes, the former slaves used the last name of the most recent master or the first family which owned him or her. More often, however, the freedmen, especially the younger ones, selected an entirely new first and last name. Famous titles and places became popular picks: Boston, London, Washington, Duke, Count, King, and Queen. The former slaves also used famous persons and wealthy family names: Washington, Lincoln, Jefferson, and Madison.

Similar to other slave persons, Dick Gray would select his own legal name after the Emancipation of 1865. After slavery, lost family members could ask about relatives by recalling the first name, which blacks usually retained. Many young blacks dropped their slave master's last name, chose a completely new last name or adopted the name of the family who had originally owned them. Dick Gray followed these black naming practices when choosing a new name, Richard Henry Boyd, after the Civil War.

Moreover, Dick's place of birth and places of residency were affected by the forces of history. With the opening of the western lands ceded to the United States by England after 1783 and the possession of the Louisiana Purchase in 1803, plenty of virgin land rested and waited for clearing and farming west of the Appalachian Mountains. After Congress prohibited the African slave trade in 1808, a domestic slave trade developed, sending slaves by boat and wagon train into these new lands called Kentucky, Tennessee, Alabama, Louisiana, Mississippi, and later Arkansas and Texas. After 1830, a Transportation Revolution developed. New canals, roads, and railroads encouraged families to move further into frontier lands. Instead of slavery declining after the Revolutionary War, the demand for slaves increased dramatically with the westward movement, causing slaves like Indiana to be sold to the West.

Dick's mother, Indiana (Ann) (1820-1915), was born in Petersburg, Virginia around 1820. The youngest of sixteen children born to slaves Dick and Mollie, Indiana (age 7) was sold in Richmond, Virginia. Slavetraders carried young Indiana to Columbus, Georgia, and sold her to Martha Gray. The Gray family moved to Noxubee County, Mississippi, around 1835. Teenage slaves, like Indiana, walked behind the wagons which carried cargo and small black children. Like most slave females between eighteen and twenty-five years of age, Indiana began to bear children. Eight years after arriving in Mississippi, Indiana gave birth to her first child, Dick. Then the Gray family moved to neighboring Lowndes County, Mississippi, where Indiana gave birth to two daughters.[2]

Indiana's slave parents, Dick and Mollie, probably cried aloud when they learned through the slave grapevine that their child, seven-year-old Indiana, was being sold. And Indiana and the other slave cargo must have cried when they learned that the destination was Georgia, the Deep South. These young black persons represented thousands of "prime slave hands" who moved from the East to west of the Appalachian Mountains. Generally, they lost any connection with their parents and relatives when sold to the Deep South and into the western lands. For this reason, the displaced slaves often used the first name of a child to connect the lost generations.

Indiana named her first child in honor of her father, Dick (Richard). She named a daughter, Mollie, after her lost mother. Because Martha Gray acted like a kind master, Indiana named another daughter Martha.

Indiana's fate exemplified the destiny of young and healthy slaves during the 1820s when the nation had emerged from the economic panic of 1819 and embarked on a great expansion to the West. Virginia's soil, like the land of the old eastern states, had been exhausted by growing cash crops like tobacco. Soon Virginia, like Maryland and the Carolinas, had poor soil and a surplus of slaves. Virginia, Indiana's home, furnished the fourth highest number of migrants to Mississippi where strong gangs of experienced slaves worked vast cotton farms.[3]

Indiana and the Gray family were no strangers to the territory where vast amounts of raw labor turned the rich, virgin soil into productive cash crops. During the 1830s, the great planters increased their movement into Mississippi where a new, exciting frontier offered opportunities to make fortunes in white gold (cotton). When the land became worn out, the pioneer planters moved further West into newly annexed American lands.

In Mississippi, which had become a state in 1817, Indiana found a harsh world. In 1830, the settlers organized Lowndes County which lay in eastern Mississippi and reached to the Alabama state line. By 1837, Lowndes County had 12,857 whites and blacks. Negroes nearly outnumbered the whites. With 3,500 people, Columbus became the center of the county. The Natchez Trace Road, the Tombigbee River, and later the Mobile-Ohio Railroad serviced the area. The black prairie belt supported timber, cotton, corn, oats, sorghum, wheat, clover, grasses, fruits, and vegetables. More than three-fourths of Mississippi's farmers were born outside the state by 1860.⁴ Houses had to be built, forests and rocks had to be cleared for fields, and crops grown and harvested.

Mississippi was a good place to live for whites, but it was a notoriously harsh society for Negroes. The lands rose no higher than 800 feet above sea level, and the climate was warm with plentiful rain. Choctaw and Chickasaw Indians had occupied the eastern red clay hills. Marshes and flood plains existed in the western and the delta areas. But precisely because the Negro workers outnumbered the whites in much of Mississippi, the state had an oppressive society and harsh racial (black) codes. Slave persons dreaded the master's threat to "sell you to Mississippi or Alabama."

But Mississippi became just one more stop for Indiana and her children. Next, the Gray family moved the slaves to Claiborne Parish, Louisiana, where Indiana gave birth to a third daughter. From about 1835 until 1859, Indiana Dickson and her family worked the Gray plantations in Mississippi and Louisiana.

During the first ten years of his life, young Dick exercised the privileges of a child. He played and did what other children did. When Indiana and the other slaves went to the fields before the sunrise, Dick and other young slave children often remained behind with the white mistress. About twice a day, Indiana walked back to the house to nurse the child. When older, young Dick sometimes accompanied his mother to the fields, resting under a shade tree within her attentive view. Until about ten years old, he had nothing to do but be a child. Mostly he played with the white children and enjoyed the freedom of a human being. After age ten, Dick became a seasoned slave and developed into a "prime hand," a healthy teenage slave who could bring top price.

When he became fifteen years old, Dick and his siblings relieved the work requirement for Indiana. Then she turned more of her energy to weaving, cooking, and cleaning. Dick served as mule boy, hauling the cotton sacks to the weighing wagons. Sometimes he worked at the mill to help gin the cotton and bale it for hauling to market. He became a strong, tall lad who easily did a day's work. The white Gray family liked the industrious Dick, and they took a peculiar interest in this young man.

Then Martha Gray died. Members of the family and creditors partitioned the property, including the slaves, between themselves. At the age of fifteen years, Benonia W. Gray paid $1,200 for Dick and took him to Texas.

Thirty-nine-year-old Indiana and her three daughters (Mollie, Sallie, and Martha) were sold and taken to Grimes County, Texas.

After years of working the red clay soil of Mississippi and Louisiana, the Grays and others had worn the land out by growing acres of cotton and corn. They, like many other southern farmers, looked west of the Mississippi River for new lands to support a growing family of whites and slaves and to make a profit. Cotton became profitable during 1850-1860, but the prices declined during the 1840s. People called the abandoned, deep-gullied farms in Mississippi "Gone to Texas farms."[5]

After Congress worked out the Missouri Compromise of 1820, slave owners poured into the slave territories of Missouri and Arkansas where the compromise allowed slavery to exist. In 1849, great numbers of farmers and gold miners crossed the Mississippi River and headed to the new lands of California. Then as a result of the Mexican-American War of 1848, the United States gained California and Texas. Congress' Compromise of 1850 declared California a free state and Texas a slave state.

The slave farmers eagerly entered the new lands and left the worn out, less profitable lands in the eastern United States. People in Louisiana and Mississippi had supported the American war to gain Texas from the Mexicans. Really, by the late 1840s, before Congress worked out the 1850 Compromise, slave farmers began to move into Texas. Slave owners found it difficult to expand their land holdings in Louisiana and Mississippi where free farmers (half of Mississippi's farmers) blocked the expansion of slave farms. The slave-owning farmers needed more land to support a growing black labor force and replenish worn out lands.

The Gray family, Indiana and her family, moved to Texas in 1859. Dick went to work for a different master, separated from his mother just as Indiana had been separated from her slave parents in 1827. The Gray family moved the slaves to eastern Texas. Some eighty percent of the slaves taken to Texas and the Southwest were moved by their masters instead of by domestic slave traders.

Likely the Gray family traveled by wagon, making about thirty miles a day. The young slave children and the white children rode in the wagons, and Indiana and the older slaves followed on foot. Dick's sisters saw the mighty Mississippi River. Entering Texas they saw tall pines, prairies, hills, and grass lands. Somewhere in Texas, sleeping under the open skies at night, fifteen-year-old Dick wondered about the whereabouts of his mother and sisters. Too, he wondered about the universe, God, and man. He dreamed what all children dreamed.

Dick's owner settled on rich lands in Washington County, Texas, the western outpost of the Cotton Kingdom. Texas became more a southern state than a part of the West when more slaves, slaveowners, and non-slaveholding southerners poured into the region. By 1860, Texas had 182,921 blacks and 420,891 whites.[6] Farmers and speculators purchased some lands for one dollar an acre.[7]

Near San Antonio, where Dick would relocate after the Emancipation, many Mexicans and anti-slavery Germans settled the area where grassy prairies, rare oak trees, and ranches could be found.[8] Cotton lands extended from San Antonio to Houston and throughout the eastern part of the state.

Again the Gray family and the slaves worked hard to clear land, grow and harvest crops, build shelters, and generally do slaves' work. The slave usually received two pairs of pants, two shirts, a hat, and a pair of shoes each year. The black bondsmen lived in log huts chinked with mud, and their diet included many peas and sweet potatoes. Dick's owners had a reputation of being "good masters"' who adequately fed and clothed their slaves.

But the slaves believed that no man who held another in bondage represented good. A former slave said: "Massa was pretty good. He treated us just about like you would a good mule."[9] In nearby Grimes County, Indiana and her three daughters worked from "can see to can't see" under the hot Texas sun. Another former slave recalled the death of the master: "We was glad he was dead."[10]

The Baptist religion also influenced Dick and Indiana Gray. Just prior to 1860, Indiana professed the Baptist religion and received baptism. Influenced by their paternalistic masters and benevolent white patrons, most southern black Christians became Baptists and Methodists before 1860.

Probably the Grays became Baptists because slave owners joined the Baptist and the Methodist churches in greater numbers than other denominations. Master Gray was a relative of an important official in the Home Mission Board of the Southern Baptist Convention. The southern Baptists took part in a southern evangelist movement after 1830 when slave masters encouraged their slaves to attend church and convert to Christianity. The southern evangelist movement, like the Methodist revivals already raging in the South, intended to counter the northern abolitionists' argument that slavery and its current expansion were evil and inhumane. But the southern white Baptist ministers preached that if a man was a slave when he became a Christian, let him remain a slave; and if he was a slave owner when he professed Christianity, let him remain a slave owner.

Dick, his siblings, and mother Indiana resented the harsh life of slavery. The master fed the slaves cornmeal, fat pork, molasses, sometimes coffee, greens, and vegetables. Sometimes the slaves hunted for animals and grew a small garden to supplement their diet. The female slaves, including Indiana, customarily worked the fields with the men until their children could take their places. Cotton had a long growing season of about 200 frost-free days. Picking lasted from August until December. Owners expected the slaves to pick 200-

300 pounds a day and work through Saturdays. A slave's life expectancy reached about forty-five years.

Dick became a strapping young slave person by 1860. He drew close to Master Gray and his three sons. Being constantly around the Grays, Dick became articulate in his ideas and organizational skills, even though he had not mastered reading and writing. But he had been exposed to the Gray boys' learning. These experiences would make Dick thirst for learning, knowledge, and the mastery of skills. He believed secretly that blacks could match the accomplishments of whites. Master Gray and the boys went hardly anywhere without Dick. Even when the masters participated in the Civil War, they involved Dick Gray, their slave.

The 1856 and 1860 presidential elections ripped America apart and convinced the southern nationalists to create a new nation predicated on slavery. Dick and other slaves stood on the edge of huge crowds of white men who debated openly the question of secession from the United States. Dick recalled that when he had reached thirteen years, the local white men discussed the meddling of the North in the South's right to retain slaves. These discussions had become prevalent during the heated presidential election of 1856 when the new Republican party fielded its first presidential candidate. Dick heard some southerners proclaim "the Union be damned." Abraham Lincoln, an anti-slavery candidate, won the election of 1860, causing most of the southern states to secede from the American Union. President Lincoln determined that the Union would not be torn apart.

Master Gray and his three sons put on home-sewn uniforms and prepared to go into town to join the Texas Confederate regiments. It seemed natural for them to take Dick along to serve as their body servant. Dick had reached eighteen years old. Like thousands of teenage slave persons, Dick marched off to war with his Confederate masters whereas older slaves remained behind to help the white mistress tend the plantation.

Dick met dozens of teenage black body servants in the Confederate camps. Later, in 1912, he would argue that a tax should be passed to give pensions to the Negroes who had to serve in the Confederate military.[11] The General Assembly in Tennessee, Boyd's new home, passed such a bill around 1921 and gave pensions to former Confederate black servants. All body servants were expected to be loyal "darkies," "faithful to the end," and cheerful and prompt in obeying the white soldiers' commands.

Dick and his fellow black Confederates attended to the masters' needs, herded horses and cattle, raised the tents, cared for the horses, cooked meals, and cleaned clothes. The body servants dug trenches, built military fortifications, and served as teamsters to drive the supply wagons.

Indiana Gray remained in Texas, not knowing that her son had gone to war. In 1861, Indiana married Sam Niblett, who changed his name to Dickson (sometimes spelled Dixon). Sam Dickson became a deacon at the Midway Baptist Church in Prairie Plains, Texas. He and Indiana had six boys: Samuel, William, Henry, Louis, Richard, and Jim. Sam, the father, died nine years after the youngest son was born. Nine of Indiana's ten children, except Richard Dickson who died in 1912, survived her. By 1914, the children, including Richard H. Boyd, lived in Texas, Tennessee, and Missouri.

Meanwhile, the units moved across the Mississippi River to help stop the Yankee army's advance after February 1862. Some Texas units traveled to Virginia to reinforce General Robert E. Lee's Confederate army. In late 1863, Texas' troops found themselves reinforcing the Confederate Army of Tennessee in the mountains surrounding Chattanooga. By water, rail, and land, Dick and his companions traveled thousands of miles. He did not know that someday Tennessee would be his home.

In November 1863, around Lookout Mountain and the Tennessee River, Confederate and Union armies prepared to challenge each other for the possession of Chattanooga, Tennessee. Chattanooga became the gateway to Atlanta, less than 150 miles south. The Union army had taken Nashville in February 1862, pushed the Confederates out of Murfreesboro in 1863, and now controlled Chattanooga and Knoxville in East Tennessee. The Union Navy controlled the Mississippi, Tennessee, and Ohio Rivers. So the Confederates had to stop the Yankees from massing forces at Chattanooga for a campaign into Georgia, Alabama, and the Deep South, the heart of slave territory. From Lookout Mountain, the young slave, Dick, and his fellow black body servants could see what seemed to be the whole world. Several states could be seen from Lookout Mountain.

Suddenly, the scenery turned to a bloody hell. Thundering booms and flashing cannons could be seen and heard. The federal artillery pieces sounded like they tore the world asunder, Dick and his fellow young slave persons thought. The shells came whistling through the air, cutting trees to splinters, breaking human limbs and leaving dead and wounded Confederates on the ground. The Confederates fought bravely, but the Union forces overwhelmed them. The commander of the Confederate Army of Tennessee ordered the Texans to cover the retreat. The regiments fought hand-to-hand combat and lost heavily when the Confederate Army of Tennessee retreated into northern Georgia.

Master Gray and two sons died near Chattanooga. The youngest Gray son suffered bad wounds. The body servants, including Dick, gathered and buried the dead. They helped to man the Confederate hospitals, burying sawed-off arms and legs, carrying away the dead, even helping to defend against Yankee attacks. Dick cared for his young master, nursing him to health when the army fled south before a powerful Yankee force. In the distance he could still hear the thunder of the victorious Union army guns. And Dick saw hordes of Georgia slaves headed into the Yankee lines to gain freedom and work for the Union army.

Dick continued to care for his master when the retreating Texas units traveled by road and train toward Texas. When Dick came down the road with his crippled master, the entire Gray family, black and white, rushed toward them in bewilderment. Mrs. Gray learned that her husband and two sons had been killed. Indiana must have prayed for her son, Dick, although she had not seen him since 1859. Neither Dick nor Indiana knew where the other person lived. Dick had reached twenty-one years old, and he was tall, handsome, and now a mature man who had seen death and dying firsthand. In fear of the powerful Yankees, young master Gray took Dick and fled to Mexico until the war ended.

After returning to Texas, Dick worked and managed the Gray plantation. Dick hauled the cotton by oxen, creeping to the Mexican markets at two miles an hour. This became dangerous business because outlaws and ruffians burned and pillaged Texas between 1864 and 1866. Some 486 Texas Negroes died at the hands of outlaws, vindictive whites, and the Ku Klux Klan between 1865 and 1868.[12]

Life After Slavery

Emancipation of the slaves became a reality by 1865. But many southerners and some northerners disliked the Emancipation idea, especially in Texas. The free movement of the slaves helped to cause a tremendous increase in white violence, particularly in the black belt counties of East Texas where the Grays, transplanted Mississippians, and many rednecks and hillbillies lived. The southerners became angry that 178,000 black men had served the victorious Union army. Expressing typical local white disdain for blacks, one federal agent said "Negroes were everywhere ignorant, lawless and starving."[13]

Dick was not ignorant, lawless and starving. He continued to work for the Gray family after the Emancipation. He worked hard to make the farm profitable. But the economy collapsed with the end of the war. In 1866 the Gray family broke apart. Mrs. Gray went to live with her daughter. Like so many other freedmen, Dick and the other former slaves scattered through Texas to find work.

Emancipation of the slave persons in Texas and throughout the United States came officially with the thirteenth amendment to the national Constitution, adopted December 18, 1865. Word about emancipation reached Texas through federal officers on June 19th. The black Texans began an annual celebration called "Juneteenth" to commemorate the Emancipation Proclamation and freedom. The Boyds became prominent in later Juneteenth celebrations, frequently making the journey from their new home in Tennessee to take part in Texas' Juneteenth celebrations.

Dick, like most of the freedmen, stayed in Texas after the Emancipation. Some 94.9 percent of the freedmen stayed in Texas. For example, only 12.3 percent of the Negroes left the state after Reconstruction in the 1890s.[14] To the contrary, thousands of former slave persons fled Mississippi, Dick's place of birth. Dick spent much of his early adult life in Washington, Grimes, and Montgomery counties which bordered each other in central-east Texas, part of the black belt. Later, he moved into southwest Texas to the San Antonio area, not far from the Mexican border.

Dick Gray secured a job on a ranch. Nearly 5,000 other black men became cowboys in the West. The cowboys drove cattle to railroad terminals for loading and shipping the animals to the East for slaughter and sale. The penny-paying job required the cowboy to sleep out in the open and work in dusty and hot conditions. Then Dick got a job in a mill in southeastern Texas. He became a foreman in Montgomery County. Here, around age 22, he began to teach himself to read by using a *Webster's Blue Back Speller*. According to the Nashville *Globe* (April 12, 1940), a young white girl helped Dick to learn his alphabets.[15]

In 1866, like so many other "lost" former slaves, Dick Gray searched for his mother and sisters. He found Indiana, her new husband and family living in Grimes County. Indiana eventually moved to the Houston area. But Dick kept in touch with his mother. When Indiana was seventy-five years old and widowed in 1895, Dick brought Indiana to live in his home in San Antonio. Indiana continued living with the Boyds until her death in Nashville in 1915.

Young Dick was a thinker, an ambitious fellow. He maintained a level head even though Texas was full of cowboys, ranchers, railroad men, prostitutes, gamblers, and saloons. In 1868, he married Laura Thomas, who died within eleven months. Dick joined the Hopewell Baptist Church in Navasota where he was baptized on December 19, 1869, by the Reverend J. J. Rhinehart. Dick Gray changed his name to Richard Henry Boyd, after discovering that his father was a Mississippi slave.[16] He also decided to enter the ministry of the gospel.

Richard Henry Boyd: The Preacher

Richard H. Boyd married Harriett Albertine Moore in 1871.[17] She became his chief supporter, financier, and business partner. Harriett washed and ironed clothes and sacrificed to send her husband to Bishop College. At the age of forty-five years, Boyd attended Bishop College, an American Baptist Home Mission Society school. This northern missionary society financed many freedmen's schools in the postwar South, including Nashville's Roger Williams

University (1864-1907); and, like Bishop College, Roger Williams trained blacks for the Baptist pulpit.

Ironically, an affiliated agency of the American Baptist Home Mission Society, the American Baptist Tract Publication Society, would ultimately oppose the Reverend Boyd's attempts to publish black Sunday school literature. Until Boyd's efforts to supply the black Baptist churches during the 1890s, the American Baptist Tract Publication Society had supplied the Negro Baptist churches. Many Baptist preachers had attended the freedmen schools sponsored by these northern white Baptists. And most of their black graduates remained loyal to the Society.

Because of lack of money, Boyd had to drop out of Bishop College to support his growing family. Although he did not continue his formal education, the Reverend Boyd received honorary doctorate degrees from Guadalupe College and Alabama Agricultural and Mechanical State College.[18]

The Reverend Boyd raised a large family. Six children survived to adulthood: Henry Allen, J. Garfield Blaine, Theophilus Bartholomew, Lula, Mattie, and Annie. All but one of these children later accompanied their father to live in Nashville, Tennessee. Annie remained in Texas and married a Galveston undertaker, becoming proprietor and operator of two funeral homes after her husband's death. The other children followed their father to Nashville where two of the boys worked at the National Baptist Publishing Board, and J. Blaine worked at the local African Methodist Episcopal Church's Sunday School Union publishing house. Lula Boyd-Landers became a Nashville housewife. Mattie also became a housewife in Nashville.

During the early Reconstruction period, 1864-1880, formerly white-controlled black congregations declared their independence from the whites. Black ministers like Boyd and others busied themselves organizing more churches and black religious associations. Boyd and other black preachers became the black community's most important and respected leaders. The churches became the freedmen's first and most influential institutions, and the religious associations frequently became, unfortunately, political battlegrounds for black leaders.

The Reverend Boyd tirelessly worked to organize churches and the freedmen Baptists across Texas. The Reverend I. S. Campbell was the first educated black minister to arrive in Texas in 1865 when he headed a church in Galveston. Campbell helped to form the Negro Baptist Association in Texas. Boyd and a southern white minister helped to organize the Texas Negro Baptist Convention. The Reverend Boyd organized and headed several churches in various towns including Waverly, Old Danville, Navasota, Crockett, Palestine, San Antonio, and Grimes City. He headed Ninevah Baptist Church in Grimes City, Union Street Baptist Church in Palestine, and Mount Zion Baptist Church in San Antonio. Cooperating with a local white minister, Boyd and others organized the Lincoln District Baptist Association at Navasota in 1875, the same year the Western Baptist State Convention was formed. Believing that former slaves should gain economic independence, Boyd and his wife purchased many acres of land in Montgomery County, San Antonio, and Palestine.[19]

Boyd became notable through his work in Texas' Negro Baptist associations. During the 1870s, he lived in Grimes County where his son, Henry Allen, was born. Boyd impressed the freedmen with his honesty, articulation of the issues, and organizational skills. He served as a district missionary between 1870 and 1874, and he became educational secretary of the Texas Negro Baptist Convention, traveling through Texas in a buggy. Boyd became a moderator for the Central Baptist Association (1879) and pastor of San Antonio's historic Mount Zion Baptist Church (1891).

The following year, the Texas Negro Baptist Convention convened in the Mount Zion Baptist Church where the meeting ended in controversy and discussion about another state black Baptist convention. The Reverend Edward W. D. Isaac, pastor of Dallas' New Hope Baptist Church, was the Convention's president. He favored a plan to create a unified and a highly centralized Baptist state organization.

Encounters with the Northern White Baptists

During the Mount Zion convention and through 1893, heated discussions also centered around a "unification plan" that would give allegedly the American Baptist Home Mission Society (ABHMS), the northern white Baptists, control of freedmen's colleges and schools. The ABHMS wanted to close and consolidate some freedmen schools. Boyd and others opposed the scheme, and they resented the attempt by the white American Baptist Publication Society, the northern white Baptists, to dominate the writing and distribution of black Baptist Sunday school literature. These black Texas Baptists expressed concern that the American Baptist Home Mission Society, not the Negroes, really owned and controlled Bishop College in Marshall, Texas. The blacks did not want to lose control over Hearne College at Hearne, Texas, and Guadalupe College at Seguin, Texas. As the educational secretary for the Texas Negro Baptist Convention, Boyd continued to resent the paternalistic attitude that the northern white Baptist officials had displayed toward the black Baptist officials.

The largest faction of the Texas Negro Baptist Association, led by Boyd and David Abner, Jr., formed another association, the "new convention," the General Missionary Baptist Convention of Texas in 1893. Boyd resigned from Mount Zion to become the superintendent of missions for the "new convention." The Reverend H. H. Williams succeeded Boyd at historic Mount Zion Baptist Church.[20]

The creation of a "new convention" and the existence of the "old convention" in Texas proved to be significant events in Boyd's life. Many of the "old convention" preachers became Boyd's enemies. They remained allies of the white American Baptist Publication Society and the American Baptist Home Mission Society, organizations that opposed Boyd's later attempt to establish a black Baptist publishing board. This feud lasted from 1891 until the National Baptist Convention split in 1915.

Many knew that Boyd resented the white northern American Baptist Publication Society's treatment of black preachers. The white Publication Society had refused to publish and distribute tracts by black preachers. Boyd felt that the northern Baptists wanted to continue paternalistic control of the freedmen's education. Yet many black preachers, including ones in the Texas Negro Baptist Convention, remained loyal to the northern American Baptist organization. But Boyd, Abner, and others joined a separatist movement and decided to assert black independence and end the paternalistic relationships between the northern white Baptists and the black Baptists.

After Boyd learned that the missionaries, the colporters, and the American Baptist Publication Society's employees had taken active roles in the controversy that had divided the state's black Baptist association, he contacted the manager of the American Baptist Publication Society's branch house at Dallas and asked him to order the missionaries and colporters to cease the interference. The American Baptist Publication Society official said that he could do nothing about the matter.

Boyd's First Efforts to Supply Sunday Literature

During his tenure as educational secretary for Texas' "old convention," Boyd had thought deeply about the idea of blacks publishing their own church materials. Now the Reverend Boyd viewed his new job of superintendent of missions for the "new convention" as an opportunity to test his ideas about blacks supplying their own churches with literature.

Boyd's occasional conversations with white Baptist ministers in San Antonio fueled his desire to pursue the ideas. Some local white Baptist preachers proudly told Boyd about the Southern Baptist Convention's newly organized Sunday School Board. Boyd began to view the southern Baptists as alternatives to the northern Baptists' American Baptist Publication Society. Maybe the southern Baptists would meet the needs of the black Baptist churches in the General Missionary Baptist Convention of Texas, Boyd thought.

The local southern white Baptist ministers, who knew Boyd as a trusted former Confederate military servant, helped Boyd to contact the Southern Baptist Convention's Sunday School Board in Nashville, Tennessee. In March

1895, Richard H. Boyd wrote to T. P. Bell, the secretary of the Southern Baptist Convention's Sunday School Board in Nashville. The letter partly read: "The colored Baptists of Texas have not been accustomed to using your publications but as I travel over the state, I hope to do much by way of introducing them."[21] Boyd requested that the Southern Baptist Convention's Sunday School Board send all orders through him, although he intended to teach the black Sunday school superintendents and pastors to order directly from the Southern Baptist Convention's Sunday school publishing house. The southern Baptists stood to gain much business. Boyd said: "Our territory is very large and uses quite a supply of literature in the course of a year."[22] He concluded an unofficial agreement with Bell to ship church literature to Texas where Boyd's son, Henry Allen, a postal clerk in San Antonio, would ship the materials to black churches throughout the state.

This Texas venture became Boyd's first lesson on how to establish a network to supply black churches with Sunday school literature. Later, the Reverend Boyd reflected that the National Baptist Publishing Board began in San Antonio, Texas. Here, Boyd perfected his skills and techniques to secure customers and effectively service that clientele.

On April 25, 1895, Boyd sent a letter to the pastors, the super-intendents, and the Sunday school teachers in the Palestine District Associa-tion. The letter called for a convention of the Sunday School Executive Committee of the Central Baptist Association to discuss Sunday school literature. The meeting took place at the True Vine Baptist Church in Navasota near the Navasota River in Grimes County. He persuaded the Reverend E. W. Adkins, the president of the Sunday School District Convention, to send the district's Sunday Schools requests for literature to Boyd.[23] The Texas-styled Sunday school convention sought to educate and train black Baptist Sunday school personnel and pastors. But maybe Boyd was moving too fast to implement his ideas in Texas.

The Southern Baptist Convention's Sunday School Board had misgiv-ings about starting a fight with the powerful northern Baptists and their American Baptist Publication Society. During a meeting at Fortress Monroe, Virginia, September 12, 1894, the Southern Baptist Convention initially had resolved to work cooperatively with the northern Baptists [ABHMS] who had more money and already had established freedmen colleges for the Negroes; and at its May 10-14, 1895, annual session, the Southern Baptist Convention had confirmed these cooperative relations. In May 1895, T. P. Bell became worried that the American Baptist Publication Society's secretary would "make a strong fight for his hold on Texas Baptists both white and colored."[24]

Yet the Reverend Bell wanted to help Boyd and the Negro Baptists. Instead of taking Boyd's money, for now, Bell donated $120 worth of Sunday school literature for Boyd to distribute to black Sunday schools. The Southern

Baptist Convention had set aside some five hundred dollars to buy Bibles and distribute some free literature to the Negroes and others. Bell's action made it appear that he and the Southern Baptists had conducted simple missionary work among the black churches. Bell did not intend "fighting the [American Baptist] Publication Society...."[25]

Although Boyd knew about the Fortress Monroe conference between the southern and the northern white Baptists and he knew that Bell wanted no war with the northern Baptists' Publication Society, Boyd pushed ahead with his plan to make the black Baptist Sunday schools independent of the northern-based American Baptist Publication Society. This plan to divorce black Baptists from being dependents of the northern white Baptists created many enemies for Boyd.

The Palestine Baptist Association supported Boyd's efforts. A Sunday school convention convened at the South Union Baptist Church in Palestine on Friday morning, June 4, 1895. (June would become the meeting time for the future national Baptist Sunday School Congress, organized by Boyd.) The Reverend J. W. Waters, moderator for the Palestine Sunday schools, gave Boyd his support, and the Reverend A. E. Ealey helped Boyd to organize the meeting. Sunday school teachers gave papers on "The Negroes' Relation to the Bible," "How Best to Teach It to Grown People and to Children," and other related topics.[26] The papers helped Boyd to further crystalize his ideas about the needs of black Sunday schools. And the meeting helped many Negro Baptists to see the wisdom of directing their own Sunday school education.

Through the summer of 1895, Boyd solidified his ideas among the black Sunday school superintendents and pastors in Texas' General Missionary Baptist Convention. This convention remained faithful to Boyd's efforts. By fall 1895, Boyd had laid the groundwork to implement his plans.

On their way to the National Baptist Convention's annual session in Atlanta, September 1895, Boyd and a delegation of black pastors from the General Missionary Baptist Convention of Texas stopped at Nashville to see the corresponding secretary for the Southern Baptist Convention's Sunday School Board. They expressed satisfaction with their reception by the southern Baptists. On behalf of the Mission Board of the General Missionary Baptist Convention, Boyd thanked the southern Baptists for their help and the literature given to twelve of the twenty-two association districts. Boyd told the Sunday School Board's head that if we did not start a series of our own, the Southern Baptist Convention's Sunday School Board literature would spread rapidly in Texas' black churches. Boyd, David Abner, Jr., Isaac Tolliver, and others headed to Atlanta to join a huge, militant Texas delegation and other separatists at the newly organized National Baptist Convention.[27]

Whatever promises the southern Baptists made to the black delegation, they did with great care. Boyd and his Texas delegation were told to get the black Baptist convention's approval before the Sunday School Board would back the project.

Texas' General Missionary Baptist Convention's Missionary Board had already started a Baptist book depository in cooperation with the Herald Publishing Company which printed minutes and other jobs for black Baptists. Boyd had suggested that Bell deposit the southern Sunday School Board's literature in the depository to be distributed to black churches on demand.[28] The latter plan would allow the black Baptists in the General Missionary Baptist Convention to have a distributorship center, a branch of the Sunday School Board of the Southern Baptist Convention. Again, however, this was not the intention of Bell and the southern white Baptists who did not want to take on the northern Baptists over this issue, at least now.

In November 1895, Boyd held one more consultation with his Texas colleagues. They decided to push the idea of a publishing house with the newly formed Negro National Baptist Convention. The idea could be carried to the September 1896 session.

In early 1896, Boyd called a conference of his missionaries and Sunday school workers in Texas. He acted smart and involved local white Baptist preachers, members of the Southern Baptist Convention. He also involved some key black ministers including the Reverend L. L. Campbell of Austin, the Reverend P. H. Collier of Houston, the Reverend William Beckham of Austin, the Reverend W. B. Ball of Seguin, and others. Born in Georgia in 1866, Beckham became general Sunday school superintendent of the General Missionary Baptist Convention and later field secretary for the National Baptist Publishing Board. The conferees agreed to accept more literature from the Southern Baptist Convention's Sunday School Board. By July 1896, the black distribution venture's revenues totaled $2,000 per year.[29]

The volume of the distribution business and the black churches' demand for books and literature astounded even the Reverend Boyd. Now he thought that black Baptists had greater potential to sustain their own publishing operations than they realized.

Boyd knew that the Negro suffered from lack of self-confidence after slavery. Few blacks willingly challenged white enterprise and took initiative on their own, especially during the turbulent 1890s when white radicals openly used lynchings to put an "uppity" Negro in his place. Boyd felt strongly that black and white Baptists in the South should work together to help solve the region's racial problems, although the black Baptists should run their own denominational affairs. Boyd smartly reasoned that the conservative southern white Baptists instead of the Yankee Baptists would prove better allies for a black publishing venture in the segregated and racially violent South.

Implementing Plans for a Publishing Board

In July 1896, Boyd rode the trains to Helena, Arkansas, and spoke with the Reverend E. C. Morris, newly elected president of the National Baptist Convention. Boyd spent a day and a half with Morris to gain his support for the publishing venture. Then Boyd returned home and prepared a resolution for the September 1896 National Baptist Convention's annual session.[30]

Morris became an important player in the history of the NBPB and the convention. Unlike the previous president of the American National Baptist Convention, Morris wanted the black Baptists to assert greater independence from the white Baptists. As early as 1893, Morris had supported the idea of a black Baptist publishing board.

Elias Camp Morris was born on May 7, 1865, in Murray City, Georgia. His parents, Cora and James Morris, were slaves. Elias pursued a career as a shoemaker before attending Roger Williams University in Nashville, Tennessee. He became a minister in 1874 and then headed churches in Arkansas where he helped to organize the state Baptist association. Morris presided over this state association for thirty years. For a time, he did mission work for the ABPS and the ABHMS. Morris headed the Centennial Baptist Church in Helena from 1878 to 1922. Like Boyd, Morris too earned honorary doctorate degrees. Morris involved his church with the Republican party's efforts to politicize the freedmen during the Reconstruction period. He became an elected delegate to the Republican National Convention between 1884 and 1900. Morris said: "I have never been with that class who hold that ministers of the Gospel should have nothing to do with politics."[31] Having political experience became an asset to leaders in the National Baptist Convention.

When Boyd arrived at the September 1896 session of the National Baptist Convention, even he found it necessary to engage in political maneuvers to promote the publishing board idea. One political problem encountered by Boyd was his lack of position in the NBC. This problem was solved quickly when the election for the Home Mission Board was held. The Home Mission Board had an elected corresponding secretary from Arkansas in 1895, but the Home Mission Board moved too slowly to get organized and become productive; after all, the new convention gave the new board no operating funds. But R. H. Boyd saw promise in the Home Mission Board. With the help of the large Texas delegation, Richard Henry Boyd won election as corresponding secretary of the Home Mission Board. This feat represented a triumph for the Texan and deserves further explanation.

In September, 1896, Boyd helped to head Texas' General Missionary Baptist Convention's delegation at the National Baptist Convention's annual meeting. The national convention met at St. Louis' First Colored Baptist Church. Mobile, Alabama's A. N. McEwen presided. With 125,000 members in the Texas state conventions, in spite of the differences between the "old convention" and the "new convention" of Texas, Boyd had enough support to gain election at the annual session of the National Baptist Convention. The large Texas delegation placed Boyd on the board as their representative. And with the help of sister Fannie Todd of Saint Paul, Minnesota, Boyd gained the job of corresponding secretary or director of the Home Mission Board, replacing the original secretary. With his background in directing missionary work in Texas, Boyd became the logical choice for the job. But a few friends of the American Baptist Publication Society and a few persons from the Texas Negro Baptist Association resented Boyd's sudden elevation to leadership in the National Baptist Convention. Fannie Todd argued, however, that Boyd was an experienced man with vision, an asset to the new National Baptist Convention. To quiet dissension, Boyd offered to resign the position, but the delegates insisted that he retain the job. Boyd had until November 1896 to resign his job of superintendent of missions for the General Baptist Missionary Convention of Texas.[32]

Making the argument that a people without a literature of their own can never have the respect of their contemporaries or achieve the recognition commensurate with their ability and capabilities, Boyd presented his resolution to create a Negro Baptist publishing house. Naturally, the American Baptist Publication Society's friends opposed the idea. The Convention sent the resolution to a committee, possibly to die. Somehow, Boyd's friends and the Texas delegates helped elect him to the committee which included Charles H. Parrish of Kentucky, E. K. Love of Georgia, and others. When a stalemate developed, the committee referred the matter to a sub-committee consisting of Boyd, Love, and Parrish. The subcommittee recommended adoption of the resolution. The Reverends S. N. Vass of North Carolina, R. J. Temple of Mississippi, E. W. D. Isaac of Texas, and others opposed the recommendation. These men, especially Vass, directly affiliated with the American Baptist Publication Society and proposed that the NBC cooperate with the ABPS. The large committee agreed to refer the issue to the newly created Home Mission Board.[33]

For the next twenty-five years, S. N. Vass would oppose the National Baptist Publishing Board. Samuel Nathaniel Vass worked as Superintendent of Colored Work for the American Baptist Publication Society. A mulatto, with no distinguishable black features, he was born May 22, 1866, in Raleigh, North Carolina to slave Anna Victoria Vass and a locally prominent white man. S. N. Vass graduated from St. Augustine Normal and Collegiate Institute and Shaw University by 1885. He worked as a school teacher before beginning his career with the American Baptist Publication Society in 1892. After the denominational split of 1915, he would join the staff of the National Baptist Convention, United States of America, Incorporated, and become R. H. Boyd's outspoken critic.[34]

Meantime, at the 1896 NBC session, when the Home Missions Board convened for a business meeting, Boyd, the newly elected corresponding secretary, requested a printing committee to prepare and publish a black series of Sunday school literature. The board agreed and authorized Boyd to appoint a five-man printing committee. The committee set the date for publication as January 1, 1897. Boyd carefully selected G. W. D. Gaines of Little Rock, J. Geter of Little Rock, J. M. Moore of Kentucky, E. R. Carter of Atlanta, and the Reverend E. C. Morris. Gaines became chairman of the Home Mission Board. Boyd nominated Morris, the president of the National Baptist Convention, to be editor-in-chief of the new publishing venture. Secretary Boyd received a salary figure of $2,800 a year and encouragement to plan the publication series.[35] Really he received no convention money for salary and expenses.

In October, 1896, the Reverend Boyd attended the General Missionary Baptist Convention's meeting at Fort Worth, Texas, where he resigned his superintendent's job. Boyd went to San Antonio and made preparations for his family. He visited local banks, obtaining cash and letters of credit. Leaving his family behind, he took a small bag and boarded the train to Arkansas. The publication committee had scheduled its meeting there.

Boyd had decided to establish the publishing operations in Nashville, Tennessee. Boyd's decision to move his activities to Nashville proved a smart one, although the National Baptist Convention's boards usually headquartered in the town where the secretary resided. The Reverend Boyd reasoned that San Antonio was too far from the black population centers of the country. Still, for several years, Boyd continued to be a part of Texas' General Missionary Baptist Convention's delegation when attending the annual sessions of the National Baptist Convention. Nashville had men at the Southern Baptist Convention's five-year-old Sunday School Board who could help Boyd establish a publishing operation. The African Methodist Episcopal Church's Sunday School Union publishing house had operated in Nashville since 1882. Nashville offered many printing and publishing companies. Blacks represented some 38 percent of Nashville's population. The black community included dozens of churches, a medical school, a law school, a nursing school, and three colleges: Fisk University, Roger Williams University, and Central Tennessee College.[36]

Boyd had done his homework. He had already visited the National Baptist Publishing Company in St. Louis to view their operations. The white manager explained that the company served Baptists in the western states. But the company struggled because of keen competition from the American Baptist Publication Society and the Southern Baptist Convention's Sunday School Board. Boyd boldly offered $3,000 for the company's plant only to find later that the American Baptist Publication Society had bought the operation. Then Boyd approached the American Baptist Publication Society about printing ten thousand copies of Sunday school lessons for the National Baptist Convention's churches and other Negro Baptist churches, but they naturally declined an offer that would eventually break the American Baptist Home Mission Society's ties with the Negro churches. The Southern Baptist Convention's Sunday School Board became Boyd's last chance.[37]

Boyd's efforts to establish a black publishing house encountered opposition from ABPS officials and black preachers who remained pro-ABPS. Some officials of the American Baptist Home Mission Society and the American Baptist Publication Society blamed Boyd and other black separatists for "exciting the race issue" and causing the northern Baptists to lose influence in freedmen and Negro church affairs. They also resented Boyd for not giving support to the Fortress Monroe agreement. And some blacks within the black Baptist conventions criticized Boyd for not supporting this cooperative movement.

Boyd was not alone in attempting to shake off northern missionary paternalism by the 1880s and 1890s in America. Even though the American Baptist Home Mission Society's schools had trained many black preachers, most of the Negro Baptist pastors had no affiliation with the American Baptist Home Mission Society. Besides, after 1880, young blacks started a "home rule" movement on the American Baptist Home Mission Society's freedmen's college campuses where they demanded more black professors and black administrators. Nashville's Roger Williams University nearly closed in 1888 when a black student rebellion forced the white president to resign. Because of the "home rule" issue, black Texans resented the American Baptist Home Mission Society's control of Bishop College in Marshall, Texas. For the next five years, the ABHMS reacted to the black "home rule" movement by proposing to close its freedmen colleges and schools and consolidate them into a "national freedmen's university."

The ABHMS' educational problem (the proposal to consolidate freedmen's colleges) had spread beyond Texas and Tennessee and into the American National Baptist Convention's (ANBC) forums during the period 1891-1893. Michael Vann, president of the ANBC, supported the northern Baptists' consolidation proposal, but Vann's credibility was destroyed because he was a missionary for the ABHMS. The Reverend Jessie E. Purdy, pastor of Nashville's First Colored Baptist Church, opposed the ABHMS' scheme and brought the issue to the ANBC's 1892 annual session. Purdy argued that black Nashvillians had helped to organize and finance the freedmen's schools, including Nashville's Roger Williams University. Local black Baptist pastors, including Nelson G. Merry and Randall B. Vandavall, helped to open the school in 1864 and served on its board of trustees until their deaths. Throughout the South, blacks had helped to build and finance the freedmen's schools whether the white northern Baptists (ABHMS) admitted it or not.

Indeed, because of the whites' segregation practices, a black separatist movement had already begun by 1890, and the ideas of blackness and black pride had surfaced during this time. Many persons suspected that these and other factors influenced the second generation of northern missionaries (i. e., ABHMS) to want to abandon black colleges. Moreover, by 1896, Booker T. Washington's Atlanta Compromise speech (1895) and the Supreme Court's *Plessy v. Ferguson* decision (1896) both recognized the reality of America's Jim Crow society and its intent to maintain separate institutions for blacks and whites. These factors also influenced many young black pastors and Sunday school superintendents to accept Boyd's ideas and plans to break away from the northern Baptists, strike an alliance with southern white Baptists who were willing to help the blacks establish separate institutions, and establish a black Baptist Sunday school publishing board.

Pulpit Furniture, Pews, Communion Tables, Tithing Boxes and Lecturns are made in this department of the National Baptist Publishing Board.

Chapter 2

The Creation and Success of the National Baptist Publishing Board, 1896-1905

Chapter 2

The Creation and the Success of the NBPB:
1896-1905

During the fall of 1896, the Reverend Richard H. Boyd quickly moved to unfold his plans to establish a black Baptist publishing board. He had to move fast before the opposition could organize fully. Boyd had to prove that a black publishing operation could be successful, and he had to prove this quickly.

On October 15, 1896, Boyd met with the Reverend J. P. Robinson in Arkansas. Robinson agreed with Boyd's plans and pledged his loyalty. A meeting of the Mission Board was scheduled for November 4, 1896, but because of a lack of a quorum it did not meet. Instead, the meeting convened on November 5 in the offices of the Little Rock *Baptist Vanguard.* Only two members of the Home Mission Board, the Reverends G. W. Gaines and J. Geter came. Boyd learned that Geter had converted to the Holiness Church. Without a quorum, an official meeting could not be held.[1]

Still full of energy and determination, Boyd took the trains to Memphis, arriving there on November 6. He ate breakfast at the Reverend T. J. Searcy's home before taking the twelve noon train to Nashville. Arriving in Nashville at 9 p. m., he made his way to the Reverend Charles H. Clark's home at 1013 High Street. Although Clark had gone to Kentucky, Mrs. Clark fed Boyd and prepared a bed for him. Clark arrived home the next morning, before the weary Boyd had arisen.[2] Incidentally, Clark was a friend to J. M. Moore of Kentucky and E. R. Carter of Georgia, men who could help Boyd deal with the National Baptist Convention.

Charles Henry Clark headed the Mount Olive Baptist Church near Cedar (Charlotte) Street. A faction of the First Colored Baptist Church founded Mount Olive in 1887 when the controversy over the local campaign for a temperance amendment to the state constitution divided the large congregation. A learned pastor, Clark came aboard around 1892 and increased the Mt. Olive congregation to 1,800 members. By February 1897 the congregation officially incorporated and built a brick edifice on Ninth and Cedar Streets by sponsoring fairs and picnics where the price of admission was either money or some building supplies including lumber, bricks and eggs to make mortar.

Charles H. Clark was born on October 15, 1855, in Christian County, Kentucky. His father escaped slavery and fled to the North. The mother married Jerry Clark, a black Union Army soldier. The family farmed in Trigg County, Kentucky, before moving to Hopkinsville to enter Charles and his brother George in school. Charles joined the Green Hill Baptist Church and became a church clerk, a deacon, and then a licensed preacher. He taught school and married Maria Bridges. They had five children: Grant, Marie, Mary, George,

R. H. Boyd and Family. Back row: Lula, Annie, Mattie, Mrs. H. A. Boyd.
Seated: Albertine Hall-Boyd, R. H. Boyd, Theophilus B., J. Blaine,
Hariett A., young Boyd-Hall, Katherine, Henry Allen (NBPBLA)

Charles H.
Clark (NBR)

and Willie. Until 1884, Clark served the Rolling Mill and Center Furnace Baptist churches. Then he came to Nashville to pastor the Mount Olive Missionary Baptist Church. He received an honorary doctorate from Cadiz Normal and Theological College. C. H. Clark became Richard H. Boyd's right hand man, serving as trustee of Roger Williams University and Citizens Bank, treasurer of the Stones River Baptist Association in Nashville, and a director and chairman of the National Baptist Publishing Board.[3]

On the morning of November 7, 1896, Clark and Boyd discussed plans to publish black Baptist literature. Clark, who had lived in Nashville for several years, agreed to introduce Boyd to the Reverend James M. Frost of the Baptist Sunday School Board and S. W. Meek of the University Printing Company. After breakfast, the men set out to meet these and other printers and publishers.

First, Boyd talked to the Reverend C. S. Smith, director of the African Methodist Episcopal Church's Sunday School Union publishing house. The AME Church had moved its publishing operations from Indiana to Nashville in 1882. Although Smith had no printing plant, he offered to introduce Boyd to his printers at the white Methodist publishing house and lease space to Boyd in the African Methodist Episcopal Church's publishing facility. Thinking that his critics would use such an arrangement to destroy his efforts, Boyd declined to share quarters with the black Methodists. Smith understood Boyd's dilemma and respected his position. Then Smith offered to be an adviser and told Boyd not to postpone his plans because of the failure of the printing committee to meet. Boyd had no intention of doing so.

Boyd arrived in Frost's Nashville office. Right away, Boyd informed Frost that the Negro Baptists intended to publish their own materials. Frost went further than his predecessor, Bell, and agreed to permit the use of the Sunday School Board's literature printing plates until the Negro Baptists had the ability and the resources to establish their own publishing board, possibly a few years in the future. Frost gained permission from his board of directors to help Boyd. Later, Frost accompanied Boyd to see local printers and introduced him to the owners. "It was an eventful moment and lives in my memory as one of the points of the history of people who are seeking their own advancement," Frost said later.[4]

On the next day, Frost and Boyd held conferences with two other men: S. W. Meeks of University Printing Company and C. H. Brandon of Brandon Printing Company. The men agreed to print materials for Boyd. Again, Frost graciously offered the Baptist Sunday School Publishing Board's printing plates. Boyd would furnish engravings and cover designs to the printers. Boyd was delighted, and he offered to pay Frost for the use of the plates. But Frost refused to take Boyd's offer of money to use the Sunday School Board's printing plates because he earnestly supported the ideas of progress and success for the former slaves. Later when reflecting on Boyd's efforts, one writer said: "It was a distinct movement of Negroes, by Negroes, and for Negroes—a great venture born of a vision for the future."[5]

Boyd still had a problem. The printing committee was not operational. No meeting had taken place since the September, 1896, National Baptist Convention session. Boyd needed the sanction of this committee to affiliate the publishing effort with the black Baptists because, without this official sanction, the factions which opposed the publishing idea would boycott Boyd's efforts when the next National Baptist Convention convened. It was now or never if the publishing venture was to be started. Boyd thought that somehow the printing committee must convene.

The Long Journey

Through sheer energy and genius, Boyd arranged to reorganize the printing committee. Clark replaced his friend, J. M. Moore. Then Clark advised Boyd to go see the Reverend M. Vann in Chattanooga. If Vann supported him, then Boyd should see the Reverend E. R. Carter, a friend of Clark's in Atlanta. Boyd took the train to Chattanooga and met with Vann who was holding his "Ten Nights in the Wilderness" campaign to raise money to retire the church's debt. Boyd accepted Vann's invitation to preach a night service. So impressive was the Reverend Boyd that the worshippers contributed $30 and a train ticket for Boyd to travel to Atlanta.

Boyd arrived in Atlanta before sunrise. At sunrise, Boyd left the station with a hand-grip and walked to the Friendship Baptist Church. Some early risers directed him to the Reverend Carter's home. When the Reverend Carter seemed to be enjoying his breakfast, Boyd persuaded him to agree to allow the Reverend Vann to replace him on the printing committee. Carter agreed because of the difficulty and the expense of getting to the meetings in either Arkansas or Nashville. When Boyd learned from some local preachers that the Alabama Negro Baptist State Association was in session, he used another donated ticket to travel to Birmingham instead of returning to Nashville.

Boyd wired ahead to give the Reverend Lewis G. Jordan notice of his trip to Birmingham. No sooner than the Reverend Boyd had arrived in Birmingham, a friend of the publishing idea, the Reverend Jordan grabbed Boyd and rushed him into a waiting buggy. Jordan told Boyd that a leading black preacher, S. N. Vass, who worked for the American Baptist Publication Society, was leaving the convention and headed to the train station. If he had seen Boyd, the man and his supporters would have turned back to the convention to oppose Boyd's presentation. After speaking to the ministers, Boyd was given twenty-five dollars for his travel expenses and a resolution of support from the Alabama Negro Baptist State Association. Because he stayed and preached a stirring sermon, the audience gave Boyd another twelve dollars. On his way back to Nashville, Boyd stopped in Chattanooga to tell

Vann about his appointment to the printing committee. Vann agreed to arrive in Nashville by the next Tuesday.[6]

Back in Nashville, Clark persuaded Boyd to preach at the Mount Olive Missionary Baptist Church's Sunday night services where Clark announced his unqualified support for the publishing venture. The worshippers were told to thank God for sending Boyd to Tennessee to do something positive for the race. The next day, Boyd met with Frost, Meeks, and Brandon to complete plans to print the materials. Boyd believed so strongly that he would gain approval for his plans, that he asked Frost for a letter of support.

The important day of Tuesday arrived. Vann traveled from Chattanooga. After Boyd and Clark escorted Vann from the train depot, they found that Gaines, the chairman of the Home Mission Board, had sent a telegram to direct Boyd not to proceed further with the publishing project without a quorum and approval of the printing committee. But Boyd knew parliamentary rules, and he knew how to use his power as secretary of the Home Mission Board which had given him the authority to appoint the members of the printing committee. Boyd and Clark had no intention of sending Vann back to Chattanooga without having a meeting. Boyd had to have his dealings with Frost and the printers sanctioned by the black Baptists. Boyd convinced W. L. Cansler, secretary of the Tennessee Negro Baptist Convention and a local public school teacher, to take Geter's seat. Boyd, Vann, and Clark sent a clever telegram to Gaines stating that Geter's seat on the committee had been filled and the committee would meet. They also informed Gaines that he must vote by proxy or agree to a replacement.[7]

The complex and quick maneuvers worked. The printing committee opened its meeting at ten o'clock with four members in Clark's office. Boyd gave a heart-stirring prayer. Then he read a telegram from Gaines, giving Boyd proxy to vote for him. Clark was elected temporary chairman. By common consent, Boyd was elected secretary and treasurer of the publishing venture. And Nashville became officially the site of the operations. Boyd briefed the printing committee about his failed efforts. He suggested that he try the Southern Baptists who had agreed through Frost to help the Negro Baptists. Frost had already agreed to give Boyd a letter to read to the committee, showing the southern Baptists' support. Encouraged by the reading of this letter, the printing committee agreed with Boyd's plans. After warning the members that Morris, Gaines, and maybe other preachers would try to stop the plans, Boyd asked the committee to approve a name for the operations. They selected the National Baptist Publishing Board as the official name.[8]

Boyd impressed all with his preparedness and organizational skills. He had laid the ground work to legitimize his dealings with the printers and the Reverend Frost. Now, Boyd's plans to publish black Baptist literature began to unfold.

Boyd had spent a week at Clark's home. During this time he had several visits with Frost, Bishop Smith, and others. To prevent wearing out his welcome at Clark's home, Boyd sought another place to board. He found a room at the home of the pastor of the Summer Street Baptist Church.

That night, Boyd boarded on High (9th Avenue North) Street at a local Baptist preacher's home where the pastor learned that Boyd had $6,000 worth of letters of credit from D. Sullivan and Company Bank of San Antonio and W. E. Robinson Brothers Bank of Palestine, Texas. Until now, Boyd had kept this information secret from all but his close friends. The credits were secured by land owned by Boyd and his wife, Harriett Albertine Moore. Mrs. Boyd had gained $1,000 through an injured brother who divided a two thousand dollar settlement with her. She gave Boyd the money to save and invest. Boyd placed properties and businesses in Harriett's name and took only living expenses from the profits. All Boyd's business enterprises were financed apparently by him and his family.[9]

The Longest Day

During the first day, Boyd and the Reverend Allen D. Hurt discussed plans to establish an office for the National Baptist Publishing Board. Hurt headed the First Colored Baptist Church on North Spruce (8th) Avenue. This church was Nashville's oldest and most influential black Baptist Church.

Boyd established a temporary National Baptist Publishing Board office in the parlor of the house where he boarded. The pastor's secretary, Lula I. Hobson, helped Boyd with the first day's work in the front room until 10:00 that first night. On the next morning, Hurt brought Lena Randal (DeMoss) to begin a long secretarial career with the National Baptist Publishing Board. Randal held membership at the First Colored Baptist Church. Hurt asked Boyd to pay Randal a weekly salary, but if he could not make the payments the First Colored Baptist Church would pay her. Hurt entered his buggy and drove away, leaving behind Boyd and Randal, the original National Baptist Publishing Board staff.[10]

The Reverend Boyd said that he liked order and good organization. Boyd also told Randal that he was irritable, high-tempered, mean, cross, snappish and short, "but if ever I hurt your feelings, all you have to do is to convince me that I did wrongfully, and you will find me as ready to apologize as a little child."[11] After briefing Randal about other assignments, Boyd left for his meetings with Frost and the printers. Randal began opening Boyd's mail.

After seeing Frost, Boyd went to C. S. Smith's office. Through careful diplomacy, he informed Smith that the printing committee did not accept the gracious offer to house the Baptist operations in the AME building. Smith offered to introduce Boyd to the printers at the Methodist publishing house, if necessary. Boyd thanked Smith and left to continue his visits.

The Reverend Boyd visited the Brown Building at 408 Cedar Street in the middle of the traditional black business district. The custodian, Dr. J. B. Singleton, agreed to show Boyd two vacant rooms. Recently, in 1892, Singleton had received his degree in dentistry from Meharry Medical Department of Central Tennessee College, and now he struggled to establish a practice. He would become a successful businessman and a deacon in the First Colored Baptist Church. Boyd agreed to rent the rooms. A First Colored Baptist Church deacon supposedly owned the building. The Reverend Hurt became Boyd's security for the lease. Singleton contacted First Colored Baptist Church deacon, William T. Hightower, about placing some matting on the bare floors to improve Boyd's office.[12]

Some nineteen years later, however, Hightower joined the anti-NBPB faction within the National Baptist Convention. Hightower was a junk dealer and a powerful force in the First Colored Baptist Church. He led the ouster of the Reverend J. E. Purdy in 1893, helped to reorganize the First Colored Baptist Church after the congregational split, and mortgaged his properties to help finance and sustain a new church edifice in 1896. For now, Hightower, like Singleton, understood Boyd's struggles and sought to help him get established in Nashville.

After doing business with Dr. Singleton, Boyd went to Meeks' office at University Printing Company. They arranged to print sixty thousand pieces of stationery including letterheads and envelopes. Meeks also presided over the Southwestern Printing Company. He arranged to have Boyd's handwritten signature printed on the letters so that "it would take an expert to know that it was not handwritten."[13] This action saved Boyd from having to sign every letter by hand.

Boyd offered his letters of credit to Meeks to guarantee payment because the National Baptist Convention, the Home Mission Board and its printing committee had given him no money for the operations. Boyd also told Meeks that he and Harriett owned a one hundred acre farm in Longstreet, Texas, property in San Antonio, twelve city lots and a funeral home in Palestine, and some property in Spokane, Washington. Meeks agreed to keep the information confidential.

Boyd informed Meeks about the opposition within the National Baptist Convention, the American Baptist Home Mission Society, and the American Baptist Publication Society. Boyd said: "I am Secretary of the Home Mission Board of the National Baptist Convention, and that Board has not one dollar in its treasury; hence, they have not put a dime in my hands. As to this Publishing Committee or Board, as we are now going to call it, I suppose if it were put to a vote today in the convention, it would be voted down by an overwhelming majority."[14] Meeks, a former member of the southern Baptist Sunday School Board, acknowledged the opposition and signaled his eagerness to defeat the northern Baptist "Yankees." Especially, Meeks seemed amazed about Boyd's use of his wife's name for business deals and his business sense. The two men agreed to print ten thousand intermediate quarterlies, ten thousand primary quarterlies, and eighty thousand primary and intermediate leaflets. The Reverend Boyd agreed to pay Meeks no later than January 15, 1897.[15] All who met Richard H. Boyd truly were amazed at his energy and determination for a man of 53 years.

Leaving Meeks' office, The Reverend Boyd visited the head of Marshall and Bruce Printing Company. This was a notable company with state contracts. Boyd ordered blank books, pens, pencils, ink wells, and other supplies. He asked that the order be held until the publishing board was ready to begin operations in the Brown Building.[16]

Now Boyd walked to the Cumberland Telephone Company and bought telephone service for the Brown Building, a three story structure. Other Negro professionals, including Singleton, lived and worked in the Brown Building but had no telephone. They gladly agreed to use Boyd's phone and help pay the bill. Now all arrangements had been made to open the offices of the new National Baptist Publishing Board.

Arriving at the Brandon Printing Company, Boyd met with the owner and Meeks who had come over to reintroduce Boyd. Boyd ordered 72,000 copies of publications, periodicals, and covers. Meeks arranged for the engravings to be made at the Methodist publishing house. Possibly because Frost and Meeks personally took Boyd to the printing and publishing houses, Boyd was not cheated like some white merchants customarily treated black customers. Frost explained to the white business owners that he had a special interest in Boyd's "serious business."[17]

Next, Meeks introduced Boyd to the cashier (manager) of the City Savings Bank. The president personally invited Boyd into the office to discuss opening an account. They also stopped in the Merchants' Bank where Boyd opened an account with $400 cash and a letter of credit. The president told Boyd to "walk into the president's office anytime and sit at the desk and write without anybody bothering you."[18] The first day's work had ended.

When Boyd arrived at the boarding house, Lena Randal appeared to be disturbed because of the late hour. Boyd told her to leave and take the $100 received in the mails. "You are my private secretary, my bookkeeper, and my cashier," Boyd said.[19] To insure her safety, Boyd gave Lena a dime to ride the streetcar. He sat down and ate the supper that the lady of the house had prepared. Before going to bed, Boyd wrote a letter to Morris to explain the printing committee's decision to locate the publishing house in Nashville and the arrangements with Frost, Meeks, and Brandon. Now he went to sleep. The day was over, and a new black American company, the National Baptist Publishing Board, had been started.

NBPB's Office Operations Begin

On the next day, Boyd worked at the Brown Building. He met with the building's professional occupants: Singleton, T. G. Ewing, and W. R. Baker. Ewing worked as an attorney and held membership at the First Colored Baptist Church. Ewing agreed to have the telephone number (1236) placed in his name. The telephone was installed in the hall for all building personnel to use. Baker was a physician. Professor Cansler brought a lamp and two split-bottom chairs to help Boyd furnish the bare rooms. A deacon from the Mt. Olive Missionary Baptist Church gave Boyd a table. Lena hired a girl from the church to help address five thousand envelopes.[20] She and Boyd also hired Lillie Lawrence, the daughter of the Reverend Emanuel M. Lawrence, to help address the envelopes. A notable preacher in the National Baptist Convention, the Reverend Lawrence (1861-1929) became a trustee of local Roger Williams University.

Within a few days, Morris, the editor-in-chief, arrived in Nashville from Little Rock by train. Morris, Clark, Hurt, and four other local preachers visited Boyd's crude office complex. Boyd took Morris to see Meeks, Frost, and Brandon. Morris expressed concern that the National Baptist Convention had no money to pay for Boyd's orders. The white men remained silent about Boyd's letters of credit and the bank accounts. They assured Morris that they had confidence in Boyd's ability to succeed and pay the bills.[21]

Morris must have wondered about this strange behavior for white businessmen who had known Boyd, a black man, only a few weeks. Boyd had briefed his white creditors about Morris' skepticism and the inability of the National Baptist Convention to pay the bills. The men wanted to make sure, however, that Morris, the president of the National Baptist Convention, would support the publishing venture. The sanction of the largest black Baptist convention was a precondition for Southern Baptist Convention support. The new company's business success depended on a strong affiliation with the largest association of black Baptist churches.

After the tour and the conferences, Boyd escorted the Reverend Morris to the train station. Morris returned to Helena, Arkansas, via Memphis. With this necessary business behind him, Boyd returned his attention to making the final preparations to begin the company's operations. Boyd did not know, however, that Morris immediately contacted A. J. Rowland, secretary of the American Baptist Publication Society, and briefed Rowland all about the activities in Nashville.

Later in the day, Boyd visited the local black colleges. By 1896, Nashville was a black Mecca that included three freedmen colleges, schools originally established by northern missionaries for the former slaves. Black students came to Nashville to study medicine, nursing, theology, teaching, and other fields. These schools included Roger Williams University on Hillsboro Road, established by the American Baptist Home Mission Society of New York in 1866; Fisk University near Jefferson Street, established by northern Congregationalists and the Freedmen's Bureau in 1865; and Central Tennessee College, established by northern Methodists in 1868. Boyd persuaded the presidents to subscribe advertisements in the National Baptist Publishing Board's publications. Even though the American Baptist Home Mission Society controlled Roger Williams University, the president bought advertisements in Boyd's *Advanced Quarterly* and *Primary Quarterly*.[22]

The relationship between the National Baptist Publishing Board and the local Negro colleges would prove to be a good one. The publishing board's publications frequently featured Nashville's educational institutions. The black newspapers in Nashville, the *Clarion*, the *Globe*, and the National Baptist *Union-Review*, frequently featured one or more of the local colleges, complete with pictures and histories. This national publicity helped to make Nashville a black center for higher education. For several generations, the National Baptist Publishing Board published the Baptist *Union-Review* and the *Globe.*

With Deacon Brown's permission, Boyd employed a brick mason and a carpenter to build a window in the dark room. Electric lamps furnished crude light in that day and needed to be supplemented by natural light during the daylight hours. Lena worked in attorney Ewing's office during the two-day construction project. She also stored the National Baptist Publishing Board's money in Ewing's safe.[23]

The National Baptist Publishing Board's two-room office suite opened for the public with two chairs, a pine table, an ink well, and some pencils and paper. Meeks sent over a desk, requiring Boyd to pay only the drayman for hauling it. Boyd telephoned his son, Henry Allen, and directed him to ship a typewriter and two quilts from San Antonio, Texas. To begin officially the work day, Boyd knelt and prayed. He sent Lena on errands just before he prayed. When she returned, Boyd would smile and say: "Now, we start to work in our own office."[24]

The secret ritual of prayers continued until one day when Lena abruptly returned and found Boyd kneeling and praying. She insisted that Boyd include her in the morning prayers. The daily ritual of prayers in the National Baptist Publishing Board's offices became a tradition. When he built larger quarters for the publishing board, Boyd included a chapel for meetings and prayer services.

In the meantime, the Reverend Boyd moved from the boarding room to live in the publishing board's offices. He could not afford to spend any of his money on himself. For seventy-five cents Boyd bought a sleeping cot. His food supply consisted of bread and a bologna sausage. Each morning Boyd rose and folded the cot before Lena's arrival, about 9:30 a. m. After the day's work, Boyd prepared his bologna sausage over an open grate, and unfolded his sleeping cot. He soon found that Singleton and Ewing too lived and ate in their offices. Later, the three successful black men laughed about their early struggles, living in the Brown Building, and the bologna sausages they learned to share.[25]

Within days, the envelopes, letterheads, and order blanks arrived from the University Printing Press Company. The pine table was used to store the items. Bob Woods, superintendent of the Summer Street Baptist Church's Sunday school, donated an old office chair for Boyd's desk. Woods, who worked as a laundry fireman in the next building, came to work as the NBPB's fireman and engineer some two years later, and he remained with Boyd for nearly nine years. When Lena found it impossible to fold, address, and stuff thousands of envelopes, Singleton took a buggy and brought back Lena's friend, Julia McKinney. Julia had worked several years at the bindery for the local Methodist publishing house. She agreed to a salary of only $3 a week. Julia suggested that Boyd buy a "folding knife" from the Methodist publishing house. He took the suggestion which speeded up the folding process. Another young lady came to help fill 5,000 envelopes with circular letters, order blanks, and return envelopes. Boyd bought fifty dollars worth of stamps. The little staff stamped the envelopes and stuffed the mail sacks.[26]

The form letter was unusual, a classic beginning for the National Baptist Publishing Board. The letter asked black preachers and Sunday school super-intendents to help pass the message to others that the National Baptist Publishing Board had opened for business. Boyd's letter pleaded the idea of blacks supporting their own religious publishing house. He warned them, however, that the literature would not be cheaper than that sold by the white Sunday school publishing houses. The orders had to be accompanied by money orders.

The December 1, 1896, letter read as follows:

Dear Brother, Pastor or Superintendent:

Will you read this to your Church and Sunday School? If you are not now Pastor nor Superintendent, will you hand it to some Negro Baptist who you know to be a pastor or Superintendent, and who is in favor of the Negro Baptists doing something for themselves?

The Negro Baptists have been saying for six years that we need a PUBLISHING HOUSE of our own, and that as we have separate Churches, Sunday Schools, Associations and Conventions, both State and National, that we ought to have a separate Publishing House for these Schools and Churches; but the necessity is not the question now. Your Publishing Board was appointed in St. Louis last September, and was told to publish a series of Sunday School periodicals at the same prices that they have been paying. We were not asked to publish cheaper Periodicals or to cut the prices, therefore we will keep them at the same prices.

The men who are acting on this Publishing Board are: Rev. G. W. D. Gaines, Little Rock, Ark.; Rev. J. Geter, Little Rock, Ark.; Rev. C. H. Clark, D. D., Nashville, Tenn.; Rev. M. Vann, D. D., Ex-National President, Chattanooga, Tenn.; Rev. E. C. Morris, D. D., Editor and President of the National Convention, Helena, Ark.; Rev. R. H. Boyd, D. D., Secretary, San Antonio, Texas. These men, together with other members of the Board, have spared no labor or money to give the Negro Baptists first class Sunday School Periodicals that they will not be ashamed of.

I enclose you an Order Blank and Envelope with the name and price of all our Periodicals. Will you order at once and try them this Quarter? Do you think the Negro capable of doing something for himself? Will you try to help? Will you help the young Negro to be a self-respecting man by putting the Periodicals of his father's organization in his hands?

My dear brother, don't ask us to send you a sample copy. There are 10,000 Negro Baptist Sunday schools, and to send a copy to all, would be to us 50,000 copies. Just fill out your order for January, February and March, go to the Post Office, get a Money Order payable to the National Baptist Publishing Board, Nashville, Tenn., put them in the enclosed envelope and put a two-cent stamp on it, and you will get your Literature so that you can on the First Sunday in January, 1897, open a Negro Baptist Sunday School with Negro Baptist Literature, for the first time in American history.

Remember, my brother, we have 60,000 copies on hand, and if the Negro Baptists do not take it and pay for it, we are at a great loss. Praying, hoping, trusting, and believing that the return mail will bring the order from your Sunday School, I am

Your Brother,

Signed: R. H. Boyd
Secretary of the N.B.P.B., Nashville, Tenn.

On the next day, Boyd established his reputation for frugality in Nashville. He took a nickel streetcar ride to mail the sack full of letters in the post office. The white female clerk was already amazed that a Negro man had bought fifty dollars worth of stamps and wanted to pay for them with a check. The woman had hesitated to take Boyd's check. Now, here he came with a mail sack full of letters on his back. When a few more letters had to be mailed, Boyd threw the sack over his shoulder and walked to the post office much to the amusement of bystanders.[27] Little did these persons realize that the Reverend Boyd had established America's only black Baptist publishing house in Nashville.

Around December 15, the printers had the magazines ready. Orders began to arrive. Through the Christmas holidays, Boyd and his small staff filled the orders and sent them through the mail. Boyd also sent some free copies to Negro newspapers which printed articles about this new black Baptist publishing company. Singleton and the other residents in the Brown Building became thoroughly delighted to see so much mail and many stacks of periodicals in Boyd's tiny offices. When not answering correspondence and cleaning the offices, Boyd helped Lena and the girls to wrap the packages. Boyd hired the Reverend I. J. Jordan to help ship materials and later to be a missionary to promote the National Baptist Publishing Board's Sunday school materials.[28]

The first staff for the National Baptist Publishing Board consisted of five persons. These included Richard H. Boyd, I. J. Jordan, Julia McKinney (Singleton), Lillie Lawrence, and Lena Randal (DeMoss). Through Christmas the little staff worked to build a company and its business.

On the afternoon of December 31, 1896, a box arrived by express mail. Harriett A. Boyd and Indiana Dickson, Boyd's mother, had prepared a Christmas dinner of turkey, baked chicken, pound cake, tea (sweet) cakes, homemade light bread, and other goodies. On the next day, New Year's Day, Boyd invited the clerks, Singleton, Ewing, and Baker to dine with him. They covered the table with wrapping paper; the food was served; and a prayer to eat was offered. They all dined sufficiently, and there was plenty left for Boyd to eat for two or three days more.[29]

In later years, the informal event on January 1, 1897, became a traditional New Year's dinner at the National Baptist Publishing Board. The Reverend Boyd gave the prayer and sat at the head of the table. He viewed the publishing board's employees as well as Singleton, Ewing, and Baker like a family. In future years after the event became more formal, the New Year's dinner for the National Baptist Publishing Board's employees and friends required several tables, a caterer, and the board's chapel where workers removed the chairs for the large event.

On January 10, 1897, Boyd contacted the Reverend Morris and informed him about the progress of operations and the $900 owed to the printers by the publishing board. On January 15, Morris arrived in Nashville by train. Solomon Parker Harris, an Arkansas attorney, accompanied Morris who explained that Harris was there to help Boyd in the NBPB's offices. Boyd seemed a little irritated by this, but he simply told Harris that if he came here to work then grab a broom and start cleaning the room. Harris obeyed, cleaning the adjacent

First NBPB Staff,
1898 (NBPBLA)

Richard H. Boyd,
1896 (NBR)

room which Boyd had rented to expand the board's operations. In this way, Harris became a new employee and later the founder of the publishing board's bookkeeping department. Until 1915, Harris remained a trusted employee at the National Baptist Publishing Board.[30]

Morris called a meeting of local Baptist preachers to review Boyd's request for $900. They planned a crude process of collecting donations from the poor local preachers. They found out, however, that Boyd had mailed checks to the printers on January 15, like he had promised his creditors. This really upset the preachers. Boyd replied that as secretary-treasurer of the NBPB he would fix salaries, pay bills, and operate the business or resign. The Reverend Clark strongly supported Boyd's reasoning. The preachers could say no more because they had no money, and the National Baptist Convention had no money to pay the bills. The meeting ended.[31]

On the following day, President Morris prepared to leave for Arkansas. Boyd gave Morris a $50 check to cover his last two trips to Nashville. Morris expected his expenses to and from Nashville to be paid by the publishing board. And the publishing board complied because the Reverend Morris deserved reimbursement of expenses for serving as editor-in-chief. Morris submitted an occasional editorial for the board's publications.[32]

Early Problems

Meanwhile, Boyd's actions perplexed the preachers and Morris. Where did Boyd get the money? Although the action strengthened Boyd's argument that he be allowed to manage the operation without interference, he missed the opportunity to force Morris, the National Baptist Convention, and the preachers to help finance the NBPB's operations. It seemed that Boyd was just testing Morris and the National Baptist Convention preachers and expected no real financial support from them. Boyd was prepared to finance the operations. But his strategy would backfire because the preachers began to think that the National Baptist Publishing Board was a money-making operation, a "gold mine for Boyd." How else could Boyd raise this much money, the preachers asked one another?

Boyd prepared quarterly financial statements for the Home Mission Board and sent the statements to HMB chairman Robinson in Little Rock to be reported to the National Baptist Convention. The National Baptist Publishing Board successfully met its expenses and realized excess revenues for the first quarter. Yet Boyd's venture received criticism.

Some persons claimed that the secretary of the American Baptist Publication Board began a campaign to discredit Boyd's operation. The secretary, A.J. Rowland, wrote a strong letter to the black churches and Sunday schools, accusing Boyd of deceiving the Negro Baptists. Rowland revealed that Boyd's material was really the literature published by the white Southern

Baptist Convention's Sunday School Board. Twelve thousand copies of the *Christian Banner,* a black Baptist paper, broadcast this anti-NBPB message to black America. The American Baptist Publication Society had more than two dozen colporters and field missionaries working among southern blacks, and these persons helped to campaign against the Negro Baptist publishing board's effort. The Dallas *Western Star* called Boyd's effort "Negro Backs and White Man's Brains."[33] A few friendly newspapers, the Little Rock *Baptist Vanguard* (edited by Joseph A. Booker) and the *Baptist Herald* (edited by L. L. Campbell) of Austin, Texas, defended Boyd's side of the story. Booker was former secretary of the Home Mission Board and Campbell was an official in Texas' "new convention." President Morris also continued to show visible support for Boyd's effort to publish black Sunday school literature.

True, Boyd used the printing plates from the Southern Baptist Convention's Sunday School Board. But really he intended to write, print, and publish all black Baptist literature when the National Baptist Publishing Board achieved that ability. Boyd used the Sunday School Board's literature for expediency. He needed to get Sunday school materials to the black churches right away and meet the January, 1897, publication date set by the National Baptist Convention. Boyd needed to affiliate with a large Baptist convention to give credibility to his efforts to publish literature for the Baptist denomination. Yet, his view that he was establishing a company for the "black Baptist denomination" and not specifically for the administration of the National Baptist Convention would cause problems for the National Baptist Publishing Board.

Boyd intended to go further than the white Baptist religious publishing houses and "print" the National Baptist Publishing Board's publications. Really, the Southern Baptist Convention's Sunday School Board did not own its own printing plant at the time, and even the American Baptist Publication Society used private printers to publish its Sunday school literature. Therefore, the American Baptist Publication Society's leaders set a higher standard for Boyd, a black man, than they set for themselves.

Boyd knew that he must establish a distribution procedure and build a communication network between the National Baptist Publishing Board and the Negro Baptist churches, their pastors and Sunday school superintendents. Particularly, Boyd and the publishing board had to build "confidence in colored people" to trust their own leaders to furnish the black churches with Sunday school materials. Boyd and others felt that Rowland, and many other northern white Baptist leaders wanted the former slaves and their descendants to maintain a paternalistic relationship with them and rely on the white church leaders to supply Sunday school materials and Bibles to the Negro churches.

Again, the movement by Boyd and others in Texas to abandon the American Baptist Publication Society started because the white company refused to publish essays and books by black preachers around 1890. But the ABPS temporarily defused a black national revolt against them by agreeing to publish a crude anthology of black preachers' sermons and comments. The head of the American National Baptist Convention, E. M. Brawley, edited *The Negro Baptist Pulpit* (Philadelphia: ABPS, 1890). Brawley compiled the book in Nashville where he used several local black preachers including Randall B. Vandavell [Vandavall], pastor of First Colored Baptist Church of East Nashville, and M. W. Gilbert, pastor of First Colored Baptist Church. The book did not become an important work, but it appeased many black leaders in the black Baptist convention.

To rely on black writers to compose and edit the Negro Sunday school materials became Boyd's next logical step. This step would help to disarm some of Boyd's critics who supported the ABPS. But the publication of books, tracts, and other materials by Negro preachers and other black authors became the National Baptist Publishing Board's most expensive operation, often losing money. Yet the National Baptist Publishing Board continued this department to give black authors an outlet for their works.

Boyd persuaded President Morris to name an editorial board: J. T. Brown of Montgomery; E. M. Brawley of Georgia; C. H. Parrish of Kentucky; W. A. Credit of Philadelphia; C. O. Booth of Alabama; Mrs. M. C. Kenney of Tennessee; Mrs. E. M. Abner of Texas; Miss M. V. Cook of Kentucky; R. DeBaptist of Illinois; E. R. Carter of Georgia; Walter H. Brooks of Washington; D. C.; W. F. Graham of Virginia; J. L. Cohron of Missouri; and Mrs. Lucy Cole of Virginia.[34]

Significantly, the Negro Baptists involved women in its board and committee memberships. Women comprised the largest number of black Baptist members. They operated auxiliaries which performed home and foreign mission work. And the women also wrote books, essays, tracts, and literature. Boyd carefully involved women, the Baptist denomination's key constituents, in the publishing board's work.

The National Baptist Publishing Board had to gain the ability to print its own work. This ability would be acquired within the next two years, a feat that astounded the publishing board's critics. Printing operations would cause the NBPB to have to abandon the small quarters in the Brown Building. The National Baptist Publishing Board would continue to expand its printing plant, buying the most modern machines available and building new facilities and additions. Meantime, Boyd continued to print materials by contracting with white printers and publishers.

Boyd had to get the quarterlies, the *Teachers' Monthly*, and picture lesson cards to the churches with regularity to build the National Baptist Publishing Board's credibility. Boyd sent a letter to Sunday school personnel and pastors to notify them that the first materials were white Baptist publications, but now the National Baptist Publishing Board had an editorial board (list enclosed) and could begin producing its own Negro-authored literature. Boyd also distributed circulars to announce the new development. He found that his chosen lithography company held a contract with the American Baptist Publication Society, and the company would not print Boyd's lithograph pictures without permission from Rowland. Boyd sent a check to the American Baptist Publication Society to cover the cost of the first lithographs.[35]

In February 1897, Boyd turned his attention to his family. He took the trains to Texas, stopping in Memphis, Little Rock, Texarkana, Palestine, Dallas, and Austin. Boyd used these ten days to gain support and business for the National Baptist Publishing Board. He distributed free literature along the route and made speeches at churches. Boyd had been home just two days when a telegraph arrived from S. P. Harris. Trouble! The American Baptist Publication Society would not allow the company to publish Boyd's materials! Return to Nashville, immediately![36]

Boyd headed toward Nashville. He stopped at Guadalupe College where one of his children attended school, and Boyd visited New Orleans' Baptist pastors and churches. In the latter city, he encountered the Reverend S. N. Vass, black field secretary for the American Baptist Publication Society. Boyd recalled that the Reverend Jordan had pushed Boyd into a buggy at the Birmingham train station in early November, 1896, to avoid just this gentleman, S. N. Vass. With a certain degree of boldness, according to Boyd, Vass offered Boyd a position with the American Baptist Publication Society. Boyd held his anger and quietly refused the offer. When Boyd reached Mobile, Alabama, the Reverend A. N. McEwen raised money to pay the train fare to Nashville. Instead, Boyd headed to Montgomery and the Dexter Avenue Baptist Church where another collection contributed to his efforts at the NBPB. The Dexter Avenue Baptist Church, Montgomery's most influential black Baptist Church, included the most educated local blacks. Educated blacks believed that every effort should be made to educate and bring the printed word to the black masses. Then Boyd traveled to Birmingham and stayed over for a local preachers' meeting where he gained more support and a small collection.[37]

Boyd's actions indicated his strong belief that the publishing board project was an effort to involve all Negro Baptists. He did not view the project as solely a National Baptist Convention operation. Boyd envisioned the distribution of Sunday school literature to black Baptists within and without the National Baptist Convention and even outside the United States and wherever black Baptist churches existed.

Harris and Clark met Boyd when he arrived in Nashville on a Tuesday morning. "What shall we do about picture cards and Bible lesson picture cards" they asked? Boyd calmly replied: "Let us not stop here to build bridges."[38] The meeting adjourned. Boyd engaged in private prayer.

A telephone call arrived from Frost, informing Boyd that the Wilde Publishing Company of Boston had sent the Baptist Sunday School Publishing Board five thousand too many picture lesson cards. Boyd agreed to take the surplus cards if the company would agree to print "National Baptist Publishing Board" on the next quarter's orders. This was agreed upon by the three parties. When the Reverend Clark returned the next day, he was absolutely amazed to see Boyd's office filled with packages of picture cards.[39]

Boyd's failure to get the American Baptist Publication Society's picture cards was already news in the Negro papers. The stories appeared to destroy Boyd's credibility and the blacks' confidence in the new National Baptist Publishing Board. To counter the bad publicity, Boyd sent a letter to all black Baptist churches, explaining the availability of the Sunday School Board's cards at a reduced price, 75 cents instead of $1. The strategy worked, and the literature was sold.[40] The officials of the American Baptist Publication Society were outdone.

Rowland told Frost that Boyd's publishing effort represented "a race feeling which has been excited and fostered by certain brethren [Boyd] and which we cannot but think disastrous upon the future relations of the two races in this country."[41] These words appeared in a letter to Frost on December 1, 1896. Rowland criticized Frost for helping Boyd, and told Frost that the American Baptist Publication Society had rejected Boyd's request to print his materials. Indeed "...It was difficult for the Northern white missionary establishment to see how blacks could save themselves," said James M. Washington in his book, *Frustrated Fellowship: The Black Baptist Quest for Social Power* (1986), page 81.

Boyd gained support for his publishing venture by urging blacks to publish Baptist materials for blacks by blacks. But Boyd's operation had the potential of taking much black business from Rowland's publishing society which wanted to maintain the paternalistic relationship with the freed blacks. Apparently Rowland believed that blacks were incapable of writing, printing, and publishing their own church materials. Boyd proved him wrong. Many whites, even the liberal ones, sometimes despised competent Negroes.

One white man and a leader in the Southern Baptist Convention, J. M. Frost, remained steadfast in his support of Boyd's effort. On December 8, 1896, Frost answered Rowland's letter and said: "I regret the tone and spirit which it [your letter] manifests concerning the movement of our colored brethren to publish Sunday-school literature. If you knew the facts in the case I am sure you would feel and speak differently."[42] Frost argued that by placing the National Baptist Publishing Board's imprint on picture cards, Boyd did only what the white religious house publishers, including Rowland, had done. And Frost assured Rowland that the southern Sunday School Board stood ready to help the colored brethren and wished Boyd God speed.

When the Southern Baptist Convention held its meeting in Wilmington, North Carolina, in May 1897, Frost read Rowland's letter to the audience and published it in the convention's proceedings. Frost urged the Southern Baptist Convention's delegates to refuse to be baited by such race talk. He introduced Boyd to the convention delegates, who welcomed the black secretary of the National Baptist Publishing Board. Frost said: "We were glad to see them [the blacks] undertake so momentous an enterprise, and earnestly wish them the greatest possible success."[43]

When they heard about Rowland's letter, some National Baptist Convention supporters of the National Baptist Publishing Board became disturbed particularly about three parts of the letter. First, Rowland said that the Reverend Morris had written to him about Boyd's efforts to set up a Negro publishing board in Nashville with the Southern Baptist Convention's support. Although some persons wondered if Morris truly supported the black publishing venture, others knew that President Morris merely extended diplomatic courtesy by informing the northern Baptists about the plans to work with the Southern Baptists. Secondly, Rowland's letter raised the issue of Negro conspiracy against white people. Thirdly, Rowland's letter to Frost indicated that he assumed that white people should stick together and not help Negroes to establish publishing companies and become independent of white paternalism.

Success: NBPB Weathers the Storm

For the first period, January 15-April 15, 1897, the National Baptist Publishing Board received $1,774.06 in revenues and spent $1,518.77. The publishing board earned $255.29 in excess revenues for its first effort.[44] Whatever excess revenues the National Baptist Publishing earned, Boyd and the committee members placed in a "sinking fund" or reserve. No dividends and personal profits were reaped by officers and board members. Most of the excess revenues were placed into plant modernization, new equipment, and additional employees and training.

For now, most of the National Baptist Publishing Board's assets were based on Boyd's personal finances, leases, and purchases of properties. But the company was owned neither by him nor by the National Baptist Convention. Boyd conceptualized a publishing company for "the Negro Baptists of the country." Secretary Boyd published annual statements about the National Baptist Publishing Board's financial condition, its progress, and its problems. These statements appeared in the official journals for the annual sessions of the National Baptist Convention. Boyd showed income and expenses and how monies had been used to build and sustain the operations.

The NBPB's first quarterly report read as follows:
April 17, 1987
Our circulation has been as follows:

Baptist Convention Teachers	6,000
Advanced Quarterlies	20,000
Lesson Leaflets	60,000
Intermediate Quarterlies	10,000
Primary Quarterlies	15,000
Bible Lesson Pictures	1,500
Picture Lesson Cards	78,000
Total copies of periodicals circulated	180,000

The above figures did not include the Bibles, catechisms, song books, and verse cards. Boyd estimated the first circulation at 200,500 pieces of literature. His office had sent eight thousand circular letters, eight thousand order blanks, and an identical number of addressed envelopes since January 15. Boyd had personally written about one thousand letters. More than 196 letters arrived daily at the National Baptist Publishing Board.[45]

The white printing shops in Nashville continued to produce the NBPB's materials. The NBPB's staff processed the orders and shipped the materials. Six black men and women worked in three small rooms to perform the enormous tasks associated with the communication and distribution systems for the National Baptist Publishing Board. They worked with dogmatic loyalty and dedication to the mission of supplying Sunday school literature to black Baptists in America. In tribute, Boyd said to this small staff:

> I want here to commend to you each of the faithful clerks in this office, who have shown that they have been personally interested in this work, and no hour named by me has been too early to open the office and none too late to close it. If the states were searched and the schools were commanded to produce a better corp of clerks, they could not be found; and, if you find anything about the office commendable, to them belongs the credit, especially my faithful cashier [Randal] who has been with me from the beginning, and my bookkeeper [Harris], who has laid the foundation for our future system of bookkeeping in this office....[46]

In his report to the Home Mission Board and Morris, Boyd expressed the need for a stenographer, another mail room, and a job press to print materials. Boyd expressed his desire to improve the staff's salaries. The requests found no response because the young National Baptist Convention had no money to give to the publishing project.

Now it was time to "prepare our periodicals and get ready for the quarter beginning July 1," 1897, said Boyd.[47] The publishing company in Boston kept its part of the agreement and sent the lesson cards with the imprint "National Baptist Publishing Board, R. H. Boyd, Secretary." The black members of the new editorial board had prepared editorial squibs and other contributions for the *Teachers' Monthly* and the quarterlies. The publishing board began to realize the dream to produce "Negro-authored" Baptist literature.

Boyd made plans to report to the National Baptist Convention's annual meeting in Boston, September, 1897. He selected the Reverends Vann and Gaines to give the first report. Boyd designed this tactic to keep the opposition from focusing on any one personality, Boyd. But Vann passed away. Gaines was not available. So Boyd had to give the report.

The Reverend Boyd impressed the delegates so that no distractions took place. Even Rowland, who attended the Negro Baptist convention, congratulated Boyd for the National Baptist Publishing Board's excellent report. The black masses, the common delegates at the convention, seemed impressed and proud to hear that their own Baptist publishing house had become operational and successful.

Boyd's position within the National Baptist Convention was strengthened through a reorganization of the Home Mission Board. The convention's delegates appointed the Reverend J. P. Robinson of Arkansas as chairman of the Home Mission Board. The Reverend Robinson had pledged his loyalty to Boyd, and he supported the efforts to build a strong National Baptist Publishing Board. Boyd's friend, the Reverend Hurt of Nashville, joined the Home Mission Board. The newly organized Home Mission Board supported secretary Boyd's plans to unify the operations of the HMB and the NBPB for missionary and Sunday school activities.[48] This would strengthen the publishing board but it would cause some of the pro-ABPS black preachers to find fault in Boyd and the black publishing house.

At the National Baptist Convention's 1898 annual meeting in Kansas City, Missouri, President Morris defended the National Baptist Publishing Board. He said:

> Notwithstanding we were accused of issuing 'backs which covered white men's brains,' in less than two years...we are turning out more than 2,000 periodicals each quarter.... We can no longer be regarded as mere consumers in the literary world but that we may be justly termed producers.[49]

By now the National Baptist Publishing Board had taken over the publication of the annual proceedings for the National Baptist Convention at no expense to the convention.

NBPB Begins Own Printing Operations

Boyd hired several other staff members to begin actual printing of National Baptist Publishing Board materials. Dock A. Hart, the half-brother of Evans Tyree, a Bishop in the African Methodist Episcopal Church, became the board's expert printer. Hart had worked at the Brandon Printing Company, but the whites made him do janitorial work. Boyd offered Hart fifty cents less per week than he had been paid by the whites, but he gave Hart the chance to become a master printer. Joseph Oliver Battle, fresh from school in Chattanooga, was hired as the errand boy. The young staff began printing operations in the midst of economic depressions and recessions which worked ironically in favor of the National Baptist Publishing Board.

Boyd began buying equipment. In a few years, he expanded the National Baptist Publishing Board's facilities. He heard about the foreclosure of the Southern News Printing Company on Deaderick Street and hired a white man to place the National Baptist Publishing Board's bid. For $2,100 Boyd received the equipment, including a ten horsepower electric motor, a large Cottrell flatbed cylinder press, five printers' racks, composing stones, and many other items. Boyd's creditor, the University Printing Press Company, also went broke. Boyd bought $3,500 worth of this company's machinery. He also bought the bankrupt Enterprise Printing Company. It was time for the National Baptist Publishing Board to move from the small quarters in the Brown Building.

The white widow who owned the property that Boyd had intended to use found out that Boyd, a Negro, was operating the Enterprise Printing Company. She refused to accept his check for the lease. Boyd contacted J. G. Kirkpatrick, agent for Major W. H. Leickhardt, about the Leickhardt residence on Market (Second Avenue) and Locust Streets. This property was bought for $10,000 in six percent, fourteen year bonds. The publishing board also borrowed money for another building behind the Leickhardt structure. Later the board leased the Leickhardt Drugstore across the street and property across the alley. Mrs. Harriett A. Boyd sold a lot to the National Baptist Publishing Board for $1,500. A steam plant was placed on this property in 1899. For a time, Boyd and his family lived in the plant to save money and secure the place.

At the National Baptist Convention's 1899 annual meeting in Nashville, Morris continued his attack on the northern white Baptist organizations that had accused Boyd and the National Baptist Publishing Board of racial division and deception. Morris said: "The color line has been drawn by the establishment of churches and schools for the 'colored people' and the employment of [colored] missionaries...to the colored people."[50] Morris argued that the white Baptists had divided themselves along regional lines of

NBPB's Plant (NBPBLA)

prejudice, whereas the black Baptists had united successfully into a truly national Baptist convention.

Naturally the American Baptist Home Society and the American Baptist Publication Society felt betrayed when Boyd and other black leaders dared become independent without their permission. And the southern white Baptists gladly took advantage of the situation, helping Boyd but also helping themselves by rebuilding their pre-Civil War communication network with southern Negro Baptist churches. Boyd got the help he needed from the white southern Baptists to establish the National Baptist Publishing Board, and the Southern Baptist Convention gained a victory when the northern Baptists lost influence with southern black Baptist churches.

The National Baptist Publishing Board entered the book-making business, a nearly unknown business for blacks. Between 1899 and 1901, the publishing board produced twenty-four book titles, including James H. Eason, *Pulpit and Platform Efforts: Sanctifications vs. Fanaticism* (1899); R. H. Boyd, *Pastor's Guide and Parliamentary Rules* (1900); Allen D. Hurt, *The Beacon Lights of Tennessee Baptists* (1900); *Golden Gems: A Song Book for the Church Choir, The Pew, and Sunday School* (1901); E. C. Morris, *Sermons, Address, and Reminiscences and Important Correspondence* (1901), including pictures of eminent ministers and scholars; Lewis G. Jordan, *Up the Ladder in Foreign Missions* (1901); J. Brown Garnett's *Don'ts and Woman's Influence* (1901).[51]

Between 1902 and 1905, the National Baptist Publishing Board company published many other titles including the following: Silas Floyd, *Life of Charles T. Walker, D. D. (The Black Surgeon), Pastor of Mt. Olive Church, New York City* (1902); R. H. Boyd and William Rosborough, eds., *The National Baptist Hymnal*, 3rd edition (1903); Jacob T. Brown, *Theological Kernels* (1903); Eugene Carter, *Once a Methodist, Now a Baptist* (1905).

The publishing board performed a valuable service by printing books by black authors. The early books represented a virtual storehouse of history about early twentieth century black Baptists. At least the publications brought pride to a once depressed people.

Boyd had trouble trying to sustain the expensive book publishing business, although he continued the operation. The board simply did not have the money to hire editors and staff members to publish manuscripts, sermons, and works by preachers. Too many preachers asked to have their sermons printed, and most of the writers wanted the board to bear the expenses for printing books and booklets that were not profitable. To avoid liability for the preachers' sermonizing and the contents of their manuscripts, the publishing board preferred to own publishing rights, not copyrights. Boyd eventually curtailed the book publishing operations also because the company lacked enough staff members to produce a full range of books and reprint outdated editions.[52] Yet the NBPB filled a void for black Baptist writers that the white

ABPS had refused to fill.

The National Baptist Publishing Board's business expanded faster than skilled staff members could be hired. Boyd had difficulty in hiring skilled clerical personnel and mechanics to operate the board's modern machinery. He blamed the situation on the white labor unions. He said: "Labor unions and organized societies have...shut out Negro boys and black girls from entering these places as apprentices."[53] The National Baptist Publishing Board decided to take inexperienced young men and women and train them to use the machinery. Many of the new trainees gained enough experience only to leave and work for other companies and teach at training schools. The National Baptist Publishing Board had many former employees teaching printing in the Negro schools and colleges throughout the region. To partly solve his problem of training enough blacks in printing and other mechanics, Boyd and his son, Henry Allen, supported the local movement to persuade the state to establish the Tennessee State Agricultural and Industrial Normal School for Negroes in Nashville (1909).

Boyd knew well that the issue of race affected the publishing board's ability to expand, and, it affected Negro progress in general. He said: "The race question is one of the most perplexing problems that confronts the American people."[54] Boyd believed that black-Americans were the victims of a mockery of citizenship. To counter the debilitating effects of white racism, Boyd said:

> The Negro must furnish his Sunday-school with religious knowledge, his choirs with music, and his firesides and parlors with wholesome literature, written and manufactured by his own energy. The literature that is best for the Caucasian of today is not always best for our children, under the present [Jim Crow] crisis. Whatever is taught in the Sunday-schools of this generation will be the doctrine of the church in the next generation.[55]

The National Baptist Publishing Board became a mission to help uplift blacks and educate them about the Baptist religion. Boyd directed the Baptists to teach black children to defend Baptist doctrine, obey laws and government, and become good citizens and Christians. He said that all angels were not white and all devils were not black. With this logic, Boyd published the picture lesson cards with black characters to give black children some positive images through biblical and religious stories. Later Boyd would manufacture Negro dolls in the publishing board's facilities, making him more vulnerable to his critics who claimed that the National Baptist Publishing Board was a profit-making business for Boyd. The publishing board formed Negro Doll Clubs to train young black girls and instill racial pride in them.

Because they became concerned about Boyd's alleged wealth and the lack of their involvement with the NBPB's leadership, the critics became blinded to the extraordinary mission of the publishing board. So paradoxically the progress of the National Baptist Publishing Board and Boyd's new influence became the praise and the envy of black Baptist leaders.

At the September 12-17, 1900, National Baptist Convention meeting in Richmond, the Reverend W. H. Sherwood titled his address "Why Negro Baptists Should Support Their Own Institutions," particularly the publishing board. President Morris's address included further rebuttal to the continuing attacks by the pro-American Baptist Publication Society preachers. Morris said:

> ...Allow me to say that the supplementary institutions planted by the colored Baptists do not seek to supplant those formed by our friends [the ABPS], but rather to augment and enlarge the opportunities of and for our race. It is necessary that there be mission boards, publication boards, and educational boards, colleges, seminaries, academies, etc., owned and operated by the Negroes, as it is for them to own houses to live in or to have newspapers, or any other enterprise necessary to develop the business side of the race.[56]

President Morris praised the accomplishments of the Home Mission Board and the National Baptist Publishing Board both under Boyd's leadership and management. Morris said: "As was expected, criticism came thick and fast, but our manager [Boyd], a man who lays no claim to an [extensive] education, was well prepared to receive all that came. And permit me to say that to his indomitable courage, coupled with his vast store of common sense, is due much of the success of that enterprise."[57]

Given the recent and turbulent history of the national Baptist convention organizations (1840-1894), no one knew how long the newly organized National Baptist Convention would prevail until regional factions and political cliques took charge and destroyed another national black Baptist convention. Boyd knew the mentality of many of the Negro preachers. He accordingly built protective systems into the National Baptist Publishing Board's organization to defend against the destructive tendencies of men who suffered the psychological legacy of slavery, a fear of success syndrome. No one knew how far the pro-ABPS and anti-NBPB forces within the convention intended to go.

Incorporation of the NBPB

The chief way to protect the new publishing board was to secure a charter to allow the company to become a corporation, an institution that could perpetuate itself without outside interference and continue through generations. During the summer of 1898, Boyd, his staff, the board members, and an attorney drafted a charter of incorporation. In early August, the Home Mission Board and the printing committee approved the draft. The charter was reviewed and registered in the Davidson County Court. Then it was filed and registered in the Office of the Secretary of State where the seal of the State of Tennessee was affixed on August 15, 1898.

The charter made the National Baptist Publishing Board a corporate business affiliated with the black Baptist denomination. Essentially with incorporation, the National Baptist Publishing Board became a person, one who could sue and be sued, own and sell property, sustain itself, and select its own leadership. The National Baptist Publishing Board became a separate entity to service the black Baptist denomination.

The Charter

Be it known that we, R. H. Boyd, E. C. Morris, C. H. Clark, J. P. Robinson, G. M. Moore, E. J. Fisher, J. E. Knox, and G. W. D. Gaines, and their successors chosen under the rules and regulations of the National Baptist Convention of the United States, and holding office under the rules, usages and regulations of the said Convention are hereby constituted a body politic and corporate by the name and style of the National Baptist Publishing Board of said conventions for the Baptist Churches or denomination. This corporation is organized for the purpose of establishment, support, and maintenance of Sunday School undertakings on the part of said church, and to print or purchase and disseminate by gift or sale religious literature. Said corporation shall have power to establish and support religious Sunday schools, purchase, own, or lease land on which to build houses in which to conduct the business of the board, to borrow money when necessary for conduct of business of the corporation, to employ all necessary agents, to solicit, collect or receive subscriptions in money or otherwise, legacies, or devices to be used in forwarding any or all of the proposed set out or herein provided for, to purchase, have printed, edit, conduct, and carry on for Sunday school purposes and uses, a magazine or magazines, paper or papers, books, tracts, Sunday school periodicals, together with other religious and denominational paper or papers, and doing a general missionary and charitable work, etc. to rent or purchase a room or rooms or buildings for office and work of the corporation, and all necessary appliances, fixtures, and material for conducting business of the corporation, to rent or purchase all necessary printing presses, type, material and stationery and to disseminate by sale or gift all literature deemed necessary for carrying on the work of the corporation. But in all things to be governed by the rules and regulations of the convention of the Baptist Churches or denomination, so far as same are consistent with the constitution and laws of the State of Tennessee and of these United States.

The general powers of said corporators shall be to sue and be sued by the corporate name; to have and use a common seal, which it may alter at pleasure, if no common seal, then the signature of the corporation by any duly authorized officer shall be legal and binding to purchase and hold or receive by gift, device, or bequest, in addition to the personal property owned by the corporation, real estate necessary for the transaction of the corporate business; and also to purchase and to accept any real estate in payment or part payment of any debt due the corporation, and to sell the same; to make by-laws and all rules and regulations not inconsistent with the constitution of the United States of America and the State of Tennessee and not contrary to the constitution, rules, and regulations of said conventions, churches or denomination, deemed expedient for the management of the corporate affairs, to appoint such subordinate officers in addition, and to designate the names of the officers and governing body of said conventions, churches, or denomination, as the business of the corporation may require and as are not forbidden by the rules and regulations of said convention, church or denomination, and to designate the names of the officers and their compensation.

The said five or more incorporators shall within a convenient time after the registration of this charter in the office of the Secretary of State, elect from their number a President, Secretary, and Treasurer, or the two last offices may be combined into one, said officers and the other incorporators to constitute the first Board of Directors; in all elections each member to be entitled to one vote, either in person or by proxy, and the result to be determined by the majority of the votes cast.

Due notice of any election must be given by advertisement in a newspaper, personal notice to the members, or a day stated on the minutes of the Board six months preceding the election. The Board of Directors shall keep a record of all their proceedings which shall be at all times subject to the inspection of any member. The corporation may establish branches in any other county in the state.

The Board of Directors may have the power to increase the number of directors to seven or ten if they deem the interest of the corporation requires such increase; and they or any subsequent Board of Directors may have the power to elect other members, who on acceptance of membership, shall become corporators equally with the original corporators.

The Board of Directors shall have the right to determine what amount of money paid into the treasury shall be a prerequisite for membership or, if necessary, what amount shall be thus annually paid, and a failure thus to pay shall in the discretion of the directors justify the expulsion of said defaulting member. The term of all officers may be fixed by the by-laws, the said term not, however, to exceed three years. All officers shall hold over until their successors are duly elected and qualified.

We, the undersigned, apply to the state of Tennessee by virtue of the laws of the land for a Charter of Incorporation the purposes and with the power, etc. declared in the foregoing instrument. This 13th day of August, 1898.

R. H. Boyd, E. C. Morris, J. E. Knox, J. P. Robinson, G. W. D. Gaines, E. J. Fisher, C. H. Clark, G. M. Moore.

State of Tennessee)
Davidson County)

Personally appeared before me P. A. Shelton, Clerk of the County Court of said county, the within named R. H. Boyd, the bargainer, with whom I am personally acquainted and who acknowledges that he executed the annexed instrument for the purpose therein contained.

Witness my hand, at office, this 13th day of August, 1898.

State of Tennessee)
Davidson County)

Personally appeared before me, P. A. Shelton, Clerk of the County Court of said county, R. H. Boyd, subscribing witness to the attached 'Charter' who being first duly sworn deposes and says that he is personally acquainted with the within named: E. C. Morris, J. E. Knox, J. P. Robinson, G. W. D. Gaines, E. J. Fisher, C. H. Clark, and G. M. Moore, the bargainers, and that they acknowledged the same in his presence to be their act and deed for the purpose therein contained.

Witness my hand at office, this 13th day of August, 1898.

(Seal)   P. A. Shelton, Clerk By Wm. B. Shelton, D. C.

State of Tennessee)
Davidson County)

Register's Office, August, 1898.

I, J. B. Armstrong, Register for said county, do certify the foregoing instrument and certificate are registered in said office in Book No. 197, Page 469, that they were received August 15, 1898, at 9:10 o'clock A. M., and were entered in Note Book 15, Page 370.

J. B. Armstrong, Register for Davidson County. By F. B. B'air Dep. Reg.

State of Tennessee)
Davidson County)

I, Wm. S. Morgan, Secretary of the State of Tennessee, do certify that the annexed instrument with certificates of acknowledgment of Probate and Registration was filed in my office for registration the 15th day of August, 1898, and recorded on the 15th day of August, 1898, in Corporation Record Book OO, in said office, Page 276.

In testimony whereof, I have hereunto subscribed my official signature, and by order of the governor, and affixed the great seal of the State of Tennessee, at the department in the city of Nashville, this 19th day of August, A. D., 1898.

Wm. S. Morgan, Secretary of State.[58]

The National Baptist Publishing Board could perpetuate itself and do business for the National Baptist Convention and the denomination. The board of directors could increase their numbers and elect officers without interference through religious politics. And the charter's rhetoric made the National Baptist Publishing Board the official publisher of Sunday school materials for the black Baptist denominational churches.

Boyd was ahead of his peers. Not even the white southern Baptist Sunday School Board had developed such a sophisticated charter, yet. And the other National Baptist Convention's boards had no corporation charter like the publishing board's.

At the first annual meeting of the publishing board, the members carefully reviewed the charter. They formed an organization according to the charter and elected the following officers: R. H. Boyd, secretary and treasurer; E. C. Morris, editorial secretary; T. G. Ewing, attorney; W. L. Cansler, auditor. J. P. Robinson became chairman of the committee on literature and printing. J. E. Knox headed the committee on denominational books. Moore headed the committee on missionary appropriations. Fisher headed the committee on children's day. Gaines headed the committee on business. And Boyd headed the committee on by-laws and constitution.[59]

Boyd presented the by-laws and the new corporation constitution. Nine members of the corporation constituted the board. Five of the nine "shall be resident citizens of the state of Tennessee," said the constitution. After all, this was a Tennessee corporation. The signature of the corresponding secretary became the official seal for the NBPB. The assistant secretary had the power to sign in the absence of the secretary. The secretary had authority to hire employees and nominate the editorial secretary, field secretary, district secretaries, and other important officers with confirmation by the board. The board organized itself into regular standing committees and elected an auditor on an annual basis independent of the secretary. The board fixed the salaries and expenses for the secretary and the assistant secretaries and per diem expenses for the board members.

The publishing board sent the charter, the by-laws, and the constitution to the Home Mission Board at Little Rock. This was reported to the National Baptist Convention's annual meeting at Kansas City, Missouri, on September 15, 1898. All was approved. During the National Baptist Convention's session, the Reverend J. P. Robinson, chairman of the Home Mission Board and chairman of the National Baptist Publishing Board's committee on printing and literature, called a meeting where the members agreed once more that because the Home Mission Board and the National Baptist Publishing Board had the same secretary, Boyd, the two groups would officially consolidate their activities. The Home Mission Board would have 3-4 seats on the National Baptist Publishing Board's board of directors (but not a majority of the seats). All missionary work and excess revenues for missionary literature would be credited to the Home Mission Board which would nominate the editor-in-chief, Morris, the president of the National Baptist Convention. The publishing board's corresponding secretary, Boyd, who also was corresponding secretary of the Home Mission Board, would handle all missionary work. The chairman of the Home Mission Board, Robinson, would make quarterly visits to Nashville to check the missionary activities.[60]

The Reaction

Within the National Baptist Convention, Boyd and the National Baptist Publishing Board faced a large faction of jealous and envious men. Slavery had left much discord among some blacks who feared racial success, and slavery had encouraged blacks to have great distrust in the credibility of men. Many persons criticized, murmured, and spread insinuations that Boyd was getting rich and the National Baptist Publishing Board was his personal business. They saw the National Baptist Publishing Board's success as Boyd's personal triumph over those men who had argued that a Negro Baptist publishing house could never work. Too many National Baptist Convention leaders had been humiliated by Boyd's success, and Boyd's power and influence among black Baptists had grown with the consolidation of the Home Mission Board's programs with the National Baptist Publishing Board's extensive operations. Later, Boyd would learn that the leaders of the "old convention" in Texas had watched these developments with envy and resentment.

Through being in charge of home mission work and Sunday school operations, Boyd and the National Baptist Publishing Board began to over-shadow all other National Baptist Convention operations and National Baptist Convention leaders. The National Baptist Publishing Board gave materials to newly organized Sunday schools, quickly gaining their loyalty to the NBPB. To cultivate good relations with the state associations, the publishing board company gave free materials for their missionary work and special Sunday school operations. In 1900, the publishing board contributed over $2,000 worth of free literature to Sunday schools.[61]

Especially Boyd's successful relations with the southern white Baptist association caused resentment from the American Baptist Publication Society and certain blacks in the National Baptist Convention who were affiliated wlth the ABPS and the American Baptist Home Mission Society. Boyd wisely gained great influence with the Southern Baptist Convention's leaders by attending the Southern Baptist Convention's annual meeting, and Boyd's Southern Baptist Convention counterpart often attended and addressed the National Baptist Convention's annual session. To dampen the criticism about his close ties to the Southern Baptist Convention, Boyd tried to patch up differences with S. N. Vass, and sometimes he visited the northern American Baptist annual meeting. However, Boyd said: "For some unknown reason..." he was "...not fraternally introduced to the body."[62]

The National Baptist Convention represented one of America's largest black associations. Any group would love to have influence and control in the National Baptist Convention because it represented 643 churches, 560 ministers, 290 Sunday schools, and hundreds of thousands of members in 1900. Even Texas, Boyd's home base, had 54 Negro Baptist associations, 163 black Baptist churches, and 135,599 Negro Baptists in 1900.[63]

In 1900, Boyd attended the National Baptist Convention's annual meeting as a member of the Texas delegation. Boyd avoided attention by permitting E. D. W. Isaac to recite the National Baptist Publishing Board's report to the Convention. The delegates learned that the publishing board had balanced the books at $49,309.37. The Reverend Sutton E. Griggs made a successful motion to endorse Boyd's new *Baptist Pastor's Guide and Parliamentary Rules.* The publishing board printed some of Griggs books, although fifteen years later, Griggs became a leading opponent and a plaintiff against the publishing board. Meanwhile, the 1900 convention delegates voted to direct Boyd and the National Baptist Publishing Board to prepare a Negro Baptist hymnal. The hymnal appeared in 1901.[64]

The NBPB, Mission Work, and Women

With the help of the Southern Baptist Convention's Home Mission Board and Sunday School Board, Boyd made the Home Mission Board and the NBPB reputable in home mission work. The Southern Baptist Convention agreed to sponsor two Negro missionaries for the Home Mission Board after Boyd and Frost had met in Chattanooga on November 28, 1900, to work out the details. Frost and the Southern Baptist Convention agreed to pay $1,800 in

Shown in this picture are four of the five linotype machines owned by the National Baptist Publishing Board. From left to right are shown, Mrs. Alberta Houston, Mr. John McCullough, Mr. T. B. Boyd, Sr., and Miss Charlyne McHenry.

salaries for the two men, and the National Baptist Convention's Home Mission Board authorized Boyd to pay the missionaries' travel expenses. The missionaries operated out of the National Baptist Publishing Board's facilities, teaching scriptural knowledge to preachers and developing better Sunday schools in the black Baptist churches. Before the agreement with Boyd, the Southern Baptist Convention had planned to have a superintendent and three district field workers in each of the heavily black states to preach, help locate Negro preachers for remote black churches, and educate the Negro pastors. The Southern Baptist Convention's Home Mission Board wanted to "uplift the [black] race to a higher plane of social, moral and religious life."[65]

Boyd used the Baptist publishing board's literature to train the superintendents and conduct the Sunday school lessons. Male and female field secretaries helped to distribute and popularize the National Baptist Publishing Board's publications. The publishing board's excess revenues helped to finance the missionary work.[66]

The 1901 National Baptist Convention delegates seemed astounded about the National Baptist Publishing Board's success. The National Baptist Publishing Board contributed $16,425 to National Baptist Convention missionary work and programs, and the NBPB earned excess revenues of $2,423 after meeting expenses and buying new machinery and buildings. The delegates unanimously adopted a resolution that read: "That the manner of conducting the Publishing House at Nashville, Tenn., by Rev. R. H. Boyd, D. D., or General Manager and Secretary, meets the unqualified support and endorsement of the National Baptist Convention, and that we will stand by him and by his work with renewed courage and interest."[67]

In 1902, the NBPB continued to expand its mission work. The Home Mission Board, which received much of its funds from the NBPB's revenues, helped to finance the two missionaries and gave funds to state associations to carry out missionary work. Secretary Boyd used this approach to avoid any conflict with the state associations. He also hired fellow Texan, William Beckham, to be the field secretary for the Home Mission Board, giving Boyd some relief, and using a younger, more vigorous man to travel extensively and disseminate the National Baptist Publishing Board's literature. Beckham had headed similar work for the General Missionary Baptist Convention of Texas, the "new convention."

Boyd's Home Mission Board work clashed with the white American Baptist Home Mission Society's missionaries in the field. In the November 15, 1902, issue of the *National Baptist Union,* Boyd wrote an editorial critical of the ABHMS. The corresponding secretary for the ABHMS assailed Boyd for the attack. Boyd denied he meant it as an attack. The 1902 National Baptist Convention delegates appointed Boyd, A. R. Griggs and J. P. Robinson to meet and iron out the differences with the ABHMS. Nothing came of the meeting.[68] The American Baptists knew that Boyd had accepted money from the Southern Baptist Convention to expand his mission work and distribute Bibles.[69]

For a good reason, President Morris placed A. R. Griggs on the committee. Griggs served as an ABHMS agent, and he supported the cooperative movement and better relations between the American Baptist Publication Society and the black Baptist convention. The Reverend Griggs served as a mediating force in the convention, and he expressed no animosity toward Boyd and the publishing board.

The Reverend Griggs' life had paralleled Boyd's life. According to the National Baptist *Union* (April 26, 1902), A. R. Griggs was the sixteenth son of Sutton and Brazelia Griggs, Alabama slaves who were moved to Grimes County, Texas, in 1859. Griggs married Emma Hodge in 1869. Griggs did missionary work for the Negro Baptist Association in Texas and edited and published a black Baptist newspaper. Boyd also was taken to Texas as a slave, lived in Grimes County, and did missionary work for a Texas Negro Baptist convention.

Griggs advised Boyd to tone down his criticism of the ABHMS. This Boyd did. In spite of the problems with the ABHMS' field people, Boyd continued to extend the NBPB's home mission work.

The black Women's Convention became another fertile field for the publishing board and the Home Mission Board. When the Women's Convention became a recognized board of the National Baptist Convention in 1900, Boyd became unofficial adviser to the women. Mrs. Boyd was a Tennessee delegate to the Women's Convention sessions. The Women's Convention simultaneously met with the National Baptist Convention's annual sessions, although the women held their meetings in another church building. The Reverend Boyd became particularly close to Mrs. Virginia W. Broughton of Nashville, the recording secretary for the Women's Convention. Broughton published several booklets through the National Baptist Publishing Board and worked with Nashville's Fireside School. Boyd contributed literature and free printing to help the women get started, although they were attached to the Foreign Mission Board in Louisville, Kentucky, home of the *The Missionary Herald* newspaper. He advised the women to incorporate as a separate board, but the National Baptist Convention's leaders discouraged the move.

In August 1901, Anne Armstrong, the Southern Baptist Convention's Women's Auxiliary secretary, visited Boyd at the National Baptist Publishing Board where they agreed on a project with the National Baptist Convention's Women's Convention. In September 1901, Armstrong attended the National Baptist Convention's annual session and pledged $250 to match $150 from the black Woman's Auxiliary to finance two black female home missionaries. Boyd gave the black women the $150 matching funds through the Home

Mission Board and the publishing board. The black women raised another $75. Boyd answered the critics who opposed closer relations with the southern white Baptists. He said: "Their [the Southern Baptist Convention's] only objective is to help us to help ourselves."[70]

Although Boyd could not develop friendly relations with the white men in the ABHMS and the ABPS, some female leaders in the Women's American Baptist Home Mission Society, another northern white Baptist group, worked cooperatively with the Reverend Boyd and the publishing board. The female leaders of the Fireside School gave business to the National Baptist Publishing Board, and they helped to distribute Bibles and Sunday school literature through their work. White female missionaries from the Women's American Baptist Home Mission Society founded and operated the Fireside School which focused on religious training for black women, the home, and the family. The Fireside School distributed books and literature for families to hold their own religious fireside chats and biblical lessons in the home. The National Baptist Publishing Board published the tracts, pamphlets, and books for the black and white Fireside School women who wrote their own works.

Joanna P. Moore, a white northern Baptist missionary and head of the Fireside School, and other female Baptist leaders wanted to break the legacy of slavery and sexism which had left many blacks and women in opposition to intellectual studies. Moore proposed that parents should read daily to their children and make home life "a purer and more intelligent atmosphere."[71] Moore, a friend to Boyd, published essays through the NBPB and edited *Hope,* the newspaper for the Fireside School. After Moore's death, the Fireside School eventually placed the *Hope* magazine under the control of the publishing board.

Not only did Boyd cultivate good relations with the southern and the northern white women Baptists, he continued to attract the black women of the National Baptist Convention. Boyd helped the woman's executive committee to plan a study course for women. Broughton was appointed editor of the series. The women were so pleased with their relationship to Boyd that they wanted to move their headquarters from Louisville to Nashville, but the National Baptist Convention leadership would not allow it. The Woman's Auxiliary's executive committee visited the publishing board's facilities on June 2, 1902, through an invitation from the secretary of the Home Mission Board. The women reported that "The system and thoroughly businesslike methods of operation reminded us of the large eastern business house. Dr. Boyd is, indeed, one of the greatest men of the age. Our Publishing House at Nashville should receive our hearty support by way of liberal patronage."[72]

The women eventually appointed two missionaries, E. E. Whitfield and L. S. Edwards. The Women's Conventions also debated community reform, race discrimination, temperance, and responsibilities and opportunities for Negro women. They agreed with Boyd and Sutton E. Griggs that the race problem was America's most serious issue. Moreover the women built a missionary house in Africa and eventually established a school for black girls in Washington, D. C.

Promoting Black Culture

The National Baptist Publishing Board went beyond the functions of sponsoring mission work and publishing Sunday school materials for black Baptist denominational churches. The publishing board played a significant role in the intellectual history of Nashville and the nation.

Between 1890 and 1915, Nashville experienced a literary Renaissance. This black Renaissance preceded the Harlem (Black) Renaissance of 1920-1945. Blacks eagerly sought to tell their story and persuade whites to respect them as equals. Like other black printing companies, freedmen schools and colleges, the National Baptist Publishing Board contributed to this black intellectual history partly because of its location in Tennessee's black cultural center, Nashville.

Since Emancipation, black Nashville had been Tennessee's cultural center. The state's first Negro newspaper, the *Colored Tennessean* (1866-1867), was published by a free Negro, William B. Scott, in Nashville. Nelson G. Merry edited the *Baptist Sunday School Standard* (1874) for the Negro Baptist Association of Tennessee. The *Tennessee Star* newspaper was published in Nashville by black attorney George T. Robinson during the period 1887-1891. The *Citizen* newspaper was published during the 1890s. Local black colleges published their own newspapers, including the *Fisk Herald*. The Fireside School published *Hope*. As early as 1880 in Nashville, Charles E. Roberts published his *Negro Civilization in the South*. Nashville's Southwestern Company published *Rising Race...Colored Americans* (1913) for a black author, Joseph R. Gay. The African Methodist Church's Sunday School Union in Nashville published several works: Daniel Payne, *History of the African Methodist Episcopal Church* (1891); Sarah W. Early, *The Life and Labors of Reverend John Early* (1894); James Haley, *Thoughts, Doings, and Sayings of the Race: Afro-American Encyclopedia* (1896).

The objectives of the Negro Renaissance writers fit perfectly the Reverend Boyd's concern about America's racial conservatism. Southern black Renaissance writers became concerned about the terrible tide of racial violence and lynching that swept the region after 1890. Some black writers believed that whites simply needed education about the black man's culture, history, and achievements. Boyd too argued that whites had familiarity only with the criminal class of blacks. By 1902, the National Baptist Publishing Board had expanded its book listings to 58 titles, an amazing feat for a black company during the early 1900s. Not all the books were about religious topics. Some books related to black history and race relations.

Sutton E. Griggs began printing his works at the NBPB. He wrote thirty-three books and tracts and formed the Orion Publishing Company to promote and sell his works. The Reverend Boyd became impressed with Griggs' "vigorous style" of writing. Griggs wrote in a militant style, opposing Jim Crowism and attempting to educate white people about Negro problems and aspirations. The National Baptist Publishing Board produced two of Griggs' books: *Unfettered* and *Whose Principles Shall Die - Vass or Boyd's*. The latter book attempted to answer the pro-ABPS faction's arguments against blacks having their own publishing board.[73]

Griggs, a Texan and son of A. R. Griggs, moved to Nashville to head the local First Baptist Church of East Nashville in 1901. He eventually moved to Memphis to pastor a church before returning to his native Texas. His first book, *Imperium in Imperio: A Study of the Negro Race Problem,* appeared in 1899, followed by *Overshadowed* (1901), *Unfettered* (1902), *The Hindered Hand: or, The Reign of the Repressionist* (1905), and *Pointing the Way* (1908). Griggs became fed up with white America's racial conservatism. In his book, *The One Great Question: A Study of Southern Conditions at Close Range* (1907), Griggs concluded that American racism overshadowed racial equality. He published a series of pamphlets, *Wisdom's Call* (1911), essays that pleaded with whites to honor the principles of accommodationism and grant blacks respect, mercy, justice, and kindness.

Boyd became mortified when the brilliant Sutton E. Griggs joined a vicious opposition against the National Baptist Publishing Board in 1915. But after Boyd's death, the Reverend S. E. Griggs ironically changed his militant attitude. He became an environmental determinist, believing that blacks could change their environment and through self-help remove even the obstacles of racism. Again, Griggs became an accommodationist, a person who cooperated willingly with moderate whites to advance the black man's cause. Richard H. Boyd too practiced this philosophy for years.

Not all the books produced by the publishing board pursued cooperative and accommodationist themes. In 1909, Boyd published his own book in protest of the Jim Crow (racial segregation) laws of the land. And the NBPB produced Maurice Corbett's *The Harp of Ethiopia* (1914), which called for violence to counter racial lynching and Jim Crowism. One of Corbett's poems partly read:

And blood the means will ever be, By which men gain their liberty. Not blood of some one in their stead. But blood which themselves have shed.

Besides books on the race issue, Boyd plunged the National Baptist Publishing Board into the business of printing and distributing circulars and religious tracts. He reasoned that a low black literacy rate limited the sale of books among adult Negroes. However, many black adults could read enough to understand short circulars and tracts. In 1902, the National Baptist Publishing Board gave away forty thousand tracts and circulars.[74]

The NBPB also printed and published newspapers. The publishing board assumed control of the *National Baptist Union,* a newspaper published by the Baptist Young People's Union and edited by E. W. D. Isaac. This paper suffered decline before Boyd assumed control of it. Boyd envisioned a single newspaper to represent the views of black Baptists, publicize the activities of the black Baptist denomination, and serve as official organ for the NBPB and black Sunday school news.

The black Baptists had a highly decentralized structure, regional and state associations, and several black Baptist papers. The list of many black Baptist newspapers included *The American Baptist* (Louisville), The Christian Banner (Philadelphia), *Baptist Vanguard* (Little Rock), The *Organizer* (Richmond), and *Baptist Herald* (Austin). The Foreign Mission Board and the Woman's Convention shared offices in Kentucky and published *The Missionary Herald.* The black Baptists published more than fifty newspapers and magazines by 1904. Seven of these papers were printed at the National Baptist Publishing Board.[75]

Boyd and Isaac agreed to combine the activities of the Baptist Young People's Union, the publication of the *National Baptist Union,* and the Home Mission Board's operations with those of the National Baptist Publishing Board. Already, these activities were located in the facilities of the National Baptist Publishing Board. Isaac remained editor of the newspaper. Boyd became the business manager and treasurer. The National Baptist Publishing Board became the publisher for the paper. Boyd enlarged the size of the paper and increased circulation to four thousand copies. The National Baptist Convention session delegates approved the merger agreement but failed to appropriate any money to help publish the newspaper as Boyd had requested. The National Baptist Publishing Board lost $1,601 on the venture but gained new business and a new audience, the young adult black Baptists.[76]

Expansion and Problems

In 1902, Boyd asked the National Baptist Convention for $10,000 in building funds. The National Baptist Publishing Board's operations spread through six separate buildings; the rooms were dark; and the employees had to cross alley ways and streets to transfer one operation to another process. The quarters became cramped enough that Boyd had to sell older equipment to make way for the newer machinery. Still many persons believed that the National Baptist Publishing Board was reaping huge profits and Boyd was getting rich.

Boyd asked Editor-In-Chief Morris and James M. Frost to help address the rumors about the publishing board being a money machine. The Reverend Frost addressed the Negro Baptist convention and urged the delegates to support Boyd and the publishing board. Frost said that the publishing house was a missionary industry with a missionary purpose and making money was not its chief function, but it had to make money to operate itself. Also at the 1902 convention, president Morris said: "The impression has gone out that the Publishing Board is 'a money machine,' hence, many expect it not only to do their work for a small price, but expect the house to aid them financially."[77]

Although Morris gave Boyd some help with the criticisms, Morris had his own problems. The Lott Carey Baptist Foreign Mission Convention remained separate from the National Baptist Convention. The *National Baptist Union* (September 27, 1902) reported that Morris' convention message included words about Lott Carey:

> A considerable number of Colored Baptists have organized what is known as the Lott Carey Foreign Mission Convention..., and this Board is doing the same class of work that is being done by our Foreign Mission Board. We concede that the brethren...have the right to do their Foreign Mission work independently of the National Baptist Convention, but it is neither intelligent nor wise to have such a division in our ranks. It has been my purpose to seek for a better understanding and a more fraternal feeling among the brethren to the end that some plan may be agreed upon which will enable us to do our foreign mission work through and by the direction of one Board. Morris believed that a settlement was near and the Lott Carey people would return to the National Baptist Convention.[78]

Morris had another problem. This problem involved the Home Mission Board under Richard H. Boyd. The Home Mission Board and Boyd had successfully concluded a cooperative agreement with the Southern Baptist Convention. Some members of the National Baptist Convention pushed for a cooperative agreement with the northern Baptists. After being stunned by the stupendous task of establishing a National Baptist Theological Seminary, the Educational Board held talks with the American Baptist Home Mission Society to gain northern white Baptist support. But H. L. Morehouse informed the black Baptists that the ABHMS had committed already $125,000 per year to twenty-five freedmen colleges and schools and could not afford more financial commitments. Boyd and others were not eager to continue ties to the northern Baptists.[79]

A *National Baptist Union* (December 13, 1902) editorial said:

For thirty years the Negro Baptists of this country have sustained the most friendly relations to this society, and reaped from it labors of love and many profitable rewards. [But] the fact still remains that some of its officers [i.e., A. J. Rowland] have made serious and damaging mistakes in dealing with our people.[80]

The article praised H. L. Morehouse and asked for unity and cooperation based on manly equality, not white paternalism.

The Reverend Morehouse became infuriated about the article. Morehouse said that the article was fatal to any hope of truly fraternal cooperation between the National Baptist Convention and the northern Baptists.[81] The Reverend A. R. Griggs warned Boyd that he should avoid opposing the cooperative movement between the black Baptists and the northern white Baptists. Griggs believed that Boyd's opposition was based on the old Texas split in 1892 when Boyd had accused the American Baptist Publication Society of aggravating the division between Texas' black Baptists. Griggs argued that by opposing the cooperation talks with the American Baptist Home Mission Society and accusing the American Baptist Publication Society of dividing the Texas convention, Boyd ran the risk of generating many enemies against the publishing board.[82] More criticism did come because of Boyd's successful efforts to conclude agreements with the southerners only.

Speaking like Booker T. Washington, R. H. Boyd defended his acceptance of help from the southern white Baptists. He said:

This is encouragement of the proper kind. The interests of the races in the South demand that the kindest and most sympathetic relations should exist. The races should strive in every manner possible to help each other. The white man is our big brother in this country.[83]

The Morehouse cooperation controversy, the problem with the Lott Convention, the opposition to courting the Southern Baptist Convention, and the Texas split, all would generate an anti-Boyd and an anti-National Baptist Publishing Board faction within the National Baptist Convention during the next five or six years. Boyd became less able to manage these complex politics when the publishing board expanded rapidly and demanded more of his time.

Boyd believed strongly in placing excess revenues into reserves and modernization of equipment and facilities. The National Baptist Publishing Board company earned $74,408 in 1902. It spent $23,655 in printing, mission work, new machinery, and travel expenses for missionaries. Boyd and the NBPB placed $5,352 into a reserve fund. Boyd said: "Our institution is compelled to make its way, get only Negro trade, find only a market for its production among Negroes, and yet compete with its [white] competitors for the same trade."[84] He directed his remarks toward the American Baptist Publication Society. Boyd suggested a "Negro tariff" to protect black businesses from unfair white competition.[85] The Congress had passed tariffs to protect young American companies from the older, more experienced European and foreign companies.

The NBPB continued to grow. The publishing board had to hire or train its own machinists, engineers, electricians, and other skilled workers to maintain six buildings, gas, electric, and steam facilities. It was the only Negro company to bind, engrave, emboss, and manufacture its own publications. The board published 6,717,825 pieces of literature in 1902 compared with 5,609,000 pieces in 1901. Because of the expense of producing Bibles, the board contracted with the American Bible Society to print plain, cheap Bibles with neither comments nor notes to save the black congregations money. The National Baptist Publishing Board placed its imprint, NBPB, on the Bibles.[86]

By the end of 1902, the National Baptist Publishing Board had developed a large, lucrative business in the sale of chapel and parlor organs and other church furniture. William Rosborough, the manager of the board's program, concluded a contract to install a $2,000 organ into Nashville's Mt. Olive Missionary Baptist Church. The NBPB installed this massive pipe organ around the first of 1903 and featured a photograph of it in the *National Baptist Union*. Additionally, the publishing board's advertisements in the *National Baptist Union* featured church bells, call bells, pulpit podiums, and other church supplies and fine furniture.[87]

During the last of 1902, the publishing board announced that the remodeled Chapel was ready. Visitors could attend the daily 9:30 morning services with the Reverend Boyd and his employees. Boyd said: "Prayer is the grace that seasoneth all. Prayer moves the hand that moves the Universe; it knocks till the door opens; and like Jonathan's bow returns not empty."[88]

In 1903 when the National Baptist Publishing Board earned $81,627 including a $1,307.67 surplus, the National Baptist Convention gave some support to the National Baptist Publishing Board by directing its Educational Board to relocate from Washington, D. C. to Nashville, and "...cooperate with our Publishing Board."[89] The Educational Board was incorporated on March 1, 1902, to support and establish black Baptist seminaries and schools.

In the meantime, Boyd began to reorganize the NBPB's mission work. He told field secretary Beckham to cut his travel and work from an office at the National Baptist Publishing Board, and Boyd directed Beckham to notify the district missionary directors to organize large general missionary Sunday school meetings with superintendents, deacons, and pastors. Boyd also instructed Beckham to involve local white Baptist ministers in these meetings, get more local support from the Southern Baptist Convention, and generate more cooperation between local black and white Baptist churches. Boyd said: "This work will be the beginning of a better era between the races in this country.... The white Baptists will have a better opportunity to understand the changed and improved conditions, the educational qualifications, moral and religious development, financial growth, and loftier ambitions of the Negro Baptists living among them."[90]

The Home Mission Board had six district secretaries who performed missionary work. These men helped display samples of the National Baptist Publishing Board's materials. The district and field secretaries helped poorly educated pastors and Sunday school teachers place orders to the National Baptist Publishing Board. This work, including Beckham's, proved crucial because the National Baptist Publishing Board did not have branch bookstores and a catalog of publications like the white religious publishers.

The mission work became an important program for the National Baptist Publishing Board. When the Home Mission Board's activities extended into new territories, so did the publishing board's publications and Sunday school materials. Boyd anticipated expanding the National Baptist Publishing Board's materials into Canada, the West Indies, South America, Hawaii, and the Philippine Islands via the Home Mission Board's field personnel. He toured the Pacific coastal areas and established relations with the black Baptists there in July, 1903.[91]

Incidentally, when they realized later that the Home Mission Board represented part of the National Baptist Publishing Board's program strength, the anti-NBPB faction pushed a resolution within the National Baptist Convention to separate the Home Mission Board from the National Baptist Publishing Board. This move would hurt the NBPB and Boyd.

The publishing board expanded its business into the music field. The Reverend Boyd knew that music represented an important part of the black religious experience and Negro church services. In 1903, Boyd decided to gain board approval to expand the National Baptist Publishing Board's *Hymnal*. Boyd hired a musical director and directed him to prepare musical productions for church choirs and write music for Sunday school lessons. The National Baptist Publishing Board also used mass and local choirs to highlight its huge annual Sunday School Congress sessions throughout the country.[92]

To expand further the National Baptist Publishing Board's territory, Boyd attempted to solve problems with the ABPS and the pro-ABPS factions within the convention. Boyd and members of the Home Mission Board met with Lott Carey Convention representatives in 1900 without results. Again, in 1903 they met at the National Baptist Convention's annual session in Philadelphia, and no compromise was agreed on. Boyd and National Baptist Convention representatives also met with American Baptist Publication Society representatives at the September 16, 1903, National Baptist Convention session. Again they reached no compromise.[93]

Boyd continued to expand his activities with the Southern Baptist Convention. He and Frost developed an elaborate memorandum of agreement for cooperative programs between the Southern Baptist Convention's Home Mission Board and the National Baptist Convention's Home Mission Board. Boyd and his southern Baptist Home Mission Board counterpart met in Atlanta on April 6, 1904, and agreed to leave all missionary work among black Baptists to the National Baptist Convention's Home Mission Board. The Southern Baptist Convention agreed to appoint a superintendent to represent its interests and spend $15,000 a year for black missionary work. The pro-ABPS faction introduced a resolution at the 1904 National Baptist Convention session to denounce the agreement and forestall any expanded relations with the Southern Baptist Convention.[94] Boyd defended his actions and explained to the delegates:

> We have, it is true, since our emancipation from slavery, because of the deep interest manifested in or educational and religious welfare by Northern philanthropists and their friends in Baptist ranks, and on account of the many grave and deep political questions rising out of the reconstruction period, enfranchisement of the Negroes, and his rights and privileges to citizenship, together with certain sociological problems, allied ourselves more fully and closely with the Northern Baptist Family."[95]

But the "...Southern Baptist Family has given its aid more in a local way, assisting pastors, individual congregations, and has made these gifts as individuals rather than as an organized body," Boyd said.[96]

President Morris saved the day. Morris said: "This Convention knows no North, no South, no East, no West in its religious work...."[97] He persuaded the convention to continue the Articles of Agreement between the National Baptist Convention and the Southern Baptist Convention on an experimental basis.[98]

Growth of the Anti-NBPB Forces

The pro-ABPS faction began a campaign within the National Baptist Convention to separate the Home Mission Board from the National Baptist Publishing Board and thereby destroy Boyd's plans with the southern white Baptists. In 1904, the National Baptist Convention delegates unsuccessfully voted to make the Home Mission Board distinct from the publishing board. The Reverend W. L. Dickson of Texas led the successful debate against the resolution. Boyd won reelection as a member and the secretary of the Home Mission Board. But the attempted resolutions revealed the growing strength of the opposition that wanted to decrease Boyd's power and influence.[99]

In October 1904, for example, Boyd said:

Since 1896, when the National Baptist Convention ordered its Home Mission Board to begin the publication of a series of Sunday school literature, there has been the 'battle royal' waged in the Negro Baptist camp, as to the wisdom of the Convention passing such an order and the propriety of the [National Baptist Publishing] Board attempting to execute it.

The white publishing societies have been the 'lazzaroni' poor houses for Negroes so long that their [blacks] intellect has become impoverished. For want of mental exercise we have produced only a few acceptable authors; we must produce some more. We must make books and write literature in order to furnish this mental exercise and stimulate its corresponding mental activity. The race that desires to make a place in the economy of men and things to stand forth amid the activities of other progressive peoples, and have its name and its deeds fully and accurately recorded in history, must make a literature that is *distinctively* and *peculiarly* its own.[100]

The anti-NBPB faction had gained enough strength to launch a series of "reviews" or investigations of the publishing board's operations. As directed by resolutions of the convention, Morris and a delegation visited Nashville in early 1905 and inspected the National Baptist Publishing Board; and for the appearance of objectivity, they also inspected the Home Mission Board, the Baptist Young People's Union Board, the Educational Board, and other operations. This action at least satisfied some of the critics about Boyd's combined operations. The team's report said: "Dr. Boyd is commended as a tireless and a faithful servant of the Convention." In his 1905 Convention address, President Morris said: "The Home Mission and Publication work has been directed and managed by Dr. R. H. Boyd, who has shown superior ability in the management of great concerns."[101]

Some delegates at the fall,1905, convention prepared another resolution to separate the Home Mission Board from the National Baptist Publishing Board, although they were warned that the National Baptist Publishing Board supplied all funds for the Home Mission Board and Boyd's salary.[102] Whatever salary Boyd received, it was paid by revenue from the publishing board's operations. The issue of separating the two boards did not give the anti-NBPB faction the ammunition they needed.

At the 1905 National Baptist Convention session, the opposition extended its attention to focus on the publishing board's relationship to the National Baptist Convention. The Reverend A. T. Stewart of Arkansas introduced a resolution and argued that "much controversy" had gone on for years and threatened to divide the Baptist ranks. Morris appointed a committee to look into the matter and report to the next convention, although he had already recommended some action to quiet the discord. However, the anti-NBPBfaction began to overwhelm Morris. The highly respected W.H. McAlpine, the first president of the Baptist Foreign Mission Board (1880), introduced Resolution No. 3 to place the Home Mission Board and the National Baptist Publishing Board under different managers. None of Boyd's supporters served on the resolution committee which recommended that the convention adopt the resolution. [103]

The year 1905 represented the visible beginning of a ten year controversy about the National Baptist Publishing Board and its autonomy. For the period 1907 to 1915, the NBPB underwent tremendous growth. Meanwhile, the anti-NBPB faction was growing in strength. This faction successfully forced the separation of the Home Mission Board from the National Baptist Publishing Board. The controversy about control of the publishing board led to a denominational split.

Chapter 3

The NBPB and the
National Baptist Convention,
1906-1915

Chapter 3

The NBPB and the National Baptist Convention, 1906-1915

In spite of harsh and often unjustified criticism, the Reverend Boyd supported the development of an effective National Baptist Convention. He said:

> The National Baptist Convention has passed through another year of prosperity. The days of the ward, the beneficiary, the helpless, penurious [miserly], thriftless, shiftless beggar Negro are numbered. The National Baptist Convention has become the exponents of self-reliance, self-assertiveness and self-maintenance. It is not seeking to alienate the races or to perpetuate racial conflicts. It has discovered that the Negro must work in a different groove to that of the white man.[1]

A proponent of black self-help, Boyd urged the readers to support the National Baptist Convention by attending the annual session.

By 1906 the National Baptist Publishing Board had become America's largest Negro publishing firm. Books, booklets, and Sunday school materials flowed constantly from its presses. The National Baptist Publishing Board had the most modern equipment and current business practices among black business firms. And its reputation in publishing and Baptist missionary work had become national and international.

Under Richard Henry Boyd's management, the National Baptist Publishing Board (NBPB) became an umbrella for some other Negro businesses in Nashville. These included the National Negro Doll Company, the National Baptist Church Supply Company, the Union Transportation Company, and the Globe Publishing Company. Boyd and other National Baptist Publishing Board officials helped to open Nashville's first black bank since 1874. Through autonomous but affiliated companies, the publishing board's customers could buy dolls, organs, sewing machines, pianos, banners, books, leaflets, training courses, songs, and more.

But the publishing board's success and Boyd's influence generated jealousy and criticism from some members within the National Baptist Convention and angered the most egotistical of the Negro preachers who gained eventual control of the Baptist convention. They accused especially Boyd of operating a profit-making machine, neglecting mission work, using the publishing board's facilities and resources for his private companies, and placing all members of his family on the National Baptist Publishing Board's payroll.

By 1907, the National Baptist Publishing Board's business had increased about thirteen percent per year. In December, 1907, the National Baptist Publishing Board ordered new printing equipment at a cost of twenty thousand dollars and announced the completion of a building expansion program. The NBPB was housed in six buildings, 2-3 stories high. The complex had new printing presses with automatic continuous paper feeders and a capacity of 15,000 impressions per hour. Workers installed a new Michle Press and a book printing press to keep pace wlth the great demand for reading materials. The second floor housed the proof-reading department, a new Washington hand press for taking impressions and making banners, and two new linotype machines. The main building included an elevator and a 45-horsepower engine to run the machinery. Another two-story building included mail rooms, counting rooms, editorial rooms, a chapel, and secretary Boyd's offices.[2]

The construction program, installation of new equipment, the deadlines for annual publications like the *Sunday School Lesson Commentary*, and traveling caused secretary Boyd to leave much of the correspondence and the daily plant operations to assistant secretary, Henry Allen Boyd.

The publishing board concluded a project to publish a pocket-size hymn book. Boyd's staff collected and selected some 632 old meter hymns from thousands of hymns. The publishing board had been publishing hymns, tunes, and song books since 1897 when a hymnal committee was appointed. A larger hymn book had been published in 1903 after the 1900 National Baptist Convention session directed the publishing board and Boyd to compile such a manuscript. By 1905, the National Baptist Publishing Board had sold ten thousand copies of the *National Baptist Hymnal*. Some persons suggested a pocket-size book which Boyd published in a 1906 edition. It included songs for all church functions.

In spite of the critics who argued that Boyd was too busy directing the publishing board and other businesses to function effectively as secretary of the Home Mission Board, the mission work of the Home Mission Board and the National Baptist Publishing Board impressed many persons. The National Baptist Convention's churches contributed a small amount of financial support for that work. To augment the mission work, Boyd proposed to use some of the publishing board's surplus funds and donations and contributions from the churches' Bible Day and Children's Day programs. Even though Boyd and the Home Mission Board preferred to allow state, district, and territorial associations to select the missionaries, the National Baptist Publishing Board and the Southern Baptist Convention's Home Mission Board paid the salaries. Boyd said: "In this way it is the hope of the Board to have friendly, united, fraternal, and co-operative relations with each State, Territorial and District organization." However, Boyd said that many of the men and women selected by these associations were "...either incompetent, incapable, unacquainted with the work, or they are too indolent to perform the tasks assigned them. In many instances they feel that they owe their election to some influential friend, or they are appointed on account of their great influence."[3]

Operating with funds obtained by Boyd from the National Baptist Publishing Board and the Southern Baptist Convention, the Home Mission Board had many missionaries and colporters appointed by the associations. The colporters traveled into rural areas, visiting homes to convert individuals to Christianity, and distributing Bibles and church literature for the National Baptist Publishing Board. But Boyd needed competent men and women to work diligently in mission work.

An effective and competent group of female mission workers operated with the Woman's Auxiliary Board. The women helped the publishing board with mission work, and the publishing board helped the women with their work. During their 1907 convention at the Vermont Avenue Baptist Church (Washington, D. C.), the women discussed dozens of topics, including "The Race Problem from Magazines and Daily Papers," "Home Happiness and How to Promote It," and "A Plea For our Boys." The women's creative topics influenced Boyd and the National Baptist Publishing Board to develop certain products and organize activities for black boys who suffered many problems by 1907. Boyd, the publishing board, and the Southern Baptist Convention's Home Mission Board funneled some money through the National Baptist Convention's Home Mission Board to continue to pay the salary for a field missionary for the black Woman's Auxiliary. That particular field missionary distributed 1,448 books for the National Baptist Publishing Board. To promote its mission work, advertise its Sunday school work, and help the women with their work, the publishing board also sent Virginia W. Broughton of the Woman's Auxiliary and J. E. Ford to the International Sunday School Congress in Rome, Italy, where the National Baptist Publishing Board displayed an elaborate exhibit of its literature and activities. The secretary of the Woman's Auxiliary said: "We feel obligated for this [NBPB] kind of help."[4]

The women's group engaged in many other activities. They supported the temperance movement. The Woman's Auxiliary helped 150 children's bands and worked in rural districts. The women's group raised money to operate a national Baptist training school for women and girls.

Meanwhile, summer began to come to an end, and Boyd and the board members prepared to travel to the annual NBC session. Considering the anti-NBPB resolutions introduced in the recent conventions' sessions, Boyd and his staff and board members could not afford to miss the convention.

The first meetings of the National Baptist Convention's 1907 session appeared to be peaceful and harmonious, and all persons seemed to be pleased with the progress of mission work by the Woman's Auxiliary, the Foreign Mission Board, the Home Mission Board as well as the work of the National Baptist Publishing Board. At the September 11-16, 1907, National Baptist Convention session at the Metropolitan Baptist Church in Washington, D. C., the delegates resolved to fight Jim Crowism, and they directed the NBPB and

Boyd to organize a publication to show the widespread nature of segregation laws in America. The delegates proposed to develop a Negro history book and resolved to support the temperance movement. They voted to force the boards to reimburse the convention president for his expenses to attend the various conventions and meetings of the boards. And the 1907 National Baptist Convention session petitioned Congress to reimburse black Americans and their descendants who lost money in the failed Freedman's Savings and Trust Company Bank (1865-1874).[5]

Then the delegates turned their attention to resolutions related to the National Baptist Publishing Board. President Morris said: "Contrary to the specific order of this Convention, the Home Mission Board and the publication work [NBPB] is still being operated under one and the same management [Boyd]."[6] Yet the National Baptist Convention had no money to give to anyone to take control of the Home Mission Board's activities which were financed effectively by the NBPB. So Morris recommended to the delegates that the separation order be rescinded if they thought that it was a bad idea. Morris also suggested that Boyd suspend publication of the *National Baptist Union* because the National Baptist Convention could not meet his requests for funding.[7] Otherwise, the publishing board and Boyd ended 1907 without having to host another investigation committee.

New Year's 1908 began with the publishing board's annual dinner. Boyd offered the prayers, as usual. The audience rendered a song. The staff prepared an elaborate dinner, spread it on banquet tables in the chapel, and removed the chapel's seats to make room for the feast. The employees presented the Reverend Richard H. Boyd with a gold watch in appreciation for his excellent leadership and managerial skills.[8]

In September 1908, Boyd presented the publishing board's annual report to the National Baptist Convention session. The National Baptist Publishing Board's magazine issues illustrated excellence. *The Teacher* had grown to a 64-page monthly. The *Senior Quarterly* numbered 48 pages per issue, and the *Advanced Quarterly* numbered 32 pages. Really popular were the Boyd's Class Collection Envelopes which sold for three cents each. "By using Boyd's Class Collection Envelope, your secretary can report in one-third of the time.... Do away with the old scrap paper system," the National Baptist Publishing Board's advertisement said in the Convention's *Journal*.[9] The annual report pleased the convention delegates.

Boyd's introduction of the assistant secretary of the Southern Baptist Convention's Home Mission Board gave his critics something to discuss about the publishing board. Again the anti-NBPB men urged the convention and Morris to "investigate the publishing board." And in spite of Morris's attempt to compromise the issue, these men insisted on repeated attempts to separate the Home Mission Board from the National Baptist Publishing Board, arguing that Boyd could not do both jobs effectively.

Word spread through the 1908 convention that Boyd was using the National Baptist Publishing Board to get rich. By now Boyd was treasurer of the Union Transportation Company, president of the Nashville Globe Publishing Company, founder and chief stockholder of the National Baptist Church Supply Company, president of One-Cent Savings Bank, business manager of the *National Baptist Union* newspaper, and soon-to-be business manager of the National Negro Doll Company. Except for the bank, these companies were housed at the National Baptist Publishing Board's facilities. Frustrated because they had not been successful in getting the convention to separate the Home Mission Board and the National Baptist Publishing Board, some of the opposition suggested that the black Baptist churches boycott the National Baptist Publishing Board.

Some preachers and President Morris quieted the opposition to the publishing board. Morris said that the Reverend Boyd was "a master mind" in creating and directing the publishing house. When pleading with the delegates to support the Educational Board's efforts, D. S. Klugh, corresponding secretary, said:

> Columbus was called a fool, but he discovered the New World. They said Lincoln was a fool, but he saved the American Union and freed the slaves....They said Boyd was a fool, but he has built out of nothing our great publishing house which is one of the marvelous achievements of the age.... No one ever disgraces himself when trying to do a noble deed; it will not hurt us to try."[10]

Boyd rose and made his reports for the Home Mission Board and the National Baptist Publishing Board. Boyd said: "We are thankful that our Heavenly Father has continued his unstinting blessings on our labors...."[11] In spite of the 1908 economic panic, the National Baptist Publishing Board had paid all creditors and floated a bond issue to finance expansion of the facilities, Boyd reported. He explained how they had moved the machinery at night from old quarters to new buildings to prevent disruption of production. Boyd made three major recommendations: (1) that the convention support missions to blacks in the West Indies and Panama; (2) that a church edifice fund be established to help small and rural churches build facilities and save failing mortgages; (3) that the publishing board begin an apprentice program to train young black printers.

The convention made no financial obligation to Boyd's three recommendations. Nevertheless, Boyd made the missionary project in Panama an immediate goal for the National Baptist Publishing and the Home Mission Board. And the National Baptist Publishing Board implemented an apprenticeship program.

The publishing board's 1909 New Year's dinner was held in Building No. 6, the woodwork and cabinet department. Employees moved the machines aside to make room for the feast and the guests. The meal consisted of roast pig, baked turkey, chicken, boiled ham, corn bread, light bread, potato and salmon salad, and cranberries. The employees honored the Reverend Boyd. Solomon P. Harris, the oldest National Baptist Publishing Board employee, sketched the history of the accounting department, which he headed. Next, Boyd directed each department head to recite the history of each unit of the National Baptist Publishing Board.[12]

Between January and September 1909, the National Baptist Publishing Board operated without any major problems. The Sunday School Congress was a success in June. Then the NBPB's staff and Boyd prepared to journey to the September session of the National Baptist Convention.

In September 1909, the National Baptist Convention's session opened in Columbus, Ohio. The two thousand delegates endorsed the temperance movement to prohibit the use and sale of alcoholic beverages. The convention's resolutions opposed racial discrimination, lynching, and denial of black rights.[13] Generally, the convention's sessions remained quiet.

The Reverend Boyd reported that the Home Mission Board had built a church in the Panama Canal Zone. He requested donations to buy a bell and furnishings for the building. The United States government had secured the Canal Zone through a 1904 treaty with Panama. The canal, which linked the Atlantic and the Pacific Oceans, was completed on August 15, 1914, after thousands of workers labored to dig the canal and build its locks and dams. Many of the workers were blacks. Boyd felt obligated to extend mission work to convert these black Panamanian citizens. Within years, the publishing board and the Home Mission Society would build a school and four churches in the Zone as well as sponsor two missionaries there.[14]

The Reverend Boyd reported that the National Baptist Publishing Board had bought new, rotary book presses costing $18,000. The Walter Scott Printing Press Manufacturing Company of Plainfield, New Jersey, had scheduled the installation of modern equipment. Already the National Baptist Publishing Board owned flat bed presses and two job presses; but employees could not keep up with the orders. The new equipment would be faster and less costly in man-hours. The National Baptist Publishing Board employed some 150 workers by now. Additionally, the National Baptist Publishing Board had bought the D. E. Dortch Publishing Company's song books, plates, and copyrights, giving the board control of more Baptist denomination songs (4,000) than any other Negro company.[15]

The publishing board expanded its editorial offices and book publishing. The book inventory was impressive, although not all the books were printed by the National Baptist Publishing Board. Some books had the NBPB's imprint but merely to indicate the publishing board's endorsement of the books. The National Baptist Publishing Board's inventory listed $178,429.49 in machinery, books, periodicals, and office equipment and supplies. Secretary Boyd said that he required the employees to "be steady, punctual, and accurate in the services they give."[16]

The publishing board also began to expand its training programs in 1909. The Reverend Nathaniel H. Pius of Springfield, Ohio, became the superintendent of the Sunday school training course. Pius was college educated and twice president of black colleges. The publishing board's teacher training program offered four courses: primary, elementary, preparatory, and normal. The normal course consisted of child nature, studies of the Bible, Old and New Testament history, and general Baptist church history. Students received a diploma upon completion of a course. The publishing board furnished the textbooks, but the students could buy other books for the courses. The American Baptist Publication Society and the Southern Baptist Convention's Sunday School Board offered similar teacher training courses.[17]

The NBPB frequently became the first among local publishing companies to implement new programs. Boyd and the National Baptist Publishing Board's staff traveled widely, visiting churches and state and district conventions to learn what others were doing and what was needed to service the churches' needs. Henry Allen Boyd, the assistant secretary, spent time visiting the nation's modern printing and publishing companies to learn the latest machinery and processes because the publishing board had to modernize constantly its operations and facilities.

Again at the National Baptist Convention's 1909 session, the issue of separating the Home Mission Board from the National Baptist Publishing Board's operations came to the delegates' attention. The National Baptist Publishing Board's supporters claimed that some of the preachers had become angry because Boyd had not appointed some of them and their people to be paid field secretaries. The men insisted on pursuing the first line of attack on the National Baptist Publishing Board by proposing to have different individuals serve as the secretaries for the publishing board and the Home Mission Board.

The Reverend Walter H. Brooks, pastor of Washington, D. C.'s Nineteenth Street Baptist Church, gave an interesting presentation that quieted this newest attack on Boyd, the Home Mission Board, and the National Baptist Publishing Board. Brooks recited the turbulent history of black Baptist missionary work in America since 1866. Brooks said: "It will be a hundred years since organized work for missions had a beginning among us, and it would indeed be unfortunate if the year 1915 found us divided into little societies, warring one against the other."[18]

In 1909, two events troubled and puzzled the publishing board's staff. An attempt was made to move the Educational Board from Nashville. But the

Educational Board members voted the action down. By concentrating many boards in Nashville, the National Baptist Publishing Board became stronger. Also in 1909, the convention authorized a new "Union Publishing Committee" to go to Nashville and take control of the *National Baptist Union*. The members consisted of E. D. W. Isaac (editor), William Haynes (president), T. G. Ewing (treasurer), and W. L. Craft (secretary). President Morris arrived in Nashville to supervise the takeover. Boyd and the National Baptist Publishing Board's officers and employees watched from a distance, although the National Baptist Publishing Board had printed and published the Baptist newspaper with its own funds. Boyd had asked the National Baptist Convention's delegates to finance the paper or take it over. The publishing board started its own paper, the *National Baptist Review*.[19]

The Crucial Years: 1910-1915

The years 1910 to 1915 became crucial ones for the National Baptist Publishing Board's members as well as for other black Baptists. The American Baptist Publication Society had announced at the Northern Baptist Convention that it was closing its branch houses in the South. The American Baptist Home Mission Society had closed Roger Williams University in Nashville (1907) and had begun to limit support for black education in the South. To help fill the void, the Southern Baptist Convention resolved to expand its missionary activity and increase its educational involvement with the Negro Baptists. In the midst of these changes, it appeared that now the National Baptist Publishing Board would receive less criticism from the pro-ABPS faction within the National Baptist Convention.

At the 1910 annual New Year's dinner for the National Baptist Publishing Board, attorney J. C. Napier said: "We never hesitate to honor such an enterprising, highly respected, worthy citizen as Dr. Boyd, the founder and manager of the publishing house."[20] Napier was followed by others who praised Boyd and presented gifts to the great leader. Boyd directed the oldest department heads to recite the company's history.

In February 1910, a National Baptist Convention investigating committee arrived in Nashville. Morris returned to Nashville to participate with the investigating committee. Rumors claimed that the National Baptist Publishing Board and Boyd were the real targets of the National Baptist Convention investigators. Boyd took the rumors and the visit in stride and said: "It is only the policy of the National Baptist Convention, and an auditor comes annually anyway to audit the accounts of the National Baptist Publishing Board."[21] The committee's members equally paid visits to the Educational Board, the Baptist Young People's Union, the Home Mission Board, and the National Baptist Publishing Board.

Nevertheless, the investigating committee focused specifically on the publishing board, asking Boyd detailed questions about the operations and books. Boyd presented six deeds to the committee, showing that one parcel of property was sold to the National Baptist Publishing Board by Boyd and his wife and the other pieces were purchased from various individuals and agencies including a parcel of land from the Panamanian government. One building was leased from Boyd and Beckham after which the two men had agreed to trade the new building for the National Baptist Publishing Board's old building at 517 Second Avenue North and the difference in value. An arbitration committee would decide the difference in value due Boyd and Beckham, according to the agreement. The Church Supply Company leased a plot of land for free from the publishing board in return for placing a building on that land, and the building would belong to the National Baptist Publishing Board in lieu of rent. The other boards, allegedly under investigation, did not submit deeds to their properties to the committee.[22]

A controversy developed because the committee of nine National Baptist Convention members hired a local white attorney instead of doing business with the Negro lawyers. Nashville had many black lawyers as well as a law school at Walden University, a freedmen school operated by the northern Methodists. A local black attorney, Robert L. Mayfield, led a protest against the National Baptist Convention for ignoring the "buy black" movement by the National Negro Business League. Mayfield, a militant black man who had brought a suit against Tennessee's Jim Crow railroad laws, proposed to sue the National Baptist Convention. The Nashville *Globe* stated that the National Baptist Convention had insulted black pride. The National Baptist Publishing Board used black attorneys, including J. C. Napier and T. G. Ewing, and sometimes a white attorney.[23]

The investigating committee found nothing out of order at the publishing board. Still, the anti-NBPB faction and the National Baptist Convention sent investigating committee after investigating committee to Nashville. President Morris had difficulty trying to contain the anti-Boyd and anti-NBPB faction. Some of the preachers resented Boyd's efforts to concentrate more boards and power under the National Baptist Publishing Board.

Boyd argued that the duplication of functions caused the Educational Board, the Foreign Mission Board, the Baptist Young People's Union Board, and the Woman's Auxiliary Board, to send representatives to the same churches visited already by the Home Mission Board and the National Baptist Publishing Board's Sunday school department. The stream of visitors and beggars annoyed the pastors and confused the members. Would it not be more efficient to concentrate several functions in one place, possibly at the National Baptist Publishing Board, Boyd asked?

After the controversy about the investigating committee quieted down, the National Baptist Publishing Board continued its expansion of missionary activities through the Home Mission Board. The publishing board obtained some funds for the Home Mission Board by sending free samples to churches and printing free programs for Children's Day programs, asking only for a share of the collection for that particular day's program. The money financed the Home Mission Board's programs including an exploratory missionary to Jamaica in 1910. The publishing board also needed more funds to extend the Home Mission Board's work into black communities in Canada and the Philippines. Boyd urged the National Baptist Convention to move into Panama "where the eyes of all the world will be turned and if the National Baptist Convention loses its opportunity on this Zone it will lose a great legacy."[24]

Some two hundred employees, friends, family members, and business colleagues attended the 1911 New Year's dinner at the National Baptist Publishing Board. The feast began at 2:00 in the afternoon with the traditional prayers by Secretary Boyd. The institution's history was repeated by the unit heads. The employees presented Boyd with a walking cane and gold cuff links wlth the inscription "RHB." Boyd reported that the National Baptist Publishing Board had balanced the books with $187,754 in 1911 compared to $177,508 in 1910. To raise the employees' salaries, the publishing board had reduced the staff by leaving some positions vacant.[25]

At the National Baptist Convention's September 1911 session in Pittsburgh, Pennsylvania, President Morris said that cooperation between the Home Mission Board and the National Baptist Publishing Board "had been both pleasant and agreeable," but the two influential boards should have separate management. He said: "In suggesting a separate management for each of our Boards, I do not wish to be misunderstood as intimating that there should be the slightest divorcement in one Board from the other."[26] Morris argued that the Home Mission Board and the National Baptist Publishing Board could continue to cooperate under separate secretaries.

Morris did not resent Boyd and the publishing board. But President Morris had tired of the three-year controversy about the publishing board, and, really, he wanted to end the feuding and to prevent a division of the convention. Morris said:

> It is generally known that the National Baptist Publishing Board had the most phenomenal growth of any of the Boards of our Convention, and yet it has been under constant fire almost all the years of its existence. It has been a source of much regret that so much has been written and spoken adversely about the management [Boyd] of the Publishing House, and that the Convention has had to send so many investigating committees to the headquarters [Nashville] of the Board, so as to get such data as would give satisfaction to the curious.... We have reached

the place where the agitation may cease and all may go to work and build up and strengthen our publishing interests.[27]

The constant controversy troubled Boyd and the staff members at the National Baptist Publishing Board. It became difficult to operate a company when constantly beset by religious politics and bad publicity among the churches and the publishing board's customers. Still, the NBPB could not avoid the religious politics and the controversy generated within the National Baptist Convention and the churches.

The National Baptist Publishing Board's members became upset further by the death of Charles H. Burrill in 1911. He died at his Brooklyn, New York home. Burrill came to Nashville in 1886 to direct printing at the African Methodist Episcopal Church's Sunday School Union. He retired and returned to New York only to return to help Boyd establish printing operations at the publishing board in 1898. Burrill became vice-president of the Globe Publishing Company before returning to final retirement in New York in 1909. He had received his printing experience in Rhode Island. Burrill had prepared Dock A. Hart to take over the operations at the National Baptist Publishing Board.[28]

The publishing board experienced other problems. The National Baptist Publishing Board suffered a fire which destroyed the power house, the steam engine, and the electric plant. Boyd kept the event quiet to prevent loss of business from the National Baptist Convention's churches. The city government forced the National Baptist Publishing Board to make improvements including the installation of a seven thousand dollar automatic fire extinguishing and sprinkling system. Repairs were made on the buildings, the plumbing, the sewer system, the electric systems, and the sidewalks. The plant looked new.[29]

The publishing board circulated over eight million periodicals and handled 238,029 pieces of correspondence. Comparatively the white northern Baptist Publication Society produced thirty-two periodicals and Sunday school materials with an output of 55,897,490 copies in 1912. The NBPB bought no new equipment in 1911-1912, but it installed previously ordered equipment. The workers could only stitch eight to ten thousand magazines per day until a continuous feed-stitching machine with two stitchers produced thirty thousand to fifty thousand magazines per day. Since 1897, the National Baptist Publishing Board had spent $2,145,307.35 on processing and mailing correspondence, including personnel costs.[30]

The National Baptist Publishing Board had made many other changes by 1912. The field secretary had visited black churches in the western states at tremendous expense to the National Baptist Publishing Board. The Reverend Beckham had visited every state in the Union, Canada and Europe to promote the Home Mission Board and the National Baptist Publishing Board. The

Church Supply Department (NBR)

Early Printing Press (NBR)

publishing board had begun Bible Conferences to promote the correct idea of Bible reading. By 1912, the Home Mission Board had spent $618,481.50, mostly the National Baptist Publishing Board's money.[31]

The National Baptist Publishing Board continued to promote the Children's Day programs on the second Sunday in June as authorized by the National Baptist Convention in 1897. To encourage young people to read in the home, the publishing board created a four-book Readers' Course: *Training in Church Membership, Theodosia Ernesti or the Heroine of Faith, The Outlines of Baptist History, Conservation of National Ideals.* Designed to teach the essential things that young black people should know, the cost of the books was kept at a minimum rate of fifty cents each.

The publishing board further expanded its apprenticeship program. Still the shortages of skilled Negro workers forced Boyd to hire skilled white craftsmen to work at the publishing board. Boyd said: "It is the object and purpose of the Board in all of its departments to start young men and women at the bottom and gradually promote them in such a way as when older employees drop out, their places can be filled without great inconvenience or disadvantage to their work."[32]

Two of Richard H. Boyd's three sons, Theophilus Bartholomew and Henry Allen, were trained in this way at the National Baptist Publishing Board. They were required to work in production areas, learning the business from bottom to top. Especially, the eldest son, Henry Allen, received training in all aspects of the business after he left his good job in the San Antonio, Texas post office and joined his father in Nashville, Tennessee.

Sunday School Congress

Henry Allen Boyd came aboard at a crucial time when R. H. Boyd needed a loyal, hard working, younger man by his side. The publishing board could not afford a high priced executive. When Boyd made Henry Allen the assistant secretary of the National Baptist Publishing Board, a howl of criticism came from the opposition within the National Baptist Convention. A handsome, young man, Henry Allen married Georgia Ann Bradford at Nashville's Mount Olive Missionary Baptist Church where the Boyds held membership. Henry Allen became not only the newly appointed assistant secretary of the National Baptist Publishing Board, he also became the secretary of the Sunday School Congress, a program so crucial to the success of the publishing board.

Around 1905, Richard H. Boyd organized the Sunday School Congress to bring together pastors and Sunday school superintendents and teachers in an annual meeting to discuss Sunday school issues and train workers. The first Congress met in 1906. Under the energetic Henry Allen, the Congress became the publishing board's most important annual event. The huge mass choirs, the young people's Christian drill team competitions, brass bands, gospel quartets, booths, seminars, and animated sermons by dynamic preachers drew thousands to the annual Congress. The Congress rivaled unintentionally the National Baptist Convention's annual session. To prevent conflict with the National Baptist Convention's annual September meeting, the Congress was held in June in different cities: Nashville (1906); New Orleans (1907); Jacksonville, Florida (1908); Nashville (1909); Atlanta (1910); Meridian, Mississippi (1911); Birmingham (1912).[33] The huge success of the Sunday School Congress program attracted more critics for Boyd and the NBPB.

To disarm critics, Richard Boyd pointed out that the Congress was not a policy-making body like the National Baptist Convention. The Congress had no elected officials and governing structure, and the Congress discussed simply Sunday school issues and trained church workers. In 1914, Boyd reported to the National Baptist Convention that the Sunday School Congress was "the greatest adjunct or the greatest assistance or agency that our Board has to increase the circulation of periodicals and other Sunday-school prerequisites."[34]

The rank and file and the younger people of the black Baptist churches attended the Congress where they became impressed wlth Richard H. Boyd and his family. The Boyd children helped to administer the massive event. Katie A. Boyd and Marie Boyd helped to plan and direct the Congress' Model Sunday School. The young, energetic Henry Allen and publishing board staff members spent most of the year organizing the next Congress. Charter and excursion rates were secured from train companies to transport thousands of delegates from their home cities to the site of the Congress. The Nashville *Globe* and other NBPB newspapers advertised the Congress several months ahead of schedule and published extensive transportation rates and travel packages.

When departure time came, the Boyds boarded a chartered train, "The Congress Special," at Nashville. The train became filled with guests, National Baptist Publishing Board members, Home Mission Board members, Baptist Young People's Union Board members, secretary E. D. W. Isaac's staff, Educational Board members, and delegates from many of Nashville's Baptist churches. On the same day, the train from Louisville arrived with Kentucky delegates, Foreign Mission Board members, and Woman's Auxiliary Board members. This was similar for the departure to the National Baptist Convention's annual sessions. Perhaps the fanfare, pomp, and circumstance drew the attention of Boyd's critics.

When the Congress opened, the atmosphere reached a fever pitch. Henry Allen often entered town, dressed in a white suit with white shoes, stepping lively in a parade down the community's streets. The Congress secretary led the parade onto the floor of the convention hall. Boy Cadets, dressed in Boy Scout-like uniforms, and young girls gaily dressed, all marched to military-style music. The Congress sessions demonstrated vividly the Boyds' great organizational skills.

The delegates burst into applause when Henry Allen, the Boyd family, and guests entered the convention hall. The Congress officially got underway. "Congress-time" became the one period in each year when the National Baptist Publishing Board interacted directly with its customers—the one time when the National Baptist Publishing Board basked in the public spotlight, and the only time when the publishing board and its officers could directly influence the direction of Sunday school ideology and training on a massive scale.

When the sixth annual Sunday School Congress opened in Meridian, Mississippi, the session was headed, as usual, by the Reverend C. H. Clark, chairman of the board of directors for the National Baptist Publishing Board. The Reverend N. H. Pius, the musical director, directed a great choir which sang "Hail the Baptist Congress." Thousands of delegates and visitors flooded the town, taxing the capacity of private homes which had to house the black men, women, and children who, because of segregation laws, could not use hotel accommodations.

President Morris, who usually attended the Congress, at the expense of the publishing board, took the opportunity to hold meetings. At the Congress, Morris could meet the secretaries of the boards before the next National Baptist Convention met in September. During the Meridian Congress, for example, Morris took the opportunity to hold a conference for the many Baptist newspaper editors in an effort to get them to avoid duplicity and agree on some common ground.[35]

The session in Birmingham, Alabama during June 9-14, 1912, became a most memorable Sunday School Congress. A "Sunday School Special" with Congress officials arrived at the Union Station on the morning of June 8. A local committee met the train and led a parade through the main streets to the Sixteenth Street Baptist Church where thousands of delegates had assembled. The Reverend C. H. Clark, chairman of the publishing board, took the podium and officially opened the session. Professor H. B. P. Johnson of Muskogee, Oklahoma, the chorister and musical director for the Congress, led a mass choir and the audience in singing "Hail the Baptist Congress." The audience gave Henry Allen Boyd, the Congress secretary, cheers and the Chautauqua salute, three waves of the handkerchief. Henry Allen read the list of presenters and their topics and gave the enrollment data. The editor of the *National Baptist Union* solicited support and subscriptions for this Baptist newspaper. Then the local committee on homes gave the assignments for delegates.[36]

Many remembered the annual trip to the Congress as the greatest of times. The June meeting signaled the beginning of Summer. The arrival of the Congress generated excitement and events throughout the city. Moreover, the arrival of trainloads of visitors and delegates and the marvelous parades excited the host black community. On Sunday morning, the Reverend Richard H.

Boyd, Henry Allen, and other preachers boarded automobiles and visited Birmingham's black Sunday Schools. The Sunday schools accepted invitations to a parade with the National Baptist Brass Band and a church band. With Dr. Boyd and the Congress officials in the lead, the bands and the Boy Cadets led the crowd to the Shiloh Baptist Church where the Boy Cadets launched their anti-smoking campaign with the "Anti-Cigarette Alphabet:"

A - Stands for ACTION Against the Deadly Weed;
B - Stands for BOY whose strength and vitality we need;
C - Stands for CULTURE the cigarette cannot give;
D - Stands for DANGER, which is ahead, If you live;

The letters continued to "Z - Stands for ZEAL which will be shown by the Boy Cadets."[37]

Even though Richard Boyd explained that the Congress was an extension of the National Baptist Publishing Board's Sunday school work, its popular appeal bothered some political forces within the National Baptist Convention. Boyd invited leaders of the Southern Baptist Convention to the annual Congress' sessions. This too bothered the critics. By 1912, some black Baptist leaders had recommended unsuccessfully to the National Baptist Convention that the Congress be stopped. But when the Baptist denomination split in 1915, the National Baptist Convention, Incorporated organized its own Sunday School Congress. The Congress served to involve young people and train Sunday school teachers, superintendents, and pastors.

Before the Storm: Panama and Mission Work

In addition to the successful Sunday School Congress programs, the NBPB built an important mission program in Panama. For years Boyd had recommended that the National Baptist Convention become involved in Panama. But the convention's Foreign Mission Board focused its work and money on missions in West Africa. Panama intrigued Boyd because of its proximity to the continental United States and the large black population that lived in Panama. Like Boyd, these blacks had endured slavery, a system that died in Latin America only as recently as the 1880s.

In 1912, Boyd increased the Home Mission Board's work in Panama and Costa Rica. He left for the Panama Canal Zone on February 10, 1912. His welcome in Panama was more than expected. The black Panama residents eagerly sought books and literature from the NBPB. They had already heard of the National Baptist Publishing Board and had some copies of its literature. During his visit, Boyd preached, met with black ministers and their congregations, and investigated the treatment of blacks in the Panama Canal Zone where persons of African descent had worked for years as laborers on the construction of the American canal and as slaves in Central America before that time. When

Boyd returned to Nashville, he was met at the train depot by a huge audience, including James C. Napier and Preston Taylor, who led triumphantly a parade to the publishing house.[38]

Local black leaders marveled that a black man, Boyd, had engaged Caribbean affairs at a time when white American imperialism seemed to oppress people of color across the globe. Through Boyd and the NBPB, the black community's leaders received satisfaction that some black Americans had extended a helping hand to fellow oppressed blacks in another country.

Boyd published his report in a series of *Globe* articles. Although he knew the danger when a black man criticized whites during the Age of Jim Crow, the Reverend Boyd severely criticized the American government for racial discrimination in the Panama Canal Zone where black Panama citizens suffered racial segregation even in the post office facilities.[39]

Houston: Real Trouble Begins

The Reverend Boyd expected to enter the National Baptist Convention hall in September 1912 like a triumphant Christian warrior to be congratulated by his fellow preachers. With the Panama project and the successful Birmingham Congress under their belts, Boyd and his entourage left Nashville via the Louisville-Nashville Railroad and headed to Houston, Texas, site of the National Baptist Convention session. Aboard the train were members of the Home Mission Board, the Baptist Young People's Union, and the NBPB. Members of the Foreign Mission Board and the Woman's Auxiliary came from Louisville to Nashville and joined the special train. The sight of Boyd heading such a large delegation worried his detractors in Houston.

Right away, critics blasted the Home Mission Board's cozy relations with the southern white Baptists. Naturally, a combative Boyd took the opportunity to oppose criticism about his relationship with the Southern Baptist Convention. He argued that the southern white Baptists accepted the National Baptist Convention on black terms, and they often accepted black preachers who did not come up to their standards. Also he argued that the Southern Baptist Convention's Home Mission Board had invested more money in the National Baptist Convention's Home Mission Board's work than had the National Baptist Convention, and a great deal of work had been done in National Baptist Convention mission work in the last ten years partly because of the help from the southern Baptists. Boyd urged the convention to carry out the articles of agreement between the National Baptist Convention and the Southern Baptist Convention. President Morris tried to quiet the debate, and he suggested that the Home Mission Board also develop good relations with the white Baptists in the North and the West where many National Baptist Convention churches also existed.[40]

Boyd focused his convention report on another problem. "One of the most vexing problems for the National Baptist Publishing Board" was the *National Baptist Union,* Boyd said to the National Baptist Convention's 1912 delegates. Although the 1909 National Baptist Convention session had taken charge of the paper and appointed an editor, his salary was not paid with contributions from each board as the convention had directed. The NBPB had advanced the editor's salary and continued to print the paper, changing the name to *Union-Review.* The editor, J. D. Crenshaw, did a great job on editorials, but the NBPB's staff did all other work including advertisements, editing, proofing, and printing. Again without success, Boyd asked the convention to reimburse the publishing board for the editor's salary and to fund the paper.[41]

Right away Boyd and the members of the National Baptist Publishing Board learned that some delegates cared less about the board's glowing reports. A growing anti-NBPB faction had become well-organized. These men pushed an idea to incorporate the National Baptist Convention, giving it power to control the boards including the incorporated National Baptist Publishing Board.

On the first night of the convention, Mack M. Rodgers of Texas read a paper on "The Propriety of Incorporating the National Baptist Convention." Rodgers pointed out that the National Baptist Convention's power rested in a series of boards, some of which had been incorporated in other states and Washington, D. C. "The Convention then should correct its mistakes and place its rights and powers where they belong—in the hands of the Baptists of the United States.... Our great Convention, which, legally speaking, is half dead and half alive," because the boards are incorporated and act separately from the Convention, Rodgers pointed out. The Convention has no title right to any real estate in any state, and it has no inherent power of control over any of the incorporate boards and it cannot appoint and elect their members, Rodgers observed further. He said that the Tennessee courts had ruled in other cases, for instance, that the parent organization has no power nor control over an incorporated branch in the exercise of those powers for which the charter was expressly obtained. And incorporation made the boards a civil body politic whereas the courts cannot look to the acts of the religious society to determine the questions in contest about the acts of the incorporated body, Rodgers quoted the Tennessee court.[42]

Mack Matthew Rodgers was born in Wharton County, Texas, on July 13, 1849. He completed Prairie View State Normal School in 1881. He became principal of a city school and gained election to the LaGrange city council. Rodgers became a regular delegate to the Republican National Convention, 1888-1912. He became a deputy internal revenue collector for the federal government in 1897. Rodgers was secretary of the LaGrange Baptist Association and secretary of the Baptist Missionary and Educational Convention of Texas. Friends and colleagues respectfully called him "Professor Rodgers." Rodgers carried great influence in the National Baptist Convention because of his political skills and knowledge.[43]

Fearing insubordination and rebellion by the incorporate boards, the Convention accepted a resolution to accept Rodgers' report and ordered a study about the incorporation of the National Baptist Convention with powers to directly control the boards. The resolution was sent to a special committee, the Committee Upon the Propriety of the Incorporation of the National Baptist Convention, with few Boyd supporters on board.[44] This set of events started the "incorporation movement" rolling.

The Reverend A. J. Rowland, secretary of the American Baptist Publication Society, attended the convention. He told the delegates that although the American Baptist Publication Society had closed its branch houses in the South, the agency still held interest in the colored people. The American Baptist Publication Society continued to use the best colored workers in its mission work. The black district secretary for the American Baptist Publication Society also attended the convention's sessions. The representatives of the Southern Baptist Convention's Sunday School Board and the Northern Baptist Convention's American Baptist Publication Society had met on January 25, 1912, in Hot Springs, Arkansas to agree to work toward Christian unity and not fight over the black Baptists.[45]

On Friday, another northern Baptist leader and secretary of the American Baptist Home Mission Board, Dr. Henry L. Morehouse, attended the National Baptist Convention session. Morehouse said he considered himself and the late Reverend W. J. Simmons the Godfathers of the National Baptist Convention. Morehouse said: "Our Society has expended more than five million dollars for the uplift of your people, and given more than $400,000 to help schools and colleges owned and controlled by your people. We have set aside $65,000 to be used in connection with the re-establishment of Roger Williams University in Nashville."[46] A move had already begun to change the name of the Atlanta Baptist College to Morehouse College. "We rejoice that Atlanta Baptist College is henceforth to be honored with the name of the venerable and venerated secretary of the [ABHM] Society and to be known as Morehouse College," resolved the 1912 annual meeting of the Northern Baptist Convention.[47] Morehouse had requested that the Northern Baptist Convention begin raising a one million dollar endowment for black educational institutions supported by the American Baptist Home Mission Society.[48] Immediately after Morehouse's speech, the Reverend Richard H. Boyd moved successfully that a vote of gratitude and appreciation be extended by the National Baptist Convention to Dr. Morehouse for the long years of service to the colored people.[49]

The 1912 session of the National Baptist Convention ended with many rumors. The Commission on Incorporation had been directed to report to the 1913 session. This meant another problem and another investigating committee for the National Baptist Publishing Board.

Even though it suffered external and internal problems, the publishing board company continued to progress. Under W. S. Ellington, the NBPB's Sunday School Department increased the number of periodicals from two publications to fourteen different magazines. Ellington had a staff of seven persons and twenty-four part-time contributors. The Reverend Ellington became a full-fledged member of the International Sunday School Lesson Committee of the World, the first black to be honored in this manner. The National Baptist Publishing Board's Readers' Course issued over three hundred diplomas. The publishing board instituted its own Bible Class Movement, the Metoka and Galeda Bible Class Movement, styled on the World's Sunday School Convention held in Washington, D. C. in June, 1910. The movement united young black people into a religious and social organization to support the Sunday school missionary movements. The National Baptist Publishing Board prepared the buttons, badges, pennants, class charters, by-laws, and paraphernalia for the organizations.[50]

The year 1912 was a most strenuous fiscal year. Heavy rains in the spring caused heavy unemployment among black people and left many periodicals without orders. Revenues fell seven thousand dollars, causing the board to borrow some money. Employees demanded raises. Rising printing costs and falling orders caused the *Lesson Leaflet* to be stopped.

The National Baptist Publishing Board became heavily involved in a movement to train and discipline black children who suffered from slum conditions, lack of good schools, and poor home training by 1912. By this time, this Progressive Movement, an American social reform movement, pervaded black Nashville and urban America. The National Baptist Publishing Board joined the Woman's Auxiliary's "Save the Boys" movement and organized the National Baptist A. F. Cadets with W. H. Crawford of Austin, Texas, as commander-in-chief. The cadets rivaled the white Boy Scouts troops which blacks could not join. Similar to a Girl Scouts movement, the publishing board also organized a Girls' Doll Club with uniforms, paraphernalia, and of course Negro dolls. At the Beaumont Sunday School Congress session, "It was a sight never to be forgotten..." to see troops of the National Baptist A. F. Cadets escorting 150 Girls Doll Club members into the meeting hall with dolls on the girls' arms. The girls were between ages six and fifteen. The Galedas took care of girls over age fifteen.[51]

A New Year, 1913

At the 1913 New Year's dinner for the National Baptist Publishing Board, Boyd saluted his wife, Harriett: "This little black woman who has stood by me all these years and who is directly responsible for whatever success I have made, as she washed and ironed and helped me raise my children, and then after they were out of the way, helped to send me to school after I was over forty years old, and [is] due the thanks for this New Year's dinner."[52]

Working diligently in his community's behalf, Boyd helped secure the 1913 National Baptist Convention session for Nashville. He received the support of Nashville's Negro Board of Trade and the local white Board of Trade. Nashville's leaders had begun a booster campaign to promote the city and improve its economy. The announcement about the convention came in February, 1913, when a committee went to work to make the necessary preparations to receive thousands of delegates. After holding the Sunday School Congress in Muskogee, Oklahoma on June 4-9, 1913, Henry Allen Boyd turned his attention to prepare for the coming National Baptist Convention session.[53]

By holding the September, 1913, National Baptist Convention session in Nashville, the action helped to keep the anti-NBPB faction from taking control of things (at least for now). The *Report of the Committee Upon the Propriety* of *the Incorporation* of *the National Baptist Convention* (Nashville,1913) answered the 1912 Rodgers' paper and said: "The Committee does not see any advantages that could be derived from the Incorporation of the Parent Body, the National Baptist Convention." We recommend that..."the present relations of the Convention and its Boards be permitted to continue."[54] For now peace reigned in the convention.

The publishing board and the annual Sunday School Congress operated effectively so that the delegates did not desire to destroy the publishing board and divide the convention. The publishing board transformed the weekly *National Baptist Union-Review* into a temporary daily newspaper to keep the convention's delegates informed. Three Mergenthaler linotype machines, a Scott's rotary press, an automatic cross feeder, and a new stitcher produced the daily paper at the rate of thousands of copies per hour. At the same time, Boyd and the publishing board continued to produce the weekly *National Baptist Union-Review* and mail it to subscribers.

The meeting of the National Baptist Convention's annual session in Nashville boosted the local economy. Thousands of delegates had to be housed, fed, and transported to meetings. Local residents received one dollar per day to house each delegate. Blacks could not stay at white hotels, and Nashville had few black hotels. The Women's Convention met at the Spruce Street Baptist Church where Nannie H. Burroughs directed the meetings. To transport the delegates from homes to the meetings, private cars and streetcars were pressed into service. Blacks who owned automobiles and passenger wagons made money during the week of the convention's sessions.

Boyd presented the National Baptist Publishing Board's annual report at the meeting. The publishing board reported over $200,000 in business for the period October, 1912 to September, 1913. Two missionaries had been sent to Panama. Boyd had taken the train to New Orleans and seen the missionaries embark upon their voyage. The National Baptist Publishing Board distributed millions of pieces of literature in 1913.[55]

A Critical Year, 1914

The National Baptist Convention's September 14-19, 1914, annual session met in Philadelphia where the move to incorporate the national convention took on steam. President Morris began the session by complaining that "the five-cents theaters, so numerous in our large cities, are simply clearing our churches of young people on the Sabbath."[56] He praised the Woman's Auxiliary for opening the new Training School for Women and Girls and the Foreign Mission Board for supporting mission work throughout Africa, including South Africa. Morris repeated his statement that the Home Mission Board should develop the same relationship with the northern Baptists as with the southern Baptists. He said: "There is no reason whatever for any friction between the Convention and its Boards, for they were created for the sole purpose of doing work for and in the name of the National Baptist Convention."[57]

At the conclusion of Morris' address, men who were leaders and state association presidents stood on chairs, waved hats and hollered to suspend the rules and reelect Morris by acclamation. Protests broke out because of this annual spectacle. Besides, the large Texas delegation, with its huge block of votes, arrived two hours late at the convention hall. With the election business over, the incorporators went to work in earnest.

In 1911, Morris had recommended the appointment of a commission to take consideration of matters coming up from any board to prevent discussing the matter in open convention where heated discussions could destroy a session. He argued that he had learned that all boards had gone along with this except two boards. Morris warned the delegates that there would be no war in the National Baptist Convention. But the anti-NBPB faction had found an issue (incorporation) to attract wider support.

Even though the 1913 Commission reported negatively for incorporation of the National Baptist Convention, the incorporation group continued the pressure to get a favorable report. They measured their strategy carefully throughout the post-1913 convention months. When the National Baptist Convention's 1914 session convened, the incorporators were ready. They scheduled another incorporation report for the National Baptist Convention's 1914 session.

At the Saturday afternoon session, the reading of the Commission's report started an uproar. This report seemed clearly anti-NBPB and called for changing the National Baptist Convention's charter to give the National Baptist Convention direct control over the boards. Boyd requested a minority report. Morris disallowed the request although Boyd claimed that his ill child had prevented him from attending all the Commission's meetings at the National Baptist Publishing Board. The convention deferred the report until Monday because of the noise and uproar. But under the leadership of the politically astute Professor Rodgers, the incorporation faction would be ready to push its proposals.

On Monday, the convention passed a resolution to accept a commission report to change the charter of the National Baptist Publishing Board. The Reverend A. J. Stokes made the successful motion. The report recommended an agency to represent the National Baptist Convention between annual sessions and have authority to study and act against complaints about any board.

The report produced bitter debate at the 1914 meeting. For a lengthy thirty-seven minutes, the Reverend Sutton E. Griggs, a brilliant orator, presented the commission's report and criticized severely Boyd's management of the National Baptist Publishing Board. A noted and eloquent speaker with great power of persuasion, Griggs launched a personal attack on Boyd and his family. Reportedly, he said: "Old man, you are a liar." Griggs claimed that Boyd's entire family was on the publishing board's payroll. The Reverend Boyd gave an emotional forty-one minute speech against the report. He said: "If it had been the father [A. R. Griggs] rather than the son that has painted me as the worst criminal in history and would send me to my grave in disgrace, branded me as a thief and an embezzler of the money of the denomination, my surprise could hardly be greater. I went to Nashville without any money furnished by the denomination, I spent my own money and invested my wife's money, and have brought you a plant worth more than $300,000, and this is my reward."[58]

Griggs' claim that Boyd's entire family fed on the publishing board's payroll was not accurate. The Reverend R. H. Boyd had three sons and three daughters. The three daughters were housewives who did not depend entirely on any of the Boyd enterprises or the publishing board. Lula Boyd Landers attended stenography school and completed the academic course of study at Roger Williams University. She helped her father at the publishing board before getting married. Annie E. Boyd Hall lived in Palestine, Texas, where she operated two funeral homes. Mattie E. Boyd Bennefield served as cashier at the National Baptist Publishing for only five years. None of Boyd's sons worked at the publishing board when Griggs published his books there; the oldest of Boyd's sons, Henry Allen, worked in the San Antonio, Texas post office. He came to work for the National Baptist Publishing Board on his father's request and for less salary than he earned at the post office. J. Blaine Boyd, the second oldest son, worked as general foreman at the African Methodist Episcopal

Church's Sunday School Union publishing house in Nashville for a salary of $850 per year. Blaine attended Virginia (Union) Theological Seminary and College and received training in printing in Chicago. Theophilus Bartholomew Boyd, the youngest of Richard H. Boyd's sons, attended Morehouse College for three years. After Theophilus completed the Tennessee Agricultural and Industrial State Normal School's literary department in 1914 and trained at the Morgenthaler Linotype factory in Brooklyn, New York, he was hired as a machinist for forty dollars per month at the National Baptist Publishing Board. Watson Boyd and Joe Boyd were on the National Baptist Publishing Board's payroll, but these men were no relation to R. H. Boyd. Only one of Boyd's sons-in-law worked at the board as chief clerk for the first-class mail room. The National Baptist Publishing Board had a few hundred employees, but members of the Boyd family did not dominate the workforce.

The tactics by Rodgers and Griggs worked. The convention adopted the incorporation report by a vote of 361 to 209. Rodgers re-introduced quickly a resolution to amend the National Baptist Convention's proposed charter to give it control of all boards. With another blinding move, the incorporators persuaded the convention to suspend the rules and adopt a resolution to make the Commission the Executive Board of the National Baptist Convention. The incorporators had won the day. The heated meeting adjourned at 7:30 in the evening.[59]

Rodgers, Griggs, and others intended to move on the National Baptist Publishing Board. Because he knew that they would move to separate the HMB from the NBPB, the Reverend Boyd resigned the Home Mission Board. The Reverend Joseph A. Booker became corresponding secretary of the Home Mission Board. Moving swiftly, the incorporators persuaded the convention to give J. D. Crenshaw complete control of the *National Baptist Union- Review* newspaper. They directed Crenshaw not to mention the controversy in the newspaper. Then a great commotion took place, forcing the session to adjourn.[60]

Now that the Commission on Incorporation considered itself a real Executive Board of the National Baptist Convention, it proposed to take immediate control of all other boards. Specifically for the NBPB, the Commission appointed a committee of three receivers: William Haynes, J. D. Crenshaw, and E. M. Lawrence, all Nashvillians. They received orders to take control of the National Baptist Publishing Board's properties, if necessary. These commissioners wanted the publishing board to abolish its charter or change it to be subordinate to the National Baptist Convention. The publishing board's officers had a perfect defense, the Tennessee charter (1898), which had separated the NBPB from the Home Mission Board. The NBPB became a private, non-profit corporation who elected its own officers and board members. Yet the charter tied the publishing board to the business of publishing for the National Baptist Convention's churches and other Baptist churches.

Boyd and the publishing board's officers had no desire to separate the National Baptist Publishing Board from the National Baptist Convention. To cut the umbilical cord to the convention could destroy the publishing board's access to its customers, the black Baptist churches. But Boyd and his faction could not let the Rodgers-Griggs incorporators take control of the publishing board which had required eighteen years of personal sacrifice, hard work, and private funds. The National Baptist Publishing Board had been established to be independent and serve black Baptists regardless of Convention affiliation, Boyd and his supporters argued.

In October 1914, the National Baptist Publishing Board published a protest that the Commission had exceeded constitutional authority. The publishing board published *Protest of the National Baptist Publishing Board Against the Acts of the Commission.* Then the publishing board printed its charter in the *National Baptist Union-Review* for the subscribers to see. The Commission scheduled its visit to Nashville for December, 1914.[61]

Under pressure from the incorporators, President Morris sent a letter to the black Baptist churches, directing them to order nothing from the National Baptist Publishing Board until the question of control was settled. The *National Baptist Union-Review* retaliated and called the National Baptist Convention's 1914 session "A Woeful Failure!"[62]

Meanwhile, the publishing board introduced, for the first time, the next year's *National Baptist Sunday School Lesson Commentary* (1915) ahead of time. The new commentary went on sale at seventy-five cents per copy. It included help for readers, truths gleaned from the lessons, colored maps, a dictionary of terms, and more. Also the National Baptist Publishing Board announced the new *National Baptist Jubilee Melodies* (1914), a song book in which jubilee and plantation songs had been set to music. The book was used in the 1914 National Baptist Convention sessions. It sold for thirty cents per copy.[63]

Months Following the 1914 Convention

After returning to Nashville, the Reverend Boyd offered his resignation to the directors of the National Baptist Publishing Board. Boyd was clearly depressed and dejected. He left the room. Henry Allen Boyd, assistant secretary, read a statement for the Reverend R. H. Boyd. But the directors refused to accept the resignation. Boyd reluctantly returned to the chair. The board reelected Boyd and elected additional directors, including the Reverend L. L. Campbell of Austin, Texas. The men decided to stand their ground, hoping that the storm would die.[64] Boyd remained calm and expressed no bitterness toward his attackers.

On October 10, 1914, the Reverend Boyd published an introduction and support for the new corresponding secretary of the Home Mission Board, the Reverend Booker, president of Arkansas Baptist College and editor of the *Baptist Vanguard* in Little Rock. Booker had been the first corresponding secretary of the Home Mission Board in 1895. Boyd said: "Dr. Booker has at all times been an earnest helper and faithful cooperator with the Board and its Secretary. He has never lost interest in its work and has been at all times ready with words of encouragement...."[65]

To quiet the critics who claimed that the Home Mission Board had not been managed properly, the Reverend Boyd said:

> I tendered my resignation for the good of the work. There were those brethren connected with the National Baptist Convention who were equally and as deeply interested in the work as the members of the Board themselves who were and still feel that the home mission work could be better prosecuted separately than in co-relation with other Boards. They felt that the Secretary's time should be given exclusively to missionary work on home fields, hence, after ten years trial of the work in co-relation with the Sunday school and publication work [NBPB], it was my earnest belief that this experiment of a change should be brought about to the satisfaction of those brethren who believe that it would be for the best interest of the kingdom of Christ and the extension of our Baptist work on home fields to have this separation brought about, and I am sure that there could be found no better man to take hold of this work than Dr. Joseph A. Booker of Little Rock, Arkansas.[66]

Boyd published the results of the last eighteen years of work between the Home Mission Board and the National Baptist Publishing Board:[67]

Year	Number of Missionaries and Colporters	Churches and Associations Visited	Money Spent
1897	4	425	$ 1,900
1898	6	150	2,557
1899	10	225	4,353
1900	15	430	8,924
1901	20	950	10,997
1902	25	1576	15,741
1903	32	1676	19,859
1904	30	1450	27,520
1905	36	1852	33,337
1906	66	2234	49,622

1907	50	4234	42,577
1908	65	6297	42,396
1909	43	5191	44,296
1910	45	4094	54,844
1911	45	3014	55,677
1912	45	3011	57,943
1913	30	631	72,905
1914	36	3731	64,890

Many proponents of the National Baptist Publishing Board became upset for months at the treatment given to Boyd, his wife, and family at the 1914 convention. President Morris received criticism for allowing the convention to operate without acceptable parliamentary rules. However, many persons knew that the political sophistication of Rodgers, Griggs, and other incorporators overwhelmed even Morris who could no longer hold the anti-NBPB men back. The *Union-Review* said:

> The [Commission's] report upon the platform in the Convention, supposed to be the report of the Commissioners, was only one man's [S. E. Griggs]. And if it were the Commissioners' entire approval, it is the most damnable piece of work ever undertaken by a set of Christian men. The paint that was attempted to be put upon Dr. Boyd by one of those he had fed and one of those who still owes certain amounts of money, and by one who was there under charges of embezzling the people of their moneys, was one of the most damnable acts ever committed in a Christian body....[68]

The publishing board's friends reported that Sutton E. Griggs was arrested by the Philadelphia police on September 11, 1914, during the convention. The policemen took Griggs before a judge and placed him in jail under a $1,500 bond for illegally obtaining money for sale of stock in his Orion Publishing Company. Griggs allegedly sold stock in the company in other states too. The Orion Publishing Company only published Griggs' books, some of which were printed by the National Baptist Publishing Board. Griggs supposedly owed the publishing board $1,500 and Boyd $300. Griggs sold his books through extensive tours of the country, but apparently he did not pay his printing bills at the publishing board and the $300 bank note Boyd had endorsed. Some also claimed that Griggs left the First Baptist Church of East Nashville $2,500 in debt because of a mortgage secured for his company.[69]

The Reverend L. L. Campbell, president of the General Missionary Baptist Convention of Texas said:

> Dr. Sutton E. Griggs is a young man of great ability and of sterling worth to the Baptist denomination and the race in general. His ability,

however, should not be used to the detriment of another who has spent his life paving the way for unborn generations.[70]

Pure jealousy about the National Baptist Publishing Board's success was suspected to be part of the problem. Many preachers became jealous of Boyd's success, and other preachers, who made little money in their profession, really felt that Boyd had a profit-making machine. Under the Reverend Boyd's management, the Home Mission Board and the NBPB had outperformed all other Negro Baptist boards:[71]

Financial Reports of National Baptist Convention Boards, 1914

National Baptist Publishing Board	$200,000
Home Mission Board	65,000
Foreign Mission Board	35,000
Woman's Auxiliary Board	20,000
Baptist Young People's Union Board	2,200
Educational Board	1,500
Benefit Board	1,200

"The large volume of business done by Dr. Boyd has made for him some enemies who went away rejoicing that he no longer serves the Home Mission Board as Secretary," said the Reverend L. L. Campbell. But "Dr. Boyd has given his service free of charge to the [Home Mission] Board since its beginning," said Campbell.[72]

Reflecting on the convention's vote to take the *National Baptist Union Review* from Boyd's control, the Reverend Boyd said:

> The National Baptist Publishing Board belongs to the Negro Baptists churches and Sunday schools of the United States. Hence, the *Union-Review* is truthfully a mouthpiece of the Baptists of the United States of America, and will so continue unless changed by higher authority.[73]

The weekly newspaper cost the National Baptist Publishing Board about $7,500 per year, and the subscriptions produced only $4,000 in revenues.[74]

The publishing board needed a newspaper. The other boards had newspapers. And many of the other newspapers joined the attack against the publishing board. The Foreign Mission Board published the *Missionary Herald* (Louisville). The Baptist Young People's Union Board published the weekly *Clarion* (Nashville) through the Clarion Publishing Company. The Home Mission Board published the *Baptist Vanguard* (Little Rock). The Benefit Board published *The Reporter* (Helena, Arkansas). The Educational Board published *The Signal Index* (Memphis). The Woman's Auxiliary Board published the *Lincoln Herald* ("Lincoln Heights," Washington, D. C.).

Boyd and the NBPB continued to print the *Union-Review* until the convention actually gave the new editor money to publish the paper. This never happened. When the 1915 dispute split the denomination, the NBPB continued to publish the *National Baptist Union-Review*; and the Rodgers Griggs convention started another paper, the *National Baptist Voice.*

In November, 1914, H. W. Jones, pastor of the Green Street Baptist Church in Louisville, Kentucky, published a paper entitled "Should We Have Another National Baptist Convention?"[75] The National Baptist Convention was rushing toward another division, worst than the Lott Carey split in 1897.

Boyd needed rest and assurance from his supporters. In mid-November, he toured extensively and received big ovations at New Orleans, Louisiana, San Antonio, Austin, and other Texas towns. Large delegations waited at the railroad stations to escort him to dinners and church meetings.[76]

1914 was a tough year for the National Baptist Publishing Board and its members and employees. Time and stress took heavy tolls. Tragedies came one after the other.

On October 28, Nathaniel Hale Pius, superintendent of the board's Teacher Training Department, chorister for the Sunday School Congress and the National Baptist Publishing Board and editor of the Metoka and Galeda magazine, died after an eleven-month illness, leaving a wife and two daughters. He was a graduate of Leland University, former president of Hearne College, pastor of churches in Texas, Indiana, and Ohio, as well as former president of Memphis' Howe Institute before coming to the National Baptist Publishing Board in 1908. The National Baptist Publishing Board's Brass Band played in the funeral processional from Pius' home at 1817 Scovel Street to the First Colored Baptist Church on Eighth Avenue North.[77]

Then the Reverend Beckham passed in Independence, Missouri, leaving his wife. Services were held in Kansas City, Missouri, before the body was shipped to Nashville. The NBPB's band played the funeral processional from R. H. Boyd's house, where the body lay in review, to W. S. Ellington's First Colored Baptist Church. On the day of the funeral, December 23, the publishing board's employees constituted the choir. Boyd gave the obituary and the closing remarks, nearly breaking down each time. Beckham had been with Boyd since his Texas days, and Beckham, the Field Secretary, had been the backbone of the National Baptist Publishing Board's successful home mission work. Beckham had traveled to every state in the Union and other countries, and he remained loyal and dedicated to the work of the National Baptist Publishing Board and its home mission work.[78]

1914 ended with another National Baptist Convention Commission coming to Nashville on December 29. The members first met in the Baptist Young People's Union Board's offices where the Reverend E. W. D. Isaac gave reportedly the Commission's members practice questions to ask Boyd about the publishing board's operations. Then they dramatically walked to the

National Baptist Publishing Board's chapel, causing much excitement along the streets. Everyone knew what had happened at last September's National Baptist Convention in Philadelphia. The police even stopped by and asked the Reverend Boyd if policemen were needed to keep order. Boyd replied that a Christian meeting needed no protection, thank you. Some of the National Baptist Publishing Board's creditors called to ask if the company was being closed for good. Boyd replied in the negative.[79]

The meeting began in the publishing board's chapel. Two local white ministers, James M. Frost and the pastor of the First Baptist Church, were present. Some blacks demanded that only members of the Commission and the National Baptist Convention's members be allowed to remain in the crowded chapel. At Morris' insistence, the Reverend Frost was allowed to return. Frost said that he too received royalties from the Southern Baptist Convention's Sunday School Board for copyrights on books he had personally published. Griggs had criticized Boyd for owning copyrights on some sixteen books and booklets. But Boyd had received no royalties from the NBPB which paid no royalties to anyone as a matter of policy. The members then questioned Boyd about printing minutes and journals for the National Baptist Convention. Boyd said that the National Baptist Publishing Board had printed the reports since 1900, except on two occasions, and received no pay from the National Baptist Convention. The answers from Frost and Boyd quieted the most disruptive elements of the Commission. The meeting ended with the Commission passing resolutions to proceed with committees to revise the National Baptist Convention's constitution and change the charters of the boards. For now the Commission did not carry through with the directive to take control of the NBPB.[80]

1915: The End of the Beginning

"The year 1915, then, was truly the end of the beginning," a new era for black Baptists, said the Reverend Owen D. Pelt and Ralph Lee Smith in their book, The *Story of the National Baptists* (1961). In his book, *Frustrated Fellowship: The Black Baptist Quest for Social Power* (1986), James M. Washington said that the history of the black Baptists "...illuminates the tremendous fragmentation and frustration resulting from the various ingredients of a power struggle involving <u>personality</u> and <u>property</u> as well as <u>internal and external</u> politics."[81]

The Eighteenth Annual New Year's Dinner, a feast for several hundred persons, took place in the NBPB's chapel on the second floor of the editorial and book department. A company catered the dinner and covered the tables with white linen cloths, china, and silverware. President W. H. Moses of Guadalupe College gave the blessing. Boyd recited the history of the annual dinner, telling the audience about the first dinner in 1897 when his wife and mother sent a package of food from San Antonio, Texas. The Reverend Boyd told the employees and the guests that three NBPB traditions should continue. These included the 9:30 daily morning prayer service with all employees, the annual publishing board employees picnic in July, and the annual dinner. Mrs. Bessie Martin Thorbourne, wife of the publishing board's missionary in Panama, said a few words. Katie Albertine Boyd recited the humorous poem, "Billy," the story of a tied-tongue boy.[82] The dinner ended with the audience singing a hymn. Nothing official was said about the current controversy with the National Baptist Convention. But all was not well.

Boyd's supporters criticized the Reverend Isaac for permitting the Commission to have a closed meeting in the Baptist Young People's Union Board's headquarters. Isaac denied that the BYPU Board had any quarrel with any other board. He said, however, "We feel that it is our indispensable duty not only to submit to convention control, but to co-operate with the Commission and every other authorized agency of the Convention...."[83] The *Union-Review* claimed that Isaac had recently (May 1910) transferred the BYPU property from his name to the BYPU's board after the controversy about the publishing board had begun. Even the Southern Baptist Convention's Sunday School Board had its properties in the name of an individual trustee, and not until around 1920 did the SBC form a legal committee to deal with the issue of convention control over the boards. Boyd did not have the publishing board's property in his name.

Even though examination of deeds showed that all properties were owned by the National Baptist Publishing Board, not Boyd, the incorporation men continued their effort to change the National Baptist Convention from a loose confederation of boards into a highly centralized federal body. Later, the officers of the black National Baptist Convention of America (Unincorporated), said: "We went to Chicago with a determination to abide by the will of the majority, though we were not willing to bow to the mandates of an illegally obtained charter, secured by perjury, that placed the entire liberties of free, volunteer Baptist associations in the hands of seven men."[84]

Charges and counter-charges began to fly heavily. One writer accused the president of trying to recover his declining power by incorporating the National Baptist Convention and controlling the boards. Morris denied the charges and he said that he tried to be fair to all secretaries of the boards; besides, the issues should be settled within the denomination and not in the Baptist newspapers and the public forum. Some claimed that the president placed the Reverend L. K. Williams over the Commission, knowing that Williams belonged to the anti-NBPB faction. Williams denied any anti-NBPB sentiment, although his churches used Sunday-school materials from the American Baptist Publication Society. The Reverend L. L. Campbell, head of the "new convention" or the General Missionary Baptist Convention of Texas, was accused by Williams' people of making Boyd's appointment to head the Home Mission Board and the National Baptist Publishing Board seem like a victory over the "old convention" of Texas. Williams headed the Mount Gilead Baptist Church and presided over the Missionary and Educational Convention in Texas. Williams and his convention wanted Boyd and the NBPB to "refrain from fighting the white friends [the American Baptist Publication Society and the American Baptist Home Mission Society] of the Negro race, to advance the interests of the Board."[85]

Pro-NBPB men circulated new reports that Sutton E. Griggs, the leader of the attacks on the NBPB, had been charged with defrauding the First Baptist Church of East Nashville. A deacon brought the charges in the Davidson County Chancery Court. Griggs had left the church holding a $1,000 stock issue in his Orion Publishing Company, and he owed the church another $2,500 for a mortgage to support his private enterprises. Also the heavily indebted Tabernacle Baptist Church in Memphis was about to force Griggs' resignation because of controversy over his business deals and management of the church's financial affairs.[86] Griggs survived for years before moving from Memphis and back to Texas.

Although business had suffered because of the controversy and the current economic depression, the publishing board's staff and directors continued to advance the company's operations. The officers were pleased to report that the publishing board had installed its new automatic fire sprinkling system and electric alarms. Two officers of the publishing board took part in fund raising efforts at Roger Williams University in April. The board's officers spoke on behalf of the National Baptist Publishing Board which helped to raise nearly $1,000 at the Rogers Williams University rally.[87] The Reverend J. A. Sharp succeeded the late Reverend Pius as director of the Teacher Training Department. Sharp had been the late Pius' assistant, and Sharp had headed churches in Texas where he served as chairman of the board of trustees for Guadalupe College. He was born near Mudville, Texas, and educated in Brazos County. Sharp became superintendent of Sunday school missions for the General Missionary Baptist Convention of Texas in 1901, serving until January 15, 1915.[88]

The National Baptist Publishing Board's Brass Band developed into an outstanding musical organization by 1915. Phillip Lindsey directed the band. The other members included Fletcher Andrews, Aaron Clark, Toussant McKissack, William Payne, Howard Holman, G. P. Baker, Joseph Matthews, Watson Boyd, William Cheers, John H. Hyde, Charles Hart, Obie Jennings, Henry Pointer, and Henry Thompson. The publishing board's Brass Band had new uniforms and hats, and it played all kinds of music including classical music. Not only did the NBPB's Brass Band perform in the annual Sunday School Congress' sessions, it appeared at funerals, weddings, local churches, and community events.[89]

In the midst of the raging incorporation controversy, the National Baptist Publishing Board's officers toured sections of the country to maintain contact with the churches and the Sunday schools. The Reverend Ellington toured Memphis in March when he spoke at the Howe Institute, Gilfield Baptist Church, the historic Beale Street Baptist Church, and other local churches and Sunday schools. Huge crowds arrived to see and hear Ellington, a notable preacher and orator.[90] Henry Allen Boyd made his rounds of Baptist churches in Nashville, making speeches and giving sermons. In May, 1915, the Reverend R. H. Boyd toured Arkansas and Tennessee and headed into Louisiana and Texas, preaching and visiting churches and Sunday schools.[91]

Again, in the middle of the incorporation crisis, Boyd and the NBPB family had to deal with death and dying among its members, colleagues and their families. James C. Napier, cashier for the One-Cent Bank, lost his mother-in-law, Mrs. Caroline M. Langston, wife of the late John Mercer Langston. She passed in March 1915 in her Washington, D. C. home. Caroline Langston was born in North Carolina and reared as a free mulatto in Ohio where she completed studies at Oberlin College and married John M. Langston on October 25, 1854. Because of Napier's connection to the publishing board and the importance of John Mercer Langston, a great figure in black American history, the National Baptist Union-Review paid tribute to Caroline M. Langston.[92]

On April 15, 1915, Indiana Dickson, mother of Richard Henry Boyd, died at the family home (1602 Heiman Street). For nine days, Boyd and his half-brothers had kept watch over Indiana's bed. Boyd had helped Indiana to financially support the younger children in Texas. Four of Indiana's sons were ministers. Henry Dickson was an engineer. Samuel and William Dickson operated orphan homes in Springs and Gilmer, Texas. A dark-skinned, well-built woman with strong African features, Mrs. Dickson wore large African-styled gold rings in her ears. She was noted for charitable work, sometimes directing Boyd to send wood and coal to poor families during the winter months. After a funeral processional from Boyd's large two-story brick house with carport, a funeral was held at the Third Avenue Baptist Church, where Indiana had held membership since her arrival in Nashville. The pastor of the church, the Reverend Lester Harding, directed the funeral. The Reverend A. D. Hurt, superintendent of missions for the Negro Baptist State Convention of Tennessee, gave the prayers. The Reverend C. H. Clark, chairman of the NBPB, read the scripture. The publishing board's employees served as the choir. The Reverend J. M. Frost represented the Southern Baptist Convention and himself as a friend of the Boyd family. The Reverend E. D. W. Isaac spoke and gave tribute to Indiana Dickson, called the "mother of the publishing board." The Reverend Preston Taylor handled the funeral arrangements including shipping the body to Houston, Texas, for final rites and burial. The National Baptist Publishing Board closed for the day.[93]

Later in the month of April, news arrived that Joanna P. Moore, a white missionary and another friend to the National Baptist Publishing Board, had died in Nashville. The publishing board's newspaper carried extensive news about Miss Moore's death and the Fireside School. She organized the Fireside School which the publishing board had worked closely with. Moore was born on September 26, 1833, in Pennsylvania, one of thirteen children to an Irish born farmer. The family moved to Illinois in 1858. Joanna completed Rockford College in 1863 and headed to Island No. 10 in the Mississippi River to serve as a missionary to Negro contrabands in Arkansas and Mississippi. She returned home for the period 1868-1873. Then Moore went to Louisiana to help the desperate freedmen. She became a missionary for the newly organized Women's American Baptist Home Mission Society in 1877 and began the Fireside School in 1884 to stimulate daily Bible lessons in the homes. In 1885, Moore began editing and publishing *Hope* magazine. She moved her operations to Nashville in 1894, two years before Boyd began his publishing operations in the city. Fireside School was located on Mulberry Street before moving to Cedar Street. The institution moved into new quarters on Gay Street in April, 1915. During Moore's funeral at the Ryman Auditorium, the Reverend R. H. Boyd graced the stage and gave special resolutions from the National Baptist Publishing Board. Joanna P. Moore insisted on being buried in a black cemetery, Greenwood Cemetery.[94]

Incidentally, black women helped to direct the Fireside School in Nashville. Ada F. Morgan succeeded Moore as editor of *Hope*. Mary Flowers served as business manager for Fireside School. Flowers presided over the Women's Auxiliary of the Negro Baptist Missionary and Educational Convention of Tennessee.[95]

By late spring, 1915, almost everyone's mind became preoccupied with the coming National Baptist Convention's annual session in Chicago and the incorporation controversy. Even the white southern Baptists worried about the pending crisis and the appearance of storm clouds in the black Baptist convention.

During the Southern Baptist Convention at Houston, Texas, the officers and delegates acknowledged the Reverend R. H. Boyd and the progress of the black Baptist publishing board. The Reverend B. F. Riley included a section on "The General Condition of the Negro" in his address to the white southern Baptists. Riley said:

> A monument to Negro executive management and skill is the great National Baptist Publishing House at Nashville, Tennessee, where Dr. R. H. Boyd, a former slave, began as late as 1896 without a penny of capital, but which now covers a half block in the Tennessee capital, and is valued at $365,000. In justice, it should be said that Dr. Boyd

[depended on] our secretary of the Sunday-School Board, Dr. J. M. Frost, a sympathetic coadjutor, but he was soon able to stand alone, and now this great institution not only publishes all classes of denominational literature, but furnishes Sunday-school requisites and church furniture, and binds and prints books after the most modern methods.[96]

Alluding to National Baptist Convention officials who opposed Boyd's efforts to strike a closer alliance between the southern white Baptists and the black Baptists, Riley said: "The Negro needs to come to know that the Christian white man is his friend and not his enemy."[97]   Riley urged the delegates to support the proposal, which Boyd pushed, to support Christian education (a seminary) for Negroes.[98]

The northern white Baptists remained behind the scenes and busied themselves with finding a suitable governmental structure to allow the boards to remain independent but related to the Northern Baptist Convention. The Northern Baptist Convention began officially in 1907 as a coordinating body, not a legislative body. In May 1915, A. J. Rowland said that the general organization should represent the Baptists who are not in one of the different societies. "The principal functions of the Convention are advisory. It may legislate for itself...but in respect to the cooperating organizations it has no legislative powers...."[99] "The simple scheme for the organization of the Convention preserves the independence of the church, of the cooperating organizations, and of the State Conventions, and in no wise [ways] impairs the efficiency of any of them."[100]

Although the white northern Baptist and the southern Baptist conventions and their boards found suitable governmental structures that allowed them to live and cooperate in harmony, the black Baptist incorporation controversy heated up by summer 1915, just months before the September session of the National Baptist Convention. Rumors arrived in Nashville that Griggs, Parrish, Rodgers, and others had obtained a charter on May 17, 1915, incorporating the National Baptist Convention. The anti-incorporation group, Boyd's supporters, became upset because the incorporation issue had been voted down at the Houston session in 1912, voted down again in the Nashville session (1913), and referred to the Commission at the Philadelphia session in 1914. But the 1914 session agreed to amend the National Baptist Convention's constitution and the charters for the boards, although such amendments could have included compromises suitable to both sides. Still, the convention's delegates did not agree on "incorporation," argued the pro-NBPB people. President Moses of Guadalupe College said: "The Reverends Griggs, Parrish, Rodgers and others have split the National Baptist Convention."[101]

The incorporators began to take a radical and a fanatical approach about the issue of controlling the NBPB. To test the waters, on July 15, 1915, the Reverend Rodgers, representing the Commission, arrived in Nashville and demanded an audit of all papers and documents at the National Baptist Publishing Board. He presented Boyd with a letter and gave him until 1:00 that afternoon to reply. The executive committee of the board of directors for the National Baptist Publishing Board met hurriedly and refused to comply with Rodgers' request.[102] Rodgers retreated from Nashville.

This particular part of the controversy started on May 20, 1915, when the Reverend Rodgers sent a letter from LaGrange, Texas to the National Baptist Publishing Board. Rodgers said he had authority from the National Baptist Convention's Commission to direct the NBPB's directors to amend the charter of the National Baptist Publishing Board and state that the publishing board is controlled wholly by the National Baptist Convention. The Reverend R. H. Boyd returned a reply that the request would be presented to the National Baptist Publishing Board's directors. Chairman Clark called a special board meeting. The company's directors decided to ask the legal counsel for the National Baptist Convention for an opinion. The attorney returned no opinion. The publishing board members authorized Boyd to hire counsel, John Keeble and Company of Nashville. Meantime, Rodgers was advised by letter that the board of directors had not decided how to respond to his request.[103]

On the Tuesday preceding July 31, 1915, the publishing board decided to go ahead with the annual picnic for the employees, notwithstanding the raging controversy. The Tenth Annual National Baptist Publishing Board Picnic took place in the Greenwood Park. Some two thousand persons, including several local Sunday schools, attended the affair. A baseball game took place between the publishing board's employees and the Sleeping Giants. The activities included many contests, foot races, roller coaster rides, and other fun things to do until that evening.[104]

In August, 1915, one month before the National Baptist Convention was to meet in Chicago, the pro-NBPB group began a campaign to revoke the charter obtained by Griggs and others. One Baptist state convention in Texas passed a resolution to condemn Griggs, a native Texan, for his "personal and venomous attacks upon the Secretary of the Publishing Board, Dr. Boyd...."[105] But Morris sent an open letter to the Baptist churches, saying that he supported the incorporation and that it was authorized by the National Baptist Convention. The September 11, 1915, issue of the *National Baptist Union-Review* said: "Shall We Have Two Conventions?" Some preachers blamed "old convention" men in Texas, "...men who are in league with the American Baptist Publication Society to destroy the National Baptist Publishing Board."[106]

On September 8, 1915, the National Baptist Convention's session began at 10:30 in the morning at Chicago's Regimental Armory on 16th and Michigan Avenue. The Reverend J. D. Brooks moved to amend the program and consider immediately the charter. Sutton E. Griggs moved to table the motion after commotion broke out. The Reverend P. J. Bryant raised a point of order that no business could begin until after the report of the enrollment committee had been submitted. The point of order was sustained to the disappointment of the "incorporation men." Confusion arose, and President Morris adjourned the convention.

The session reconvened at 2:30 in the afternoon but moved to adjourn at 5:00 p.m. because of more disruptions. However, the Rodgers-Griggs faction's motion to adjourn met a resounding defeat. Perhaps because of the confusion, the convention's president ignored the vote when the National Baptist Convention's officers found themselves surrounded by rebellious delegates. Twice the Rodgers-Griggs forces made a motion to adjourn, and twice the motion met defeat by overwhelming votes.[107] The president, the other officers, and the Rodgers-Griggs people left the hall, hoping the delegates also would leave.

But the delegates remained in the hall. They elected Edward Perry Jones as the new president of the National Baptist Convention of America. Realizing that they had better respond quickly, the Rodgers-Griggs faction directed the management of the building to close the facility; they controlled the lease for the facility.

On the next morning, the Morris administration had policemen at the door, admitting only those persons with convention badges. They locked thousands of Boyd's supporters out in a cold rain. Some of the Boyd men forced the doors open and let some of the women through. Then Boyd's group retreated to the warmth of the Salem Baptist Church on the corner of LaSalle and 30th Street where the National Baptist Publishing Board's members joined the group.

President Morris proceeded to give his address in the Armory. Before he could finish his address, a court officer interrupted Morris with an order for him and the officers to appear in court. The court allowed the Morris officers to return and continue the session. The Reverend E. W. D. Isaac said:

> There is but one great issue before the Baptists of this country, and that is, shall the Baptists of this country own and control that which they, through their principal organization, have found and built up, or shall its control be left to a few to be used for personal gain? Or shall those Boards created by the Convention dominate the Convention, or shall they be subject to the parent body? The great issue before the convention is, shall these Boards that are the creatures of this Convention, control the Convention, or shall the Convention control the Boards.[108]

The Morris convention adjourned at 7:30 that evening.

On September 11, 1915, Haynes, Isaac, Morris, Griggs, and others filed suit in the Illinois Cook County Chancery Court to prohibit the Boyd-Jones group from meeting in the Salem Baptist church and using the name National Baptist Convention of America. The issue was not decided affirmatively by the court. The Haynes-Morris group also sued in Illinois on September 16, 1915, to gain control of the NBPB's books, but the NBPB officers had returned to Nashville by now, and besides, the Illinois courts had no jurisdiction over a Tennessee corporation, the National Baptist Publishing Board.

At the 1916 meeting of the National Baptist Convention of America, Unincorporated, the National Baptist Publishing Board report said:

> We desire to remind the brethren that each member of the Publishing Board was present in Chicago last year and suffered with you. We did not take an active part in the convention over the charter, but most of our members sat quietly by and watched with eagerness and earnestness the unparliamentary, the un-Christianly, the unreasonable and the unmanly attacks that were attempted upon the brethren of the convention.[109]

The Rodgers-Griggs men became angry when they found that the convention could not elect any persons to the National Baptist Publishing Board's board of directors according to the Tennessee charter of incorporation. On September 30, 1915, a suit was filed by Tennessee black Baptist residents William Haynes, E. M. Lawrence, William T. Hightower, Solomon Whitton, A. L. Bartlett, A. E. Jones, and M. W. Moore. The defendants were R. H. Boyd, H. A. Boyd, W. S. Ellington, C. H. Taylor, C. H. Clark, J. P. Robinson, J. C. Fields, and L. L. Campbell.

The Chancery Court of Davidson County, Tennessee, ruled in favor of the current directors of the National Baptist Publishing Board. No outside agency, not even the National Baptist Convention, had any right, according to the charter, to elect members to the board of directors of an independent company, namely the National Baptist Publishing Board. The Morris men, as they were now called, appealed the ruling to the Tennessee Supreme Court but lost that decision, too. The National Baptist Convention had no proof that its authority and resources had established the National Baptist Publishing Board. And there was no proof, absolutely, that Boyd or anybody else either had mismanaged the company, misused its profits and resources, or violated the corporation's charter.

The Rodgers-Griggs faction continued with the National Baptist Convention of the United States of America, Inc. and the Jones-Boyd faction continued with the National Baptist Convention of America, unincorporated.

The controversy between the National Baptist Convention of the United States of America (Incorporated) and the National Baptist Convention of America (Unincorporated) continued for a few more years with the National Baptist Publishing Board remaining at the center of the controversy. In his pro-NBC (Incorporated) book, *Negro Baptist History* (1930), Lewis G. Jordan said that on Tuesday night, September 7, 1915, the opposition met in the Salem Baptist Church where the "whole atmosphere was filled with venom."[110] Yet, Jordan praised the Reverend R. H. Boyd for his business sense and wisdom to establish a publishing board.

Several years later, the Reverend J. P. Robinson, a publishing board member and a defendant, said:

> I hope the time will come when these [incorporation] men will hands off and let us have one man whom the race can look to as a prince of preachers without nullification. What he has done is substantial, and no man can controvert it except it is done through falsehood and maliciousness. Therefore, we should allow this prince to be down and sleep, for he needs rest in these declining years, he needs praise for what he has done, and thanks from the denomination of the race for his accomplishment that he has paved the way for future generations.... The opposition printed articles to illustrate Boyd as a man of theft, lies, and trickery; They tried to degrade Boyd in his relations with white Baptists....[111]

By July 1916, the publishing board, other boards, and members of the National Baptist Convention of America (Unincorporated) had begun to prepare for the coming session at Kansas City, Missouri scheduled for Wednesday through Monday, September 6-11, 1916. Many persons speculated about which churches would attend either the unincorporated convention or the incorporated convention. The *National Baptist Union-Review* advertised heavily about the scheduled unincorporated National Baptist Convention session, and the paper mentioned the churches already committed to attend the September 1916 session in Kansas City.[112]

The period 1916 to 1922 would be a trying time for Boyd, the NBPB, and the National Baptist Convention of America, Unincorporated. These years would find Boyd, the publishing board, and officers of the unincorporated convention trying to rebuild the organizations and sustain a business. But also after 1916, a slow healing process would begin for America's two largest black Baptist groups.

Mailing Department (NBPBLA)

NBPB's Chorus (NBPBLA)

Foreman's Office (NBPBLA)

NBPB Truck and Employees (NBPBLA)

Book Bindery Department (NBPBLA)

Book Bindery Department (NBPBLA)

Press Room (NBPBLA)

Machine Room (NBPBLA)

Chapter 4

Struggle for Survival: The National Baptist Publishing Board, 1916-1922

Chapter 4
Struggle for Survival: the NBPB,
1916-1922

For eighteen years, until the 1915 convention at Chicago, the publishing board had continued to grow. The following chart illustrates that growth before the convention split.

NBPB Operations, 1897 to 1914

Year	Letters Written	No. Periodicals	Money Spent
1897	13,570	1,746,500	5,664.29
1898	43,160	1,593,150	19,426.64
1899	43,160	4,695,950	31,683.22
1900	99,886	3,366,600	49,309.37
1901	116,504	5,900,600	62,423.84
1902	39,914	5,509,000	62,4Z3.84
1903	149,914	6,717,825	87,769.95
1904	177,134	7,273,700	107,840.01
1905	204,864	7,939,949	120,533.80
1906	196,258	9,606,815	152,112.58
1907	273,181	10,233,422	160,152.14
1908	226,462	11,001,008	160,781.05
1909	294,400	11,717,876	167,741.19
1910	272,504	9,348,209	180,177.91
1911	306,559	9,035,160	187,753.27
1912	272,223	9,034,261	209,665.12
1913	284,298	8,208,104	209,665.12
1914	238,029	8,220,679	204,632.40

Beginning in 1914, the incorporation controversy caused the publishing board's business to decline. Many printed publications did not sell, and boxes of periodicals had to be destroyed. Especially after some of the churches began to boycott the National Baptist Publishing Board, revenues and sales dropped dramatically.

The publishing board survived the crisis. The National Baptist Publishing Board's secretary-treasurer said: "We have been able to hold our own" in spite of massive negative publicity in newspapers, circulars, pulpits, and pamphlets throughout the country. Secretary Boyd made this statement in the September 1917 annual report for the publishing board.[1]

The NBCI diverted some business and personnel away from the National Baptist Publishing Board because of the large number of churches its membership contained. The incorporated National Baptist Convention published the 1915 journal through a Philadelphia company instead of the NBPB. The Reverend L. G. Jordan edited the NBCI's 1915 journal. Anyway, the National Baptist Publishing Board had received no real financial return for printing the annual journal, and besides, the NBPB continued to print the annual sessions journal for the National Baptist Convention of America, Unincorporated. Attorney T. G. Ewing, one of the NBPB's early attorneys, served as the National Baptist Convention, U. S. A., Incorporated's lawyer.[2]

The National Baptist Convention, U. S. A., Incorporated, immediately made plans to establish its own publishing board. This convention too selected Nashville as the site for its Sunday School Publishing Board. Attorney Solomon P. Harris, who was brought to Nashville by President Morris in 1896, remained loyal to Morris. Harris and the Reverend William Haynes, another Nashvillian, received orders to start a publishing board for the incorporated convention.

The National Baptist Convention, U. S. A., Incorporated, opened the Sunday School Publishing Board at 409 Gay Street. Harris and Haynes started a newspaper, the *Baptist Voice,* for the convention. The Reverend J. D. Crenshaw, formerly editor of the *Union-Review,* edited the *Baptist Voice.* The *National Baptist Union-Review* remained with the National Baptist Convention, Unincorporated, under the editorship of Dr. Boyd.

The new Sunday School Publishing Board struggled along until 1920 when Arthur M. Townshend, a physician and president of Roger Williams University, became the corresponding secretary. By 1921, the Sunday School Publishing Board had thirty-two employees, cylinder presses, automatic cutting machines, wire stitchers, linotype machines, job presses, and folding machines among other modern equipment. Soon, the operation outgrew the cramped quarters. The *Baptist Voice* (August 27, 1921) said that "The forces that accomplish the most are not always noisy. Quietly the roots strike into the rich soil. Later the fruits appear." The convention authorized Townsend to buy or build a facility for the publishing operations. He employed Nashville's black architectural firm of McKissack and McKissack to design and build a facility. On May 18, 1924, they laid the cornerstone. The Morris Memorial Building opened on October 19, 1925, at a cost of $700,000. Five years later, the Sunday School Publishing Board published its denominational history, L. G. Jordan, *Negro Baptist History, U. S. A.* (1930),[3] a rough study first authorized by the convention in 1913.

America's black Baptist denomination did not disintegrate and decline because of the split. Like Pelt and Smith said in their book, *The Story of the National Baptists* (1961), the year 1915 began a new era for the black Baptists when they grew into two national organizations and two publishing houses. The black Baptist conventions each had a seminary by 1924. The two Baptist conventions and the two Negro Baptist publishing houses coexisted without any major disputes between them, and both publishing houses flourished eventually because plenty of business existed for the two publishing houses. By 1919, the southern white Baptist convention estimated some 3,018,000 black Baptists lived in America.[4]

Both black Baptist conventions and their constituent organizations began rebuilding in 1916. Both conventions launched a campaign to open a seminary, and both organizations began rebuilding their boards. The Southern Baptist Convention decided to support financially the black Baptist educational and mission programs in the Morris convention. The northern Baptists gave some support to the NBCI, although the northern Baptists practically had withdrawn from the turbulent and violent South. The National Baptist Convention of America, Unincorporated, and its boards, including the National Baptist Publishing Board, had to rebuild without financial support from the white Baptists who sided with the incorporators.

To deal with the governance issue became the first order of business for the National Baptist Convention of America, Unincorporated. During the September 1916 convention, the National Baptist Convention of America amended the 1895 constitution. The structure of the National Baptist Convention of America included the following boards:

> Foreign Mission Board
> Home Mission Board
> Baptist Young People's Union Board
> National Baptist Publishing Board
> Benefits Board
> Woman's Auxiliary Board
> Evangelical Board

Each board included an advisory board member from each state represented in the convention. The states nominated the members and the convention confirmed the nominations. For instance, the convention elected the "Publishing Board Advisory" members who had no other function than advisory. The advisory board monitored matters related "to the doctrine and policy of all Baptist publications furnished by them [the National Baptist Publishing Board] to our churches and Sunday schools under the resolution passed by this convention."[5]

According to the 1916 constitution of the National Baptist Convention of America, the boards had a second governing board, the management board. The board of management included the chairman, recording secretary, corresponding secretary, and secretary. The corresponding secretary managed the board's affairs and also served as treasurer. The board of management directed the affairs of a particular board during the convention's recess. The boards had their own charters, and the board of management controlled the operations of the institution. So the National Baptist Convention of America, Unincorporated, gave the boards the autonomy they desired, and the convention maintained a confederation-style government with little centralized authority.

The 1916 session for the National Baptist Convention of America, Unincorporated, convened in Kansas City, Missouri, during September 6-11. The turnout was moderate but energetic. Delegates came from Mississippi, Missouri, Alabama, Connecticut, California, Oklahoma, Georgia, Tennessee, South Carolina, Pennsylvania, Indiana, Kentucky, Ohio, Colorado, Arkansas, and Florida. The attendance represented a good start for the National Baptist Convention of America, Unincorporated, considering that much confusion continued to exist about the denominational division. Some churches did not know to which of the conventions to send their delegates.

The Reverend Edward P. Jones presided over the National Baptist Convention of America, Unincorporated. Jones' home church and state Baptist association stood by him and sent ninety-six representatives to the 1916 convention. President Jones began his speech by blasting the actions of the other convention at Chicago last year. He praised the Reverend Boyd and severely criticized the men who attacked Boyd's character. Jones pointed out that two attorneys had been hired in 1916 to further examine the records of the National Baptist Publishing Board and put to rest the insinuations. The lawyers certified that the property deeds were all in the National Baptist Publishing Board's name; none of the deeds were in Boyd's name or any of his heirs. Davidson Court records confirmed that Boyd and his wife had transferred machinery and supplies to the National Baptist Publishing Board by warranty deed on May 20, 1899. The National Baptist Publishing Board had $350,000 in assets, all in the name of the Baptists of America, said Jones. He also tried to rebuff the National Baptist Publishing Board's critics who continued a campaign to prove that the National Baptist Publishing Board belonged to Boyd.[6]

The National Baptist Convention of America, Unincorporated, continued the separate management of the Home Mission Board. A new corresponding secretary was selected. The new secretary moved the Home Mission Board's headquarters to New Orleans, although Boyd offered him a room in the National Baptist Publishing Board's facilities. The Home Mission Board spent just $300 for the year, compared to thousands spent when Boyd had directed the HMB. But the Home Mission Board no longer received support from the Southern Baptist Convention's Home Mission Board. Boyd did not have his usual connections in that white convention after J. M. Frost passed in 1916. Boyd's colleagues said: "We believe that when the Southern white Baptists know the facts that they will help us as they are now helping others [the National Baptist Convention, U. S. A., Incorporated]."[7]

The National Baptist Publishing Board continued to build its Sunday school activities. The Teachers' Training Department enrolled some seventy-five or more Sunday school teachers in a three month institute which met in Nashville during the winter of 1916.[8] John H. Frank of Louisville became editor of the *Union-Review*. Frank was allowed to maintain his Fifth Street Baptist Church and medical practice in Louisville and mail his editorials to the National Baptist Publishing Board where the publishing board's staff completed all other work on the newspaper. The Reverend C. T. Hume of Oklahoma became the circulating manager for the *Union-Review*. The paper's circulation had dropped to only 2,500 after the National Baptist Convention had taken control of it and gave J. D. Crenshaw, the new editor, no funds to operate the paper. The National Baptist Publishing Board announced to the 1916 convention delegates that the paper would soon reach seventy thousand copies and later one hundred thousand copies a week. The National Baptist Publishing Board continued to be the financial supporter of the paper. The 1916 convention's delegates collected ten dollars to support the paper.[9]

The Reverend W. S. Ellington remained the editorial secretary of the National Baptist Publishing Board, a decision that caused Ellington to leave the First Colored Baptist Church. Head deacon, W. T. Hightower, a plaintiff in the Davidson County suit against the National Baptist Publishing Board, and other pro-NBCI members clashed with pastor Ellington, causing him to leave and go pastor the First Baptist Church of East Nashville where he remained until his death in 1948. Ellington was a graduate of Fisk University and a popular preacher. Each year he packed his church or the city's downtown Ryman Auditorium with the annual "Prodigal Son" sermon.

In June 1918, however, the Reverend Ellington resigned his position as editorial secretary after seventeen years at the publishing board. His tenure had begun with the writing of articles for $7 a month. He became assistant to the editor-in-chief at $25 per month and later $50 per month. During the seventeen years, Ellington refused to give up his pulpit ministry, tirelessly working to perform both functions. By 1918, he decided to retire from the position as editorial secretary of the National Baptist Publishing Board. Ellington addressed the employees with a departing message and praised the Reverend Boyd and the publishing board for the wonderful years he had spent with them. In 1921, Ellington became editor of a young adults magazine for the Sunday School Publishing Board of the National Baptist Convention, U. S. A., Incorporated.[10]

Despite the negatives it received, the National Baptist Publishing Board continued to expand its horizons. The National Baptist Publishing Board handled 278,214 letters and published 8,212,131 copies of periodicals compared to 238,029 letters and 8,220,679 copies in 1914. The reorganized Baptist Young People's Union, headed by the Reverend S. R. Prince of Fort

Worth, Texas, contracted with the National Baptist Publishing Board to print its literature and paraphernalia.[11]

The National Baptist Publishing Board's Sunday School Congress met in Vicksburg, Mississippi, on June 14-18, 1916. Some twenty-two states had representatives, pastors, Sunday school superintendents, and children present at the Congress. The annual Sunday School Congress meeting helped keep the National Baptist Publishing Board active with the rank and file Baptist members. Furthermore, the Congress became the greatest promoter for the publishing board's products and services among the Baptist churches.

The National Baptist Convention of the United States of America (Incorporated) organized a Sunday School Congress and held the session in Memphis also in June 1916. Ironically, some forces within the National Baptist Convention had objected to Boyd's annual Sunday School Congress; however, most black Baptist leaders learned the value of holding a national Sunday School Congress.

Some persons felt that the 1915 denominational division would cause the Black Baptist publishing houses to lose much business to white publishers. The NBCI had not established printing facilities for its Sunday School Publishing Board, and therefore, white religious publishing houses could establish customers among many black churches. By now the American Baptist Publication Society had withdrawn its operations from the South, and the SBC's Sunday School Board had no desire to compete with the black Baptist publishing boards. The black Baptist publishing houses enjoyed a near monopoly on supplying the needs of black Baptist churches.

The Reverend Boyd and the National Baptist Convention of America's officials quickly moved to sustain the business and volume of the publishing board.

A key element in the hard work it took to sustain the National Baptist Publishing Board during the National Baptist Convention's controversy was Henry Allen Boyd, the eldest son of Richard H. Boyd. The National Baptist Publishing Board held on to a great number of its customers, the black Baptist churches. After twenty years, these churches had relied on the National Baptist Publishing Board, its quality, programs, and services. The younger Henry Allen directed the operations of the company under the wisdom and the energetic guidance of his elderly father. Now Richard Henry was about seventy-three years old.

Secretary Boyd praised the assistant secretary of the National Baptist Publishing Board for his relentless efforts to sustain the board's operations. To organize the annual Sunday School Congress, visit modern printing plants, cultivate business with churches and Sunday Schools, manage the National Negro Doll Company and the National Church Supply Company, serve on the board of directors for One-Cent Savings Bank, and edit the weekly Nashville

Henry Allen Boyd (NBR)

Nashville, Company G, Black Soldiers in France, 1918 (NBR)

Globe, the Reverend Henry Allen Boyd, who was ordained in 1904, traveled constantly and worked long hours in the offices of the National Baptist Publishing Board. He received offers for other jobs because of his experiences and effective management of a large corporation, but Henry Allen Boyd remained loyal to his father's work and the National Baptist Publishing Board. And except for taking the spotlight during the annual Sunday Congress sessions, Henry Allen faithfully performed his duties and quietly stayed in Richard H. Boyd's shadow.

For the 1915-1916 fiscal year, the Reverend R. H. Boyd reported that the National Baptist Publishing Board had an income of $151,990.17 and expenses of $152,989.79 compared to a $200,000 figure the year before the 1915 denominational split. The publishing board paid $46,633.24 in wages, salaries, and for piece work, and it suffered a loss of $999.62.[12] This loss seemed small compared to what might have been after the controversial split. In a way, however, the newly reorganized boards depended heavily on the more experienced National Baptist Publishing Board, sending most of their printing needs to Nashville and helping to rebuild the publishing board's business. In this regard women Baptists continued to support the publishing board.

Georgia DeBaptiste Ashburn became the new head of the Woman's Auxiliary. In 1916, the Women's Convention met in the Highland Avenue Baptist Church in Kansas City, Kansas also on September 6-11. Mrs. Richard H. Boyd served on the women's program committee, and she served on the obituary committee and the committee on needlework. The women's group for the Jones-Boyd convention had little money because the previous assets and leadership of the Woman's Auxiliary Board remained affiliated with the National Baptist Convention, Incorporated.[13]

Nannie Helen Burroughs, corresponding secretary of the Woman's Auxiliary and her officers decided to remain with the Morris administration during the 1915 split. Burroughs also served as president of the National Training School for Women and Girls in "Lincoln Heights," Washington, D. C. The Woman's Auxiliary had a charter that allowed it to hold the school and other properties separate from the convention. The women argued, like Boyd, that the convention had not given any financial support to establish the school in Washington. Burroughs and the Women's Convention coexisted peacefully with the National Baptist Convention, U. S. A., Incorporated, for six years after the denominational split and without giving any properties to the convention. In 1921, however, the Woman's Auxiliary yielded to the inevitable and worked out an arrangement with the NBCI to allow the convention to select half of the trustees for the training school. The Reverend S. N. Vass said:

> Everything considered, I think our Convention is treated pretty liberally in the certificate of incorporation [for the National Baptist Training

School for Women and Girls]. Of course in the time this school was chartered we had not looked into the matter, for we did not establish the school. But one thing is clear, and that is that Miss Burroughs is not in the class with R. H. Boyd by any means.[14]

Vass had left the American Baptist Publication Society to become field secretary for the National Baptist Convention, U. S. A., Incorporated's Sunday School Publishing Board in 1919.

The National Baptist Publishing Board held its Annual New Year's dinner with upbeat tempo in 1917. With first-class style, a catering company served oyster soup, celery, dressing, olives, ham, roast turkey, cranberry sauce, mashed sweet potatoes with raisins, peas, combination salad, rolls, cakes, ice cream, fruit, and coffee. The publishing board's Brass Band furnished the music. As usual, the employees gave R. H. Boyd a gift. Several persons gave speeches about the board's progress. And hymns were sung by the audience. A *National Baptist Union-Review* editorial said:

> We are about to enter a New Year, 1917. It comes fraught with meaning. No one is wise enough to forecast all the vents for weal or woe which it brings to us, but we should enter into it with full determination to make the most of it and act our part so well that we shall have no regrets at its close. The year 1916 left many duties unperformed. There were a lot of bickering and dissensions. It should be relegated to the limbs of forgotten issues; these obstacles to our progress are removed.[15]

The year 1917 signaled the beginning of the end of the downturn in business for the National Baptist Publishing Board. The National Baptist Convention, Unincorporated, and the NBPB prepared for renewed growth.

The 37th annual session of the National Baptist Convention of America (Unincorporated) convened in Atlanta, September 5-11, 1917. Some five thousand persons, including about 1,587 delegates, attended the sessions. The Woman's Auxiliary Convention met in Atlanta's Liberty Baptist Church. Georgia DeBaptiste Ashburn said: "Our convention is placed in our hands by the providence of God, but it is placed in our hands, and we must all feel the responsibility resting upon our own shoulders."[16] Reportedly, all states but Maine, New Hampshire and Vermont had citizens at the National Baptist Convention, Unincorporated's 1917 annual meeting.[17] Boyd's old Texas organization, the General Missionary Baptist Convention of Texas, overwhelmed the convention with a long list of delegates.

When the National Baptist Convention of America met in Atlanta it was evident that successful rebuilding of the convention, other boards, and the National Baptist Publishing Board had taken place. The National Baptist Chorus sang with vigor and hope. The convention included lively events such as Young People's Night, Children's Period on Saturday morning, and young people's topics: "The Boy and His Gang," "Negro Doll Clubs," and "Amusements for the Children," among other interesting themes.[18]

An official of the Southern Baptist Convention addressed the Wednesday afternoon session. He informed the delegates that the Southern Baptist Convention had appointed a committee to meet with both black Baptist conventions' leaders to attempt to reunite them. The president of the Southern Baptist Convention also spoke to the delegates and won cheers for his support of independence in Baptist churches. The convention collected forty dollars to defray the speaker's travel expenses. Then the secretary of the Southern Baptist Convention's Home Mission Board spoke and agreed to help all black Baptist organizations in their missionary work. The convention voted to make this southern Baptist official and the president of the Southern Baptist Convention members-for-life of the National Baptist Convention of America, Unincorporated. The National Baptist Chorus and the audience sang a moving version of "Soon-a-Will Be Done with the Troubles of the World."[19]

Emotions ran high when the choirs and the delegates continued singing old Negro spirituals and soulful songs. Tears flowed freely, people embraced one another, some shouting and dancing. Much had happened during the last ten years. Many black sons and daughters were about to leave for Europe to participate in America's united effort to win a world war. At home, the black Baptists were divided still, and some men continued to attack Boyd and the publishing board and to stir up controversy. Although the black Baptist denomination was indeed a frustrated fellowship, the NBC, Unincorporated session's delegates and officials refused to break under the circumstances.

On Friday evening, the historian of the Southern Baptist Convention visited the convention and urged reconciliation. The convention delegates gave twenty dollars and twenty-five cents toward the historian's travel expenses. The Reverend Boyd offered a resolution to appoint a committee to meet with Southern Baptist Convention's representatives to discuss reconciliation with the National U.S.A., Inc.[20]

Dr. Boyd was happy and pleased that the Southern Baptist Convention's officers, his old white Baptist friends, had not abandoned him and the National Baptist Convention of America. But earlier in 1916, the Reverend James Marion Frost had passed away. Boyd and the National Baptist Convention of America, Unincorporated, gradually lost favor in the Southern Baptist Convention.

Because the critics continued to attack Boyd and the National Baptist Publishing Board's officers, President Jones used part of the president's annual address to answer the critics. President Jones said: "The records at Nashville show unmistakably that from cellar to dome the Publishing House is the property of the Baptists of the United States held in trust by the National Baptist Publishing Board."[21]

Then the president turned to convention business. Jones recommended a board for church extension and aid. This was like the Northern Baptist Convention's church edifice fund which had been operating for several years. Incidentally, the Reverend Boyd had recommended a church edifice fund several years earlier during one of his publishing board reports to the National Baptist Convention. Jones also recommended a committee of three persons to meet with the Southern Baptist Convention's officials and request aid to the National Baptist Convention of America's mission work and efforts to establish a black seminary.

The Reverend R. H. Boyd presented the publishing board's report to the 1917 convention. Boyd said:

> We make everything from a post card to an encyclopedia, and from a calling card to a Bible. Our literature is written by Negroes, set up on Linotype machines owned and operated by Negroes, printed on printing presses owned and operated by Negroes, finished in a book binding plant owned and operated by Negroes, and sent out for use by Negro Baptists. A Baptist literature from beginning to end.[22]

Boyd, too, had to answer the continuous criticism about the National Baptist Publishing Board. Mainly, S. N. Vass remained embittered toward Boyd. Secretary Boyd said that the claim that the National Baptist Publishing Board "...is a 'money-making institution'...is erroneous." It is incorporated as a non-profit institution and "...cannot pay a dividend."[23]

Boyd recalled that there were no provocative questions about the publishing board until 1909. Then the questions were raised again in 1910 and 1911. Lastly, the incorporation paper read at the 1912 Houston convention really started the division.

The publishing board's continuing progress, however, quieted some of the critics and pleased the Unincorporated convention's delegates. The National Baptist Publishing Board published 7,266,270 pieces of literature compared to 6,750,063 pieces during fiscal year 1916-1917. The NBPB's receipts totaled $154,366.46, up from $152,989.79 in 1916. The company processed 275,472 letters. Comparatively, the National Baptist Publishing Board received 311,173 letters and balanced its books with $160,798.33 in 1915 before the split.[24]

The publishing board continued to produce a variety of Sunday school and church publications and training programs. The printed materials included the Baptist Young People's Union quarterly magazine, the monthly magazines for the Metokas and Galedas, and some twenty-six song books, booklets, and pamphlets in the book, Bible, and tract department. Under J. H. Frank, the *Union-Review* kept its columns dignified and generally clear of mud-slinging about the denominational split. The *Outline of Baptist History* by Nathaniel H. Pius was published in cloth in 1917. The board also published the *History and Manual of the Colored Knights of Phythias* (1917) which was marketed by the Central Regals Company of Cincinnati. The $2.50 hardback book included photographs of officers as well as biographies and information about the organization's practices and procedures. The National Baptist Publishing Board's Teacher Training Department held graduation exercises at the Mount Olive Baptist Church during the 1917 academic year when a Southern Baptist Convention editor furnished the major speech. The normal department had eleven graduates; the intermediate department had one graduate. The advanced department granted about sixteen certificates including one to Mrs. Henry Allen Boyd.[25]

Boyd reported to the 1917 convention that the Sunday School Congress had held its session in Nashville, June 13-18, 1917. Delegates came from some twenty-four states, an improvement over the attendance at the 1916 Congress. Alabama sent 133 persons compared to 111 from Tennessee. The Congress had become one of the publishing board's largest divisions with departments for Bible conferences, primary teachers, intermediate teachers, advanced teachers, Metoka and Galeda classes, Boy Cadets, Negro Doll Clubs, Sunday school missionaries, Baptist Young People's Unions, cradle roll and home classes, and sociology and applied sciences classes. Louretha V. Chambers, editor of the *Metoka* and *Galeda* magazines, planned the class meeting, and a Cadet Band of fourteen-year-old boys furnished the music for the Congress. The Rising Star Glee Club of Shreveport, Louisiana, held daily concerts, and a Congress Chorus performed songs. The delegates visited the National Baptist Publishing Board to see its eight giant presses producing ten thousand sheets of print per hour. A parade of five thousand persons marched through the streets of Nashville after a mass meeting at the city's Ryman Auditorium. Again to answer the constant criticism, the Reverend R. H. Boyd said: "Our Sunday School Congress is not held for raising money. To the contrary, our Board spends money to make this Congress what it is."[26]

After being refused the opportunity to address state conventions in Alabama and Georgia, Henry Allen and Richard Henry Boyd began more extensive trips to shore up the publishing board's relations with churches and associations. They involved President E. P. Jones in this effort because some defensive strategy was needed to counter the continuing anti-National Baptist Publishing Board offensive. Jones and Boyd visited Chicago churches where the Reverend Baston J. Prince's Providence Baptist Church sponsored the tour. President Jones said:

> Chicago will forever stand out in the eyes of Baptists of America as pre-eminently a City of redemption from autocracy and high handed

misrule. There was fought the battle of construction against destruction, a vision against blindness and progressiveness against reaction as well as truth against error.[27]

Under Richard H. Boyd, the National Baptist Publishing Board continued to produce some twenty-five books, booklets, an eight-page weekly National Baptist *Union-Review*, and pamphlets besides the annual *Sunday School Commentary*. The editorial staff grew to twelve persons, including Mrs. W. S. Ellington, Professor H. Walker, John H. Frank, and Professor C. T. Hume. Still, the publishing board had not filled the field secretary's position. The Reverend Boyd prefaced his report by saying that "Our real work began in San Antonio, Texas in 1895." He said that the National Baptist Publishing Board is a "...corporation...organized for a specific purpose; that is to carry on corporation work for a specific, religious purpose."[28]

The court suits continued when the other convention's leaders tried to gain control of the lucrative publishing board. The court suits and the constant criticism consumed time and resources. Some persons from the other convention continued to proclaim that Boyd was a thief. The *Union-Review* suggested that R. H. Boyd sue his attackers for libel and slander. Boyd endured the pain of his former colleagues attacking his character, and he refused to directly attack his critics by name or sue them. Many pastors, church congregations and Baptist associations wrote letters and passed resolutions to denounce the treatment of Boyd.[29]

Although the National Baptist Publishing Board announced in 1917 that secretary Richard H. Boyd would retire and take his deserved benefits and rest when the controversy was over, the Reverend Boyd remained preoccupied with the work to sustain the National Baptist Publishing Board and to help stabilize the National Baptist Convention of America. The following year, 1918, he worked even harder to promote black support for America's World War I efforts. Nashville and the National Baptist Publishing Board and the National Baptist Convention of America needed the old gentleman.

Boyd became notable for his untiring efforts to help uplift black people. The president of the Woman's Auxiliary Convention thanked the National Baptist Publishing Board for its invaluable help in publishing women's materials. She said:

The names of Dr. R. H. Boyd and family will ever live in the hearts of our women. So much of the good results realized in different departments of our work is due to the efforts and influence of this great man and family. God bless them and cause their hearts to rejoice amid their sufferings.[30]

Efforts to Compromise

In 1918 a joint commission met in Memphis and tried to resolve the split between the National Baptist Convention (Unincorporated) and the National Baptist Convention (Incorporated). The Peace Commission, led by members of the Southern Baptist Convention, proposed that the lawsuit against the publishing board be dropped, and a consolidated convention would appoint a committee to determine the best way to govern the boards. The Southern Baptist Convention offered to appoint a permanent advisory committee to confer with the consolidated conventions and its boards. On December 12, 1918, the Southern Baptist Convention's commissioners called another joint meeting, this time in Nashville. Again there was no compromise. President Edward P. Jones publicly proclaimed that the opposing side, the National Baptist Convention, U. S. A., Incorporated, still insisted on taking control of the National Baptist Publishing Board.[31]

The Tennessee Supreme Court completed the final review of the suits in 1919. The court concluded that the National Baptist Convention of the United States of America (Incorporated) was not a church and had no right to question the validity of the charter of incorporation for the National Baptist Publishing Board. The plaintiffs had to pay the cost of the suit.

After 1919

In 1919, the National Baptist Publishing Board had recovered from the 1915 setback. The publishing board bought a new duplex Webb perfecting printing press. This machine could print on both sides of the paper, paste, fold, trim and deliver a multi-page newspaper at the rate of twenty to thirty-seven hundred per hour. This was the first such machine installed in Nashville in spite of the city's huge printing industry. Even though it was a black-American company, the National Baptist Publishing Board had made several firsts in the local printing industry: the first to own and operate linotype machines made by Mergenthaler of Brooklyn; the first to own and operate Smythe book sewing machines; and the first company to own and operate cross paper feeders.[32]

The 1919 Sunday School Congress met in Bessemer, Alabama where large crowds waited for the "Congress Train" to arrive on June 11. The Reverend W. H. Wood, president of the General Baptist Sunday School Convention of Alabama, sponsored the meeting. The National Baptist Publishing Board transported its new thirty-six voice choral society and the Congress Band to the convention.[33]

The National Baptist Convention of America met in Norfolk, Virginia in September 1919. The delegates launched a $2,000,000 endowment fund campaign for ministers' relief work, aged ministers, and support for educational

Dr. R. H. and
Mrs. Harriett A. Boyd,
1918 (NBPBLA)

NBPB Facility, Second Avenue North (NBR)

J. P. Robinson, Chairman,
NBPB, 1923 (NBPBLA)

Henry Allen and Richard H. Boyd, 1918 (NBPBLA)

institutions. In the May 16, 1919, issue of the *National Baptist Union-Review*, Harriett Boyd issued a plea to the women to help meet their goal to raise $2,000 for the seminary before the next Convention's annual session. In November, 1919, some forty-two students enrolled at the National Baptist Theological and Training Seminary. Since 1897, the National Baptist Publishing Board had circulated over 137 million copies of literature.[34]

The year 1920 was not a bad one for the publishing board and the unincorporated convention. The Foreign Mission Board under corresponding secretary D. R. Kemp was snugly located at 503 South Eighth Street in Louisville. The publishing board experienced a decline in letters and revenues but realized a slight increase in the number of periodicals published. The National Baptist Publishing Board's Sunday School Congress convened in Little Rock, Arkansas, at the Philander-Smith College and the First Baptist Church. The publishing Board produced some new editions of books: *The Baptist Church Directory, National Gospel Voices, National Anthem Series,* and *Celestial Showers,* all hard covers.[35]

The 1920 session of the National Baptist Convention of America met in Columbus, Ohio, beginning September 8. Delegates came from North Carolina, Missouri, Oklahoma, Florida, Mississippi, Louisiana, Arkansas, Texas, Wisconsin, Michigan, Illinois, Indiana, Virginia, West Virginia, and Alabama among other places. Both the Texas Baptist State Convention and the General Baptist Convention of Texas sent large delegations. Tennessee was represented by the Missionary Baptist State Convention, the Stone River Baptist Association, and the Nashville City Baptist Association. It seemed obvious that the convention continued to rebuild itself, five years after the split.[36]

Because of his scheduled trip to Tokyo, Japan, Henry Allen Boyd became the center of attention at the convention. Richard Henry Boyd decided that he was too old to make the previously scheduled trip, so he designated Henry Allen to represent the National Baptist Publishing Board at the World's Sunday School Congress. The convention band played and the audience sang affectionately "God Be With You Until We Meet Again" when Henry Allen came to the podium. The delegates contributed a collection of $63.08 to help with traveling expenses. Henry Allen sailed from San Francisco on September 17, 1920, at noon. He took his daughter, Katherine, to serve as stenographer.[37]

President-elect Warren G. Harding (Republican) sent a message to the convention. Harding praised the 340,000 black citizens who had served in the recent World War. He said: "Your people by their restraint, their patience, their wisdom, integrity, labor and belief in God, will earn the right to that justice, and America will bestow it."[38] Of course the Republican President's speech represented mere political rhetoric. American society had become segregated by race in the North and the South. Social, political, and economic opportunities for black Americans were minimal, at best. Yet the Reverend R. H. Boyd, the convention's leaders, and most other black Baptists remained loyal to the Republican party, the party of Abraham Lincoln, the Great Emancipator.

At the 1920 convention, the delegates learned that the National Baptist Convention of America had made much progress. The Foreign Mission Board continued its work in Africa. The Home Mission Board moved toward realizing a home for the aged ministers to retire in dignity and comfort. The Educational Board reported that the National Baptist Theological and Training Seminary had been incorporated under Tennessee's laws and the National Baptist Convention had given $10,000 of the $10,676 needed for operating expenses. A goal of $2,000,000 for the school's endowment had been announced. Less than fifteen thousand dollars was owed on the seminary property. Richard H. Boyd made a plea for subscriptions to support the *Union-Review*. Again a $2,000,000 endowment fund drive was announced by the convention. Because he had great reverence for history, the convention entertained a resolution to appoint Richard Henry Boyd as the historian for the National Baptist Convention of America.[39]

At first, President Edward P. Jones said little about the 1915 division. Instead he recommended a home for aged ministers. Then as if he could not hold himself back, Jones made a plea for more compassion and support for the National Baptist Publishing Board and Dr. Boyd. Jones said: "Today five years ago, in Chicago, a liberation from attempted thraldom came as truly to the Baptists of this nation as that which followed the immortal proclamation of the preserver of a nation." Compared to the great American Civil War, "...brothers fought against brothers," he said. Speaking about the incorporation, Jones said: "That infamous charter sought unrestrained power. Its hands would grasp a denomination's printing plant."[40]

The Reverend Boyd gave the report for the National Baptist Publishing Board. During late winter of 1920, he had visited Central America where labor strikes and influenza outbreaks slowed his tour of churches. He found that the Southern Baptist Convention operated two churches in the Panama Canal Zone. Boyd visited the mission churches operated by the National Baptist Convention of America and the Home Mission Board. The National Baptist Publishing Board gave Boyd a sixty day leave with full pay in lieu of expenses for the trip; and the Home Mission Board defrayed some of the expenses for the trip.[41]

Continuing his annual report, Boyd said that the black northern migration "has caused us to be to a certain extent hampered for labor...."[42] And "Now that all of the five lawsuits have been decided in our favor, we are hoping that our customers and patrons, churches and Sunday schools will better understand our condition, and we in turn better able to give them permanent and prompt service."[43] Boyd claimed that the opposition's attorneys had offered him $3,600 a year to retire and abandon the National Baptist Publishing

Board. The final two suits had gone to the Tennessee Court of Appeals and the Tennessee Supreme Court. The latter court said: "...The National Baptist Publishing Board is still a corporation organized under the laws of Tennessee, and the title to its properties and primary control of its affairs is vested by the laws of the State in its Board of Trustees."[44] The chairman of the National Baptist Publishing Board said: "Now that the lawsuits are over, the Board is earnestly considering retiring him [Boyd] as Secretary emeritus."[45]

According to the National Baptist Publishing Board's report, the *Union-Review* became a seven-column eight-page paper. Now the publishing board printed the newspaper from a continuous roll of paper at the rate of thirty thousand copies per hour, cut, folded and bundled for immediate mailing. The paper went to press on Wednesday and reached the subscribers by Saturday. Three full-time persons looked after advertisements, correspondence, and general matters for the *Union-Review*. The National Baptist Publishing Board completed the typeset, proofs, composing, printing, and mailing of the paper. But the subscription price did not defray the production costs. Like so many years before, Boyd constantly asked the convention to support the paper and subscription drives.[46]

Compared to 7,322,479 copies in 1919, the National Baptist Publishing Board printed 7,516,522 pieces of literature in 1920. The board handled 378,430 letters, a great increase over 1915. Boyd reported that the controversy caused the board's production to decline by more than 2,000,000 copies in circulation, 1910-1916. "Since that time our periodical circulation has been gradually increasing. Our best financial year before the division was 1913, but this [1920] proves to be our banner year and the largest in our history."[47] However, the National Baptist Publishing Board's property was "greatly run down," and repairs had to be made. The board's total receipts for 1920 were $231,485.74.[48]

The National Baptist Publishing Board report detailed the wide variety of activities and programs. Since its inception, the National Baptist Publishing Board had difficulties maintaining the operation. High paper costs made it hard to get Bibles to sell at reasonable prices. The board no longer could afford free distribution of its publishing tracts. But the board hired another field secretary, the Reverend J. S. Dixon. The NBPB and the Home Mission Board jointly paid the salary for Dixon, who visited fifteen states and distributed books and subscriptions for the *Union-Review*. However, the level of mission work had not been restored to the level of the William Beckham years.[49]

Boyd also reported about the previous Sunday School Congress. Heavy rains delayed the June 16, 1920, Congress train to Springfield, Illinois. But when the train arrived, a band played the Congress song and then "America." The meeting outgrew the days when the audience could be seated in a local church building. A parade under police escort traveled to Springfield High

School, the site of the Congress' sessions. Crowds lined the streets, cheering and waving flags. The old man, Richard Henry Boyd, was cheered with reverence when the Reverend Clark, the Congress chairman, introduced him. Then Henry Allen read the list of subjects and teachers and the roll of delegates. Tokyo Night raised money to support Henry Allen's scheduled trip to Japan. On Sunday, the usual Sunday School Congress parade assembled with pennants and banners flying. The parade traveled around the State Capitol and entered the Armory for a mass meeting. Later, the publishing board's officers laid a wreath at President Abraham Lincoln's grave. The sessions ended on Sunday night.[50]

The feud between the black Baptists remained alive. When Arthur M. Townshend, secretary of the Sunday School Publishing Board for the National Baptist Convention of the United States of America, Incorporated, tried to speak in certain Ohio churches in late 1920, he was shunned. Townshend said:

> The Boyd Convention was to meet in Columbus in September, and as the State of Ohio was largely committed to the Boyd Convention it was determined that I should not be allowed to come to town and perhaps make sentiment against the Boyd Convention, and pressure of an unusual order was brought to bear to keep me out until the Boyd Convention should have a fair chance to vindicate itself. [51]

Townshend claimed that some five hundred Ohio black Baptist delegates came to the National Baptist Convention, U. S. A.'s convention in Indianapolis.[52]

The Ohio case illustrated the frustration, confusion, and disunity the black Baptists in America suffered by the 1920s. Ohio black Baptists divided their loyalties between the two conventions and several state and local associations. The Ohio Baptist General Association, the Ohio Colored Baptist State Convention, the Ohio State B.Y.P.U. Convention, the Ohio State Sunday School Convention, and district Sunday school conventions competed with one another. The black Baptists in Ohio preferred apparently decentralized, loose associations to highly authoritative, highly centralized organizations. Some of Columbus' black Baptist churches supported Boyd. Other leaders of the Ohio Baptist General Association favored the Lott Carey Convention. The Ohio Baptist General Association voted to affiliate with none of the national black Baptist conventions and directed the Ohio black Baptist churches to affiliate with the convention of their choice, if any.[53]

The old wounds were hard to heal. But the two national conventions moved on and prospered.

The National Baptist Convention, U. S. A., Incorporated, continued also its rebuilding process. Lewis Garnett Jordan, the corresponding secretary for the Foreign Mission Board 1896, reported that his board had over sixty missionaries and helpers in Africa beside a hundred congregations and plans to open a seminary there. The Foreign Missionary Board pleaded for donations from the churches.[54] The *National Baptist Voice* began advertising Negro dolls sold by the L. Landers Company of Nashville.[55] To sustain itself, the *National Baptist Voice* carried many commercial advertisements including ones for hair products. The Benefit Board was flooded with requests from impoverished and aging ministers without pensions and jobs.[56]

The National Baptist Convention of America, Unincorporated, also made progress under the leadership of President E. P. Jones whose background and education served him and the convention well. Jones was the eldest son of the Reverend George P. Jones, pastor of the King Solomon Baptist Church in Vicksburg, Mississippi. E. P. Jones was born February 21, 1872, in Cayuga, Mississippi, and educated in the Vicksburg public schools and Natchez College. He attended the Alcorn Agricultural and Mechanical College and received the honorary Doctor of Divinity degree from Rust College in 1906. He headed the Mount Heroden Baptist Church in Mississippi for seventeen years before heading the Mount Zion Baptist Church in Evanston, Illinois.[57] Jones remained loyal to the Reverend Boyd, the National Baptist Publishing Board and the National Baptist Convention. In 1920, Jones said: "Dr. Boyd and the Board deserve sympathy, not criticism, and at this meeting we must come to the rescue of this Board whose expenditures, because of the lawsuits, have been enormous."[58]

In September, 1921, the National Baptist Convention of America met in New Orleans' Freedman Baptist Association's auditorium. In spite of great labor unrest and the 1921 economic depression, the National Baptist Publishing Board survived; and "...we have kept the force of employees at work, sometimes more and sometimes less," stated the 1921 National Baptist Publishing Board report.[59]

Boyd reported many activities, developments, and some problems for the National Baptist Publishing Board. The NBPB had bought the Boyd-Beckham building when the lease expired in 1920. Boyd and Beckham had agreed to build the facility when the 1907 effort to secure a loan for the building fell through because the anti-NBPB faction started a controversy that scared off the lenders. Boyd and Beckham completed and leased the structure to the National Baptist Publishing Board with the option to purchase at the end of the ten-year lease. The board experienced problems moving books from the shelf. Some twenty-five editions went out of print. And other books remained on the shelf for one to five years, causing great profit losses. The board studied the problems it had experienced with the *Sunday School Lesson Commentary* since the first publication in 1903. The book proved expensive because every line, picture, text, and monogram had to be set anew each year, and sometimes as many as one thousand copies were left unsold because the copies became outdated within six months. The circulation varied from three thousand to ten thousand copies. The National Baptist Publishing Board continued the series because it was important to the board's Sunday school work. Boyd reported that the National Baptist Publishing Board was the only religious publishing house in America to print a Sunday school commentary until 1922 when the white Baptists followed the National Baptist Publishing Board's lead and began their own Sunday school commentary.[60]

The National Baptist Publishing Board experienced continuing trouble in moving song books. By 1921, the NBPB had over twenty-five song books including the *Baptist Hymnal,* old meter songs, old plantation jubilee and folk songs from slavery days, and contemporary music. The National Baptist Publishing Board became the first company to set the old slave melodies to music. The printing plates for these publications could not be reproduced now for many thousands of dollars. Many of the song books had been profitable, and some caused the board to suffer losses. Boyd asked the pastors to advertise the books among the members and the choir directors.[61]

By 1921, the National Baptist Publishing Board printed fifteen periodicals including three weeklies, two monthlies, and ten quarterlies. The cost of machinery, supplies, paper, and labor had more than doubled because of postwar inflation. Sometimes, as many as thirty thousand copies of literature had to be destroyed because of over-estimation of the orders. At other times, the under-estimating of orders caused the presses to be restarted two or three times to reduce customer complaints about delayed orders. The National Baptist Publishing Board produced 7,526,522 pieces of literature in 1921 compared to 7,516,522 in 1920. The number of letters dropped from 378,430 in 1920 to 306,054 in 1921. Revenues were down, and expenses were up, causing the board to have a deficit of $6,057.75.[62]

The world-wide economic depression and the influenza outbreak of 1921 closed many businesses in America. But the National Baptist Publishing Board survived.

Excerpt From NBPB Report, 1921

Year	Letters	Periodicals	Money Paid
1920	378,430	7,516,522	$231,485.74
1921	306,054	7,526,522	$219,561.10

The National Baptist Publishing neared the end of an era. Its leaders had become old men, worn through constant struggle. The Reverend Boyd and his colleagues had tired of controversy and criticism. The recurrence of economic depressions, war, and fluctuating market conditions demanded constant attention and great energy. For years, Boyd and these board members had contemplated retirement.

The Last Days

After so many years of toiling in Nashville, the Reverend C. H. Clark, pastor of the Mount Olive Missionary Baptist Church and chairman of the board of directors for the National Baptist Publishing Board, took a lucrative offer to pastor the Ebenezer Baptist Church in Chicago, Illinois.

In the spring of 1921, Professor Mack M. Rodgers, the leading incorporator in the National Baptist Convention of the United States of America, Incorporated, passed away.[63]

During the last night of the 1920 National Baptist Convention (Unincorporated) session, the Reverend Richard H. Boyd had taken seriously ill. Henry Allen had already left for Japan. Mrs. E. B. Bolton, who knew the business of the Secretary's office, took charge of the National Baptist Publishing Board's operations until Henry Allen returned in November. Then Richard H. Boyd went to Florida for December through January. He recovered and visited thirty-five churches and the Florida Progressive Baptist Convention. But the 79-year old gentleman took ill once more. The Reverend G. B. Taylor became acting chairman of the board of directors to have some leadership on site in Nashville. Henry Allen directed the daily operations of the National Baptist Publishing Board.[64]

In April 1922, R. H. Boyd had another great disappointment. His son, J. Blaine, died on April 6, 1922. He left his wife and children. The youthful J. Blaine's death stunned his parents. Even fifteen years later, J. Blaine's memory was kept alive through a memorial section in the *Baptist Union-Review*.[65]

When the 1922 session of the National Baptist Convention of America, Unincorporated, convened in September, the Reverends Richard H. Boyd and Elias C. Morris had passed away within a few weeks of each other. The Reverend Richard Henry Boyd passed away on August 22, 1922, at his home, 1602 Heiman Street. The Reverend Elias Camp Morris passed on September 9, 1922, in Helena, Arkansas. These deaths signaled the end of an era for the publishing board and the Negro Baptists in America.[66]

The great black Baptist leaders never made up with each other because the feuding factions continued the attacks on the men. Yet Morris and Boyd refrained from personal attacks on each other. The two men had more common dreams than differences. They both dreamed of uplifting the black race in America. And both men believed that a powerful national Baptist organization could guide black America to economic greatness.

Boyd knew Morris for more than 44 years and worked with him for 21 years. Boyd wrote the introduction for Morris' book, *Sermons, Addresses and Reminiscences and Important Correspondence* (1901). Boyd said:

> Whoever has attended Negro assemblages know the thorns in the way of a presiding officer. To be impartial in the midst of such conflicting

interests and diversities of opinion, to remain calm while the surround-ings are anything but calm; to pilot a body through floods of discussion to definite creditable action; is work not easy of accomplishment. And yet Dr. Morris has been a perfect master of the situation.[67]

Unfortunate historical events, jealous men, and warring factions sepa-rated two great Baptist leaders into different camps. A Holy War was fought, and the ending seemed sad and frustrating. Each convention's newspaper barely mentioned the death of the other man. The *Baptist Review* and the Southern Baptist Convention's 1923 journal gave honorable mention to Morris' death. But neither the *Baptist Voice* nor the Southern Baptist Convention's 1923 journal gave honorable tribute to Boyd's passing.

Morris' remains were interred in Helena. The members of the National Baptist Convention, U. S. A., traveled to Arkansas where dignitaries witnessed the laying to rest of a great Baptist leader.

Instead of meeting, as planned, in Denver, Colorado, the National Baptist Convention of America, Unincorporated, met in Nashville, Tennessee on September 6-11, 1922. Boyd's body was left unburied until the convention convened. The National Baptist Convention of America passed resolutions to offer condolences for both Boyd and Morris. On Saturday morning, the convention's delegates met at the Greenwood Cemetery on Elm Hill Pike for the interment of Boyd's body. The cemetery was owned and operated by Elder Preston Taylor, R. H. Boyd's close friend and business associate. Taylor was chairman of the board for Citizens Savings Bank; and nine years later, he, too, would pass away.

In explaining Boyd's purpose for establishing the National Baptist Publishing Board, President Jones said:

> It has been done because of necessity. No man could tell of the tears and sorrows in accomplishing that 'willingness' as the venerable, earnest and conscientious Dr. R. H. Boyd, upon whose brow has fallen needless criticisms, charges and countercharges, unwarranted by facts; but in the main ignorantly alleged and for reasons personally sinister, advanced and maintained.... But [like Lincoln] so clean had he washed his hands from the seductive influences of passion and hate that his immortal documents grow white in purpose with the years.[68]

The critics found no great fortune after Richard H. Boyd's death. The bulk of his estate was willed to Harriett A. Boyd, and the remainder was given to his children "to share and share alike."[69] Some real estate had been in Hattie Boyd's name since September, 1899. Four pieces of property were acquired under Henry Allen Boyd's name between 1905 and 1913.[70] Richard H. Boyd listed his home at 1602 Heiman Street and the lot next door under his name.[71]

T. B. Boyd, another son, owned a house and lot at 1600 Heiman Street.[72] Most of the real estate owned by Hattie and Richard Boyd was bought in 1899.[73] The Reverend Boyd had made a good living for his family, but he had expended his own energy and personal money to achieve his goals.

The Reverend Richard H. Boyd's life itself represented an interesting chapter. He acted the part of a renaissance man. He endured the attacks on his character and the board, maintained a stable NBPB, helped establish a seminary for the National Baptist Convention of America, and helped to sustain the National Baptist Convention of America, "Boyd's convention," after the denominational split of 1915. Not only Boyd's fortitude, but his contributions to black American history and black cultural achievement deserve further detail.

William Beckham,
Field Secretary, 1914 (NBR)

Rev. R. H. Thorbourne,
Our Missionary on the
Panama Zone, 1914 (NBR)

Negro Doll
Advertisement (NBR)

Organ For Sale (NBR)

Lula Boyd Landers, 1920 (NBR)

Bessie Thorbourne,
Panama Missionary, 1920 (NBR)

Mr. Gilbert King is in charge of the Press Room where you will find five big presses and two job presses on which all the printing of the National Baptist Publishing Board is done.

Chapter 5

R. H. Boyd: Preacher, Entrepreneur, and Leader

Chapter 5
R.H. Boyd: Preacher, Entrepreneur, and Leader

After his death in 1922, Boyd was frequently honored. The National Baptist Convention of America, Unincorporated, and the National Baptist Publishing Board devoted the month of March to commemorate Boyd's death. Hundreds of Baptist churches observed the event for many years. Boyd's Normal and Industrial Institute at Oakwood, Texas, was named in his honor. Boyd's memberships included the Knights of Phythias, the Masons, the U. B. F. Society, the Odd Fellows, the Board of Directors of the International Sunday School Committee, and life member of the National Negro Business League. Nashville's annual minority business enterprise fair and banquet used Richard Henry Boyd's name, and this annual affair continues to operate in Boyd's honor into the 1990s.

Richard Henry Boyd became a renaissance man. Not only did he plan, create, and develop the National Baptist Publishing Board into one of America's largest black business operations, but Boyd founded other companies including the National Negro Doll Company and a church furniture manufacturing company. Boyd helped to organize and direct the Union Transportation Company, the One-Cent Savings and Trust Company Bank, and the Nashville Globe Publishing Company. In Nashville, the Reverend Boyd became a leader in local politics, religion, and civic endeavors.

Boyd became prominent in Booker T. Washington's National Negro Business League movement. Promoting the black man's cause through the publishing board's activities and other ways consumed much of Richard H. Boyd's life. The Reverend Boyd was a close confidant and business partner to James Carroll Napier, Washington's chief cohort and local "Mr. Republican." And Boyd became acquainted with Booker T. Washington, who frequently visited Nashville where he served on Fisk University's board of trustees. To Boyd, Booker T. Washington was the "Champion of the People's Cause."[1] Like Washington and Napier, R. H. Boyd, too, became a "Race Man," a black leader who believed in uplifting the black race to a level of equality with white people.

Like Booker T. Washington and Nashville's James C. Napier, Richard H. Boyd too believed in accommodationism relative to race relations between whites and blacks. The white accommodationists believed in racial segregation, but these whites believed in some degree of fairness through the separate but equal concept. The southern accommodationists argued that racial harmony was necessary to attract industry and improve the Region's depressed post-Civil War economy. Accordingly, the black accommodationists became pragmatists who worked with moderate whites to establish and maintain institutions for blacks and keep harmonious race relations in the South. For black accommodationists, like Boyd and Napier as well as Washington and

v. R. H. Boyd (NBR)

others, the forming of alliances with moderate whites became an expedient thing to do if the practically illiterate freedmen would advance and prosper. Most black leaders, like Boyd and Washington, believed that the former slaves and their descendants needed their own institutions to instill confidence and prove the blacks' abilities before integrating and assimilating with the whites who had advantages and experiences through generations of living as free persons. Boyd and the black accommodationists believed that contemporary whites intended to keep whites in control of the major institutions and would never give blacks any control of American institutions and businesses. Besides, if blacks had their own schools, churches, colleges, and other institutions, they had no reason to want to integrate with whites. The southern white Baptists felt comfortable working with Boyd.

Promoting Education

The Reverend Boyd had two years of formal education at Bishop College in Marshall, Texas, a grammar and normal school sponsored by the American Baptist Home Mission Society of New York. Mostly, Boyd was a self-made man who gained his education through the informal, hands-on process. Boyd perfected his writing, speaking, and communication skills through years of preaching and writing. He gained most of his education in the real world of business and religious politics which earned him respect as a doctor of organization and management of religious publishing. He became highly respected for his business genius and leadership skills. Boyd received two honorary doctorate degrees.

The Reverend Boyd and his family recognized the value of formal education, and they promoted secondary and higher education for blacks by soliciting help from white philanthropists. Boyd was not a true elitist. He believed that educated men and women should help lead the freedmen to true equality in America. Boyd supported personally the establishment of schools, seminaries, and colleges for Afro-Americans. He even became a founder and a member of the faculty for the National Baptist Theological and Training Seminary in 1918.

Hardly eleven years after he became a resident of Nashville, Boyd became involved in the effort to save Roger Williams University. This freedmen's university was closed in 1907 by the American Baptist Home Mission Society of New York. The American Baptist Home Mission Society had proposed to close the school in 1888 when black students rebelled against a racially conservative white administration. However, local black Baptist churches successfully appealed to the northern white Baptists to keep the school open. Again the ABHMS proposed to close the school in 1891; but Nashville's Reverend Jessie E. Purdy, pastor of First Colored Baptist Church, took the issue to the American National Baptist Convention's session. For now, the ABHMS backed off their controversial proposal to close Roger Williams and other small freedmen's colleges and consolidate their black educational programs into a "National Freedman's College" in the South. But by 1905, Roger Williams University's white officials received pressure from white realtors who wanted to consume the black college campus and develop the land for the booming white suburban expansion in West Nashville. In January and May 1907, mysterious fires destroyed the main University buildings on Hillsboro Road. In 1907, the American Baptist Home Mission Society decided to close Roger Williams University, sell the land and remaining buildings, and transfer the black students to other ABHMS schools throughout the South.

Why close a college that was over forty years old? The newest generation of northern white Baptists had less tolerance for work among the southern blacks who had become more radical with their "home rule" movement. The cost of operating many freedmen schools and colleges in the South had become too expensive for the northern Baptists, specifically the American Baptist Home Mission Society. Moreover, the Jim Crow South had become a place where violence, murder, occasional anarchy, and mob action by radical whites against "uppity" blacks and liberal whites was acceptable to white authorities.

Black leaders in Nashville protested the closing. They requested that the American Baptist Home Mission Society give them part of the insurance proceeds from the burnt buildings. After the American Baptist Home Mission Society agreed to a ten thousand dollar matching fund, Nashville's black leaders and the Negro Baptist Association of Tennessee engaged in plans to rebuild Roger Williams University on the black side of town.

The Reverend Boyd and other local black Baptist preachers headed a delegation of black leaders to the Tennessee General Assembly to ask for $10,000 to reestablish Roger Williams University. The General Assembly refused to support the effort. Under the leadership of the Reverend William Haynes, the blacks raised the money. Roger Williams University opened in new buildings on Whites Creek Pike in 1909.

Boyd and other officers of the National Baptist Publishing Board continued their involvement with Roger Williams University and its fundraising efforts. In the fall of 1914, the Reverend Boyd preached the opening sermon for the cornerstone ceremonies at Roger Williams University. His topic was "The Adolescence of Man." The cornerstone for the boys dormitory was laid on Sunday, October 11, 1914, by the East Nashville Masonic Lodge No. 170, headed by the Most Eminent Grand Commander, Elder Preston Taylor, Boyd's fellow minister and business colleague.[2]

By 1915, the black Baptist denomination split on the national level. Factions that opposed the National Baptist Publishing Board controlled Roger Williams University. This development ended Boyd's participation with Roger

Williams University. Roger Williams University closed in 1929 and merged with Howe Institute (LeMoyne-Owen College) in Memphis.

In 1909, The Reverend Boyd and his son, Henry Allen, became early leaders of the movement to locate a state-supported school for blacks in Nashville. The General Assembly passed legislation in 1909 to build state normal schools in West, Middle, and East Tennessee (for whites). After protest by Nashville's black leaders, including James C. Napier, the white legislature included a fourth school, a state normal for Negroes. The site of the normal schools would be determined by bids from interested communities.[3]

Richard Boyd's experiences with shortages of skilled mechanics, printers, and clerical personnel at the National Baptist Publishing caused him to see the wisdom in having a public training, industrial and normal college in Nashville. Henry Allen Boyd, J. C. Napier, Preston Taylor, Dock A. Hart and others formed the Tennessee Agricultural and Industrial State Normal Association. Henry Allen Boyd presided over the association. Richard Boyd served in the delegation of local black leaders who approached the Davidson County Court (county government) and the General Assembly of Tennessee about the state normal school, and he headed a list of preachers and businessmen who published an appeal in the *Globe*, asking the "White Voters of Davidson County" to vote for a $25,000 bond issue to establish the Negro normal school in Nashville, Davidson County. The bond issue was defeated by the voters. Preston Taylor, the Boyds, Napier, Hart, Benjamin Carr, and other black leaders traveled door-to-door collecting money and raising thousands of dollars to help build the school's facilities. In 1911, the state awarded the Tennessee Agricultural and Industrial State Normal School for Negroes to Nashville, Davidson County. The school opened during the summer of 1912.[4]

The publishing board and the One-Cent Savings Bank as well as other businesses affiliated with Richard H. Boyd became involved in promoting the Negro normal school through the participation of Preston Taylor, Napier, Henry Allen, Richard Henry, and Hart. Dock A. Hart became involved, for example, because he directed the printing department at the National Baptist Publishing Board and needed more trained blacks in printing, mechanics, and clerical work. Possibly the new state normal school could help increase the supply of trained Negro mechanics. Boyd had sent Hart to New York to learn to operate and install modern linotype printing machines. And Richard and Henry Allen Boyd skillfully used the Nashville *Globe* to gain support to locate the school in Nashville. Richard Boyd was a major owner of the Globe Publishing Company.

Richard Boyd also had a keen interest in promoting secondary schools in Nashville. He and other members of the Negro Board of Trade persuaded the city government and the mayor to build a new Pearl High School near Fisk University. Since 1912, Boyd and other black leaders in Nashville's Negro

Board of Trade had pressured the city to build a new high school building for the black community. The old building near Fifth and Demonbreun Streets had been built in 1883, and it was overcrowded and located in the middle of the Black Bottom slum neighborhood. The school overlooked the Bottom where frequent floods from the Cumberland River left deep pools of water and black mud. In return for black support for the bond issue and the 1912 reelection of Mayor Hilary Howse, the city agreed to build a new Pearl High School. The Boyds and the *Globe* supported Howse and solicited the black community's support. A new Pearl High School opened in 1916 near the Fisk University campus.

Soon the blacks concluded that the whites had cheated them. The president of the Negro Board of Trade and other black leaders criticized the city's officials for taking most of the bond issue money to build beautiful white schools and leaving only enough to build a plain red brick school (with no stone trimmings) that was too small to hold the black high school students. The black leaders protested to the all-white Board of Education only to be told that black people don't pay taxes and, therefore, should not complain. Still it was important, said Boyd, for the students to make the best of the crowded situation and take advantage of educational opportunities. In a speech, the Reverend Boyd told the high school audience at Pearl Public High School to be punctual, correct and honorable.[5]

In 1937, the federal New Deal program's Works Progress Administration program built a large, modern black Pearl High School at the corner of Jo Johnston and Seventeenth Avenue North. Boyd did not live to see this modern black high school, but his grandchildren attended Pearl School.

The Reverend Boyd became a leader for locating a Baptist seminary in Nashville. This effort started with the establishment of the Educational Board by the National Baptist Convention in 1900. Boyd was not a member of the Educational Board, but he became highly interested in the campaign for a seminary. Boyd's interest peaked when the National Baptist Convention formally authorized the institution in 1912 and designated Nashville as the school's location. He promoted the campaign for a seminary through the National Baptist Publishing Board's publications and the Nashville *Globe.*

The Reverend Boyd solicited support from James M. Frost and the Southern Baptist Convention. In October 1914, Frost and the Reverend W. O. Weaver, pastor of Nashville's First Baptist Church, and other local white Baptist ministers formed a committee to help raise $7,500 to locate the seminary on Whites Creek Pike, next to Roger Williams University. Boyd and Frost persuaded the Southern Baptist Convention to pledge $50,000 for the seminary. The Reverend Weaver said that the influence of Negro preachers was the most potent factor in bringing about a better understanding between the races. Therefore, the education of more black Baptist preachers became important.[6]

The 1915 Baptist denominational problem separated Boyd from the seminary effort and left the Educational Board under the National Baptist Convention of the United States of America, Incorporated (NBCI). The NBCI's Educational Board eventually established the American Baptist Theological Seminary in September 1924 on nearly forty acres of land next to Roger Williams University on Whites Creek Pike. Sutton E. Griggs became president of the institution for a brief period in 1925-1926. The Southern Baptist Convention contributed some $7,500 per year to the seminary, today's American Baptist College.[7]

The National Baptist Convention of America, Unincorporated, and its Educational Board continued to work toward establishing their black Baptist seminary in Nashville. Now Boyd headed the effort to establish the National Baptist Theological and Training Seminary in Nashville, although he was not the board's corresponding secretary, and Boyd was some 73 years old by now. Under Dr. Boyd's leadership, in 1917 the National Baptist Convention of America, Unincorporated (NBCA), proposed to buy the formerly white female Boscobel College campus. The National Baptist Seminary and Training School would be established on these grounds.

When attending the Illinois Baptist State Convention, President Jones had urged Boyd to move full speed ahead with the purchase of Boscobel College's vacant facilities. Jones promised to gain the Convention's support. Boyd called the Reverend D. Abner, Jr., the new secretary of the Educational Board, to come to Nashville and look at the Boscobel facilities. Some 150 ministers, laymen, and Baptist women from twenty states came to Nashville and visited the Boscobel College campus. Then they met in the Colored YMCA building where the executive board of the NBCA endorsed the plans. Some five thousand dollars had to be raised to close the deal. On Thursday night of the National Baptist Convention of America's 1917 session, the Reverend Boyd had reported some great news—the Boscobel College campus in Nashville had been purchased for $25,000 by the NBCA.[8]

The Boscobel campus was worth at least $100,000, the Reverends Boyd and Jones said. The facility had two main brick buildings on ten acres overlooking the Cumberland River in East Nashville. One could see the Shelby Park not far away. The Boscobel College campus included sixty-five dormitory rooms with bathrooms between every two dormitory rooms. The buildings had steam heat and ventilation, a large recreation room, a chapel, eight class rooms with fine desks, five offices, and a dining hall for hundreds. Jones recommended a committee of three persons to meet with the Southern Baptist Convention's officials and request aid to the National Baptist Convention of America's mission work and efforts to establish the new seminary. After the school opened, the publishing board shifted most of the Sunday school teacher training program to the National Baptist Theological and Training Seminary.

The Southern Baptist Convention's officials became upset about the NBCA's new seminary. The southern Baptists had become disturbed particularly about the failure of the two black conventions to reunite on common grounds. The southern Baptists had formed a Peace Commission to try and merge the NBCI and the NBCA. Apparently, the Southern Baptist Convention's officials blamed the NBCA for the failure of reunion because the NBCA refused to accept the principle of incorporation. The May, 1919, Southern Baptist Convention's report read:

> The National Baptist Convention (unincorporated) has bargained for a site in Nashville, Tenn., and published the fact that they have organized a National Baptist Theological Seminary, without regard to what the Southern Baptist Convention proposed to do. How far they have proceeded in the organization, we may not be fully informed, but we have in hand the charter of such institution. And it is chartered under a Self-Perpetuating Board, and acknowledges allegiance to no other Baptist organization.[9]

The Southern Baptists praised the National Baptist Convention, U. S. A. (Incorporated) for accepting the principle of denominational control and for showing appreciation for the help of the white brethren.

Therefore, the seminary established by the National Baptist Convention of America, Unincorporated, and Boyd had to do without support from the southern and northern Baptists. Although the other seminary was not established until 1924, with annual appropriations from the southern Baptists, the NBCI's American Baptist Theological Seminary, U. S. A., survived to present times whereas the black seminary on the Boscobel campus faded away years after Boyd's death.

But Sunday school work, missionary work, publishing and education represented only some of the many involvements of Richard H. Boyd. He also involved himself in the political life of his community. Because the church became the most powerful black institution, it became impossible for the preachers and the churches to refrain from promoting black political power.

Boyd's Political Involvement

By the time Boyd had established residency in Nashville, the local black community had launched a struggle to get the county court, the city council, the General Assembly, and other political bodies to respond to its needs. For now, no blacks served in these legislative bodies. The last black to serve on Nashville's city council was James C. Napier (1885). In 1882, Thomas Sykes became the last black Nashvillian to serve in the General Assembly.

Since 1890, no blacks had served in the county court, Davidson County's government, and in the Tennessee General Assembly. Poll taxes, intimidation of blacks by white radicals at the polls, black poverty, and political legislative acts had stopped political participation for most eligible black voters. Since receiving the right to vote in February 1867, Tennessee's freedmen had remained loyal to the Republican party, Abraham Lincoln's party and the political group that freed the slaves.

By 1870, the Democratic party and former Confederates had taken control of Tennessee by forming a successful coalition of rural and urban whites who consistently defeated Tennessee's Republican party. Rural and former Confederate whites continued to be bitter about the South's Civil War defeat, and urban whites feared the huge migration of blacks into southern towns and cities. Southern whites viewed the Republican party as the "black Republicans," friends of the Negro. After constantly losing elections, except one gubernatorial campaign, the Tennessee Republican party decided that more white voters had to be attracted into the party, and the blacks should be diminished in the Republican ranks. Around 1900, Boyd and other black Tennesseans called this Republican faction's strategy "the lily-white movement."

On March 10, 1900, the Reverend Boyd sent a letter to pastors in the National Baptist Convention in Tennessee, asking them to attend political meetings. He said: "I fear [a]...destruction of our political rights as a race in this state. You are aware of the fact that there seems to be a concert of action in every Southern State to disfranchise the Negroes at the ballot box, and some of the white Republicans seem equally as eager to eliminate them from active participation in their political gatherings, both state and national."[10] Boyd advised the Baptist pastors to "carefully guard the political interest of the Negro race" and see to it that all male members of their congregations are properly informed about political issues.[11]

It was not unusual for preachers, like the Reverend Boyd, to use the black church to promote political participation. After Emancipation, the church became the most influential institution in black America. Black pastors could persuade their members to support or not support a certain candidate. From Boyd (early 1900s) to the Reverend Martin Luther King, Jr. (1950s-60s), the black church served as an instrument to enable black people to gain their rights in an American society where the white majority sought to deny those constitutional rights. Besides, Boyd did not fear white economical reprisal because he and the publishing board depended on black churches, not whites, for a living and a business.

Even though he had resided in Nashville only four years, Boyd had become acquainted with James C. Napier, black attorney and the leading black Republican in Tennessee. Boyd admired Napier and trusted his advice. Boyd,

Napier, and others in the predominantly black Davidson County Republican party intended to pressure the Republicans at the national convention that was scheduled for June 19, 1900.

Although since the 1870s the blacks had been represented in the Tennessee Republican party's state executive committee and had attended national Republican conventions, now the white Republicans wanted to exclude black delegates. Napier, Boyd's friend and later business partner, had represented blacks in the state Republican party, and he had been a candidate from the sixth congressional district in 1898 when white leaders criticized Napier for his audacity to run against white men for a seat in Congress. Boyd urged the blacks to demand representation in the Tennessee Republican delegation, and he and other black leaders in Tennessee insisted that the Republicans select Napier to attend the 1900 convention in Philadelphia.

It seemed that the Republican party, the party of Lincoln, would be an advocate for black rights. That was not the case. By 1900 the Republican party had become dominated by northern big business interests, wealthy interests, and conservative white men. The Republican party began to divorce itself from the blacks and end a political marriage that had lasted since 1867.

Boyd and other local black leaders refused to be pushed out of the party. Some local black leaders, including the Reverend Boyd and his son Henry Allen, protested when President Theodore Roosevelt (Republican) visited Nashville in 1907 but snubbed the black community. President Roosevelt's motorcade passed the black Pearl High School to view the black teachers and students lined along the sidewalk near Fifth and Demonbreun Streets. But Roosevelt did not visit a single black site, not even the black colleges, the pride of black Nashville. Black leaders were not admitted to places where the President spoke.

The Boyds used the Nashville *Globe* to protest against Nashville's all-white Board of Trade for not including any blacks on the presidential welcoming committee. "Negroes should have been represented," said the *Globe's* editor.[12] The blacks wanted to tell Roosevelt that Nashville's Fort Negley should be restored as a national battlefield and serve as a tribute to the thousands of slaves, black federal troops, and white Union Army soldiers who built and maintained the fort from 1862 to 1866. Blacks recalled that 21,133 Negro men and 30,000 white Tennesseans had served in the Union army in Tennessee during the American Civil War.[13]

Incidentally, the black community continued the *Globe's* campaign to restore Fort Negley. The federal New Deal's Works Progress Administration program restored Fort Negley in 1937 during the Great Depression. By then, the Democratic party and President Franklin D. Roosevelt had begun to attract black voters from the Republican party. Local blacks took pride in the restored Fort Negley which had a reception center and paved roads for visitors. But

Tennessee's authorities, who worshipped the state's Confederate history, allowed the historic site to deteriorate and return to ruins and weeds by 1949. Again, beginning around 1980, local blacks continued efforts to get Fort Negley restored as a "black historic site and Civil War museum."[14]

The local black leaders and Richard H. Boyd opposed outright the lily-white Republican faction which sought to exclude blacks. On the other hand, the whites resented that the Davidson County Republican party was predominantly black, because the whites believed that a party with a predominance of black members could not win elections in the South during the height of the Jim Crow period.

In May, 1908, Richard H. Boyd and the Reverend Luke Mason helped to take control of the Sixth Congressional District Republican Convention in Nashville. Boyd, Mason, and the other black Republicans elected two Negro delegates to the National Republican Convention. The Republican Convention would neither certify nor seat these delegates. The Boyd-Mason group declared the Nashville *Globe* to be the official newspaper for the Davidson County Republican party.[15] The Globe Publishing Company, which was owned primarily by R. H. Boyd., published the weekly *Globe* newspaper. The publishing board's employees, Joseph Oliver Battle and Henry Allen Boyd, edited the paper and directed a campaign to educate the black community about the "lily-white Republicans." The NBPB printed the newspaper.

Luke Mason became a leading militant about the degradation of blacks in the Republican party. Mason had headed the Lewis Street Primitive Baptist Church since 1878, and he had served on the county court (government) as a commissioner for six years and the executive committee of the Davidson County Republican party for twenty years. Richard H. Boyd considered Luke Mason to be a valuable ally. When Mason died at the age of 66 years, the *Union-Review* reported his death and funeral. Mason was born March 10, 1848, and died February 27, 1915. His funeral was held at the Ryman Auditorium in downtown Nashville where some five thousand persons, including the Boyds, attended and paid respects.[16]

The Reverend Boyd had much clout in the local Republican party conventions. But he was not a politician, and Boyd desired no political office. Boyd's colleagues and some of the publishing board's employees frequently served as delegates and leaders in those meetings. For example, present at the 1907 district convention were J. C. Napier (cashier of the One-Cent Savings Bank), J. O. Battle (head of the National Baptist Publishing Board's book department and editor of the *Globe*), and T. G. Ewing (one of Boyd's attorneys and old friends).[17]

Local blacks, the Boyds, and the *Globe* supported William H. Taft for president in 1908. President Roosevelt's Republican successor, Taft, rewarded the Nashville community by appointing Napier to the position of Register of the

United States Treasury in 1911. Boyd said that "Mr. Napier is my personal friend and has been my lawyer during all of my business and professional life. He is a Negro of whom the whole race is proud."[18] At the farewell dinner for Napier in March, 1911, Boyd toasted Napier: "Well done, thou good and faithful financier, you have been faithful in your administration over our few pennies [One-Cents Savings Bank], walk up higher to the Register of the United States Treasury and have dominion over billions."[19]

Napier served as Register of the United States Treasury until 1913 when Woodrow Wilson, a Southerner by birth and a Democrat, succeeded President Taft. President Wilson ordered the department heads to segregate their federal employees because many federal offices existed in southern territory, including Washington, D. C., where laws and customs demanded racial segregation. Napier refused the President's order, resigned, and returned to the job of cashier at Nashville's One-Cent Savings and Trust Company Bank.

Meanwhile in 1911, an employee of the National Baptist Publishing Board, Solomon P. Harris, campaigned successfully for election to the city council. Harris ran on the Democratic ticket with Mayor Hilary Howse who had strong black-support. Because the Republican party had not won a city election since the 1880s, local blacks voted for Democrats and reform candidates in city elections but continued to support the Republican party on the state and national levels. Mayor Howse had gained credibility among black leaders because his administrations granted more services, a city park (Hadley Park), a Carnegie public library, and other concessions to the black community. The *Globe*, edited by publishing board employee J. O. Battle, supported Howse and Harris. Harris was elected from the predominantly black third ward.[20] Not since 1885 had a black man served in the city council. After Harris left the council in 1913, no other black was elected to that legislative body until 1951.

By 1912, Theodore Roosevelt had formed his Progressive ("Bull Moose") Republican party faction. Roosevelt's faction blamed the Republican party's corruption and misfortune on the ignorant and corrupt blacks. Between 1912 and Boyd's death in 1922, local black participation in the Republican party continued to decline. After 1922, Boyd's son, Henry Allen, would head the local black Republican party organization until the 1950s when blacks abandoned the Republican party.

Again the Reverend Richard H. Boyd was too busy as a builder of businesses to spend much time in politics. But Boyd gave support to black leaders like Napier. The Reverend Richard H. Boyd's business success and his philosophy of leadership touched and motivated many others.

Promoting Business Development

By the turn of the century, black American leaders had begun a movement to promote and develop black businesses to help uplift black people. Booker T. Washington and other Negro leaders created the National Negro Business League in 1900. Two years later, J. C. Napier, Richard H. Boyd, and others chartered the Nashville chapter of the League. The men realized that capital must be raised to promote and develop Negro businesses and increase black real estate holdings, including home ownership.

All black businessmen in Nashville and Davidson County became eligible to join the Negro Business League of Nashville, Tennessee. The purpose of the Negro Business League was to "arouse business interests among Negroes by advocating the support of the industries and business houses already established and encouraging the establishment of new ones and such other manufacturing enterprises that will enable the world, and ourselves as well, to know of our possibilities as business men."[21] The League vowed not to lend its name for the furtherance of any movement having for its end private gain or personal profit. The League outlawed religious and political involvement within the organization. This was a black business missionary movement.

The campaign to organize a local bank, the One-Cent Savings and Trust Company Bank, became the greatest accomplishment by Nashville's black business leaders.

On November 5, 1903, Boyd, Napier, and other members of the local Negro Business League chapter decided to create a local bank. The original founders included Boyd, Taylor, J. B. Bosley, J. A. Cullom, T. G. Ewing, J. W. Grant, the Reverend William Haynes, E. B. Jefferson, and attorney Napier.[22] The One-Cent Savings Bank became black Nashville's first bank since the Freedman's Savings and Trust Company Bank had existed in 1865-1874.

The history of the Freedman's Bank helped to motivate Boyd to head the One-Cent Savings Bank effort. The Freedman's Savings and Trust Company bank was created in March, 1865, by Congress to service former slaves. The Nashville branch was organized in late 1865 and became one of thirty-three Freedman's Banks in the country and among four branches in Tennessee. The Nashville branch thrived, and it built its own three-story headquarters, Liberty Hall, at 44 Cedar Street. Liberty Hall became black Nashville's political and social headquarters where state colored conventions and other meetings were held. Near Cedar (Charlotte) and Cherry (Fourth Avenue North) black visitors stayed at the Harding House Hotel, Sumner House, and Keeble Hall, all black-owned buildings. By 1874, the Nashville Freedman's Bank had $78,535 in assets compared to $19,823 in the Columbia Freedman's Bank and $56,775 to Memphis' Freedman's Bank. Nashville's bank even had a black cashier (manager), John J. Cary, a free Negro who migrated from Canada. However, whites in Washington, D. C. controlled the Freedman's Bank and its branches, including the one in Nashville. Corrupt white men caused the Freedman's Bank and its branches to collapse in 1874.[23] Local blacks lost their money and their confidence in any black financial institution for the next generation.

NBPB Book Bindery Depart.

One-Cent Savings Bank's Director's Dinner at R. H. Boyd's Home (NBR)

Board of Directors, 1904, One-Cent Savings Bank (NBR)

James Carroll Napier, 1904 (NBR)

Since the failure of the Freedman's Savings and Trust Company Bank, only one other banking venture had been launched in black Nashville. The Home Banking and Loan Association, organized by black businessman Lewis Winters and others, began to engage in real estate and home ownership campaigns for blacks during the late 1880s. But this effort fizzled because local blacks had no confidence in operating their own financial institutions.

Napier, who knew the above history well, led the effort, with Boyd and others, to establish a new bank as a necessary mission to restore the financial confidence that black Nashvillians had lost since 1874. In November 1903, the black men agreed that a Negro bank was needed to accumulate capital and restore black confidence. Boyd argued that blacks could support a bank just like they supported a publishing house. He reminded the founders that blacks throughout the country had established recent banks to encourage racial pride and uplift the Negro's confidence in his own institutions. The number of black banks in America increased from six in 1900 to more than forty by 1911.

The men scheduled another meeting for November 12, 1903. The list of charter members grew to sixteen including William Beckham, G. I. Jackson, Charles N. Langston, J. L. Martin, Robert L. Mayfield, Lewis Winters, George W. McKissack, C. S. Randall, and W. D. Chappelle. Beckham worked at the publishing board, and he jointly owned real estate with Boyd. Langston was James C. Langston's nephew. McKissack worked as a local brick masonry contractor. Winters owned the largest poultry business in Nashville and a multi-story building at 211-213 South Cherry Street. On November 28, the men received Napier's offer to furnish space for a bank in the Napier Court office building at 411 North Cherry (4th) Street near Cedar. Napier offered three months free rent to help support the bank. Thereafter, he would charge only $25 a month in rent.[24]

The One-Cent Savings and Trust Company Bank opened on January 16, 1904, at 9:00 a. m. in a room of the Napier Court Building with $1,600 of capital and $6,500 in deposits. Each founding member invested one hundred dollars and Napier pledged one thousand dollars. The officers included R.H. Boyd, president; J. W. Bostic, vice-president; James C. Napier, cashier (manager); and Preston Taylor, chairman of the board of directors.[25]

The bank seemed bound to succeed because three of black Nashville's most able businessmen headed the new institution. These men included Richard Henry Boyd, James Carroll Napier, and Preston Taylor.

The elected Chairman of the board of directors, Preston Taylor, was owner of a funeral home and proprietor of the Greenwood Cemetery. Taylor came to Nashville during the late 1880s after building railroads and founding a freedmen's college in Kentucky. He headed the downtown Gay Street Christian (Disciples of Christ) Church until around 1892 when he and some members formed the Lea Avenue Christian (Disciples of Christ) Church in

Greenwood Park, 1912 (Globe)

Greenwood Park, 1912 (Globe)

South Nashville. In 1889, Taylor created the Greenwood Cemetery on property he bought near "Buttermilk Ridge," a dairy farm area on Elm Hill Pike. By 1905, Taylor had bought the property behind the cemetery, fronting on Lebanon Pike and Spence Lane, to open the Greenwood Park, a large recreation enterprise. Greenwood Park included rides, spraying fountains, a zoo, electric merry-go-round, skating rink, bandstand, food stands, side shows, woman's building, ticket gates, a baseball stadium, and "pleasure wagons" to bring the patrons from the nearest streetcar line to the ticket gates. Taylor made constant improvements on the park, securing bank loans to buy the right-of-way to extend the streetcar line to the gates of the park. Major black events, including the State Fair, picnics for churches and other organizations, Sunday band concerts, and baseball games by the Greenwood Giants took place at Greenwood Park. Taylor, born a slave in 1848 in Louisiana, served as chairman of the board of directors for the One-Cent Bank (Citizens Bank) until his death in 1931.[26]

James C. Napier was born free in 1845 in Davidson County. His parents were free persons. Napier attended the local free black school operated by black preacher Daniel Wadkins before it closed in 1857 because of Nashville's race riot (December 1856). The Napiers moved temporarily to Ohio where Napier attended school at Wilberforce. Shortly after the Civil War, young Napier returned to Nashville. In 1872, Napier completed the Howard University law school. Six years later, he married his former dean's daughter, Nettie Langston. The girl's father, John Mercer Langston, became the first black American to receive a law degree, and Langston, a free Negro, also became a black congressman from Virginia during Reconstruction. Napier served in various government posts during Reconstruction and in Nashville's city council from 1879 until 1885. He became a successful lawyer and owner of the Napier Court office building in downtown Nashville. Napier became U.S. Register of the Treasury (1911-1913), a member of Fisk University's board of trustees (1915-1940), a member of Howard University's board of trustees (1911-1940), and a key ally to Booker T. Washington.[27]

The selection of Boyd as president proved important to the organization. Boyd was respected highly for his "business sense," integrity, and influence with the black community. Already, he headed the largest black publishing business in the country. Boyd said that the bank became necessary because local white banks did not welcome the small black depositors, and white depositors resented the presence of black customers. Boyd insisted that One-Cent Savings Bank keep cold cash on hand to honor any depositor's demand. To further build the black community's confidence in the One-Cent Savings and Trust Company Bank, Boyd published the bank's annual financial statements in the Nashville *Globe* newspaper.

The Reverend R. H. Boyd directed the One-Cent Savings Bank with frugality like he managed the National Baptist Publishing Board. In 1906, the bank made a $2,462 profit in loans to institutions and individuals. Boyd insisted on reasonable but not lucrative salaries for bank employees. He discouraged the payment of dividends to stockholders during the early years and encouraged the stockholders to reinvest the dividends in the bank. Boyd continued to remind the stockholders and the public that a black bank was needed to keep black Nashville from falling behind other black communities where banks had been started. Henry Allen Boyd won election to the board of directors to replace the Reverend G. I. Jackson who moved to another city.[28]

The new black bank had some rough times to weather. But with excellent leadership in Boyd, Taylor, Napier, and others, the One-Cent Savings Bank survived one economic depression after another although many white banks collapsed. During the financial panic of 1907, Boyd called a special board meeting to spread the word that the One-Cent Savings Bank was solvent. Stacks of currency were available for the customers to see. The bank balanced its books with $43,907.69. Boyd praised the bank's employees including "the janitor who sweeps the floor and lights the building" who keep the institution strong and successful. Boyd argued that "Because the Negro by unjust legislation and political discrimination is robbed of every vestige of self-government, his religious and benevolent institutions are his most important agencies for uplifting the race."[29]

Some black leaders criticized Boyd's conservative approach to fiscal affairs. They argued that the bank should make more profits for the stockholders. To answer those who criticized his conservative fiscal management, Boyd said:

> It should be clearly understood by the stockholders that this institution was born out of real necessity. It was not organized as a loan company and investment company, an industrial insurance company, nor a pawn shop. The idea of 'getting rich quick' was never in the minds of the officers of this institution. The one objective of this institution has overshadowed all others and that objective was the gaining and dissemination of confidence. There is a woeful lack of confidence among Negroes themselves in the Negro's ability and his integrity collectively.[30]

Boyd recommended that the directors pay dividends to stockholders only on demand so that the bank's reserve fund could be increased. Boyd believed that banking was an honorable way to restore confidence in a former slave race. "Banking is the highest, most honorable and painstaking business of higher civilization,"[31] he said. The bank's character and reputation must be impeccable, Boyd argued to the directors. The bank must be ready to meet the demand of the depositors, dollar for dollar each day, he said. From 1904 to

1906, the One-Cent Savings and Trust Company Bank processed respectively the following sums of money: $317,743.81, $512,612.48, and $576,859.79.[32]

Feeling that Boyd's management of the bank was "too exacting" and "made money a little hard for borrowers to obtain," in 1909, a group of black leaders, led by Robert Fulton Boyd (no relation to R. H. Boyd), organized the People's Savings and Trust Company Bank. Robert F. Boyd was a board member of the One-Cent Savings and Trust Company Bank. He was a Meharry-trained physician, businessman, proprietor of Mercy Hospital, and founder of the Olympia Amusement Park on Whites Creek Pike. His former park became the site for the new Roger Williams University in 1909. The People's Bank opened at 410 Cedar Street. It had over $21,198.65 in assets by 1911. By 1917, the bank had $71,100.33 in assets and deposits. Because of the Great Depression, People's Bank closed by 1930.[33]

Robert Fulton Boyd and his fellow businessmen also disagreed with R. H. Boyd, Napier, and the other black leaders about the direction of the local Negro Business League chapter. So Fulton Boyd and his group chartered a second chapter of the League, causing Nashville to have two sets of delegates at the 1910 National Negro Business League convention. In 1912, the black leaders combined their efforts, dismantled the Negro Business League chapters, and organized the Negro Board of Trade to help promote Nashville and develop the black community. Napier was elected president of the Negro Board of Trade, and R. H. Boyd became a member of its executive committee. Robert F. Boyd passed in 1912.

Richard H. Boyd and his group had no objection to the formation of People's Bank. Boyd called the new bank a friendly competitor and said "This is the way it should be."[34] Boyd reasoned that Nashville could support two black banks, and he noted that members of the board of directors for One-Cent Bank were members of the board of directors for People's Bank. Boyd's friend, J. B. Singleton, became the second president of People's Bank. Employees of the National Baptist Publishing Board, Solomon P. Harris and Dock A. Hart, served on People's board of directors.

In spite of the criticism about being too exact, Boyd continued to guide the One-Cent Bank on a slow, deliberate path. One-Cent Savings Bank survived the economic depressions.

By 1910, the One-Cent Savings Bank was clearing $800,000 in transactions. Boyd said: "I think each stockholder invested his or her money in this institution more as an experiment than as a money-making investment. The One-Cent Savings Bank is restoring confidence among the laboring class of people and the capability and honesty of their own people to handle their money."[35] The bank showed a $3,594 profit in 1910.[36]

For Boyd, investment in the bank became a life-time commitment and a personal sacrifice to uplift the black people. Boyd said:

The 20th century will prove that he who steers the wheels of commerce will direct and control the civilized world. Some argue that the greatest needs of the Negro race are religion, morality, higher education, industrial education, and wealth. I hold that the Negro needs all of these. But if he needs one thing more than another, he needs racial confidence, racial fidelity, racial patriotism, and racial love. If the money handled by the Negroes of Nashville was handled by the Negro financiers through well-organized and safely guarded financial institutions, his treatment and his condition, together with the tone of the daily newspapers would indeed be different. If every merchant in Nashville who sold a Negro $1.00 worth of merchandise or a piece of real estate, received as payment a check on some Negro banking institution...[they] would see the Negro in a very different light.... [37]

Boyd argued that the whites were in undisputed control of everything. They kept control by placing things in the hands of whites who had education and wealth. Unless blacks did the same thing, they would forever beg the white man for handouts, Boyd reasoned.

In 1910, the board of directors agreed with Boyd not to seek new stockholders. These new owners would share the undivided profits with "those who labored so earnestly to build up the institution,"[38] said Boyd. But the new persons might not be loyal to the philosophy and the goals of the bank. Boyd feared that outsiders, especially white stockholders, would gain control of the bank and cause it to fail like Nashville's Freedman's Savings and Trust Company Bank had failed because of crooked white managers and directors. Boyd believed strongly that blacks had to establish stable leadership within the Negro-owned institutions to continue and advance them generation after generation. [39]

Even though the bank paid a six percent dividend to the stockholders, the bank placed surplus funds into a growing reserve. One of R. H. Boyd's two-year-old grandchildren became One-Cent Savings Bank's youngest stockholder in 1910. The bank processed $774,077, including $386,523 in deposits, and $387,544 in checks during 1909-1910. By 1911, the bank had processed four million dollars. The *Globe* said: "Splendid Gains Through Conservative Management." The original $5 stock was worth $6.50.[40]

In 1912, the One-Cent Savings Bank elected several new directors: Evans Tyree, a bishop in the African Methodist Episcopal Church; William H. Oden, a real estate dealer; and Henry T. Noel, a physician. Noel became Nashville's first full-time black physician in 1879 and a president of the National Medical Association of Colored Physicians. The bank balanced the books at $60,375 in 1912. The board of directors agreed to buy the Brown Building for $12,450 to be renovated and leased for office space. The Brown

Building had housed the first National Baptist Publishing Board offices in 1896. The bank remained in Napier Court Building. One-Cent Savings and Trust Bank had handled over $3,800,569 since 1908. It handled $832,968.97 in 1912 alone, and the bank had $80,000 in assets.[41]

In 1912, the One-Cent bank held its first annual banquet to acquaint stockholders with one another and promote the bank. In his 1913 address to the stockholders, president Boyd re-emphasized his philosophy about "Negro confidence" in black institutions. He said: "I believe the history of the Freedman's Bank should be constantly repeated until the children of the old ex-slaves who placed their earnings in this savings bank should be continuously told among them...."[42] Boyd frequently repeated the history of the One-Cent Bank to remind the audience of its mission. He became a reverent student of history and the lessons it so effectively taught.

The Bank inaugurated its Christmas Clubs in 1914. These accounts were designed for any person including children. The bank accepted any amount for deposit. The depositors could withdraw the funds at Christmas time. The program intended to bring young depositors into the One-Cent Savings Bank's organization and pass the desirable habits of thrift and frugality from one black generation to another.[43]

By 1914, the bank had $38,000 in working capital, and Boyd wanted to expand that amount to one hundred thousand dollars to further boost the economy in black Nashville. Boyd said: "I believe the money is in the possession of the Negro citizens of Nashville in particular and Middle Tennessee in general, if they could see the importance and could have the confidence to place their money with the One-Cent Savings Bank in such a way as that money could help others."[44] Boyd argued that more capital was needed to address the problems of the black community.

During 1915, the One-Cent Savings Bank had handled over eight hundred and fifty thousand dollars. The bank's board declared another six percent dividend on all paid-up stock. The stockholders received their checks at the annual meeting.

In 1920, the One-Cent Savings and Trust Company Bank's name was modernized and changed to Citizens Savings and Trust Company Bank. The bank moved into the Colored YMCA Building on the southwest corner of Fourth Avenue and Cedar Street on February 20, 1922.

The bank's growth and expansion continued under R. H. Boyd's son, grandson, and great-grandson, through the 1990s. The Colored YMCA building fell to urban renewal; and in 1974, the Citizen's Bank moved into the Morris Memorial Building where the former People's Bank had been headquartered on the northeast corner of Fourth Avenue and Charlotte (Cedar). In August 1985, Citizens Bank moved into a new skyscraper, Citizens Plaza, on the opposite corner (southwest corner of Charlotte and Fourth Avenue North).

Not only was Boyd a banker, he was a newspaper man. Richard Boyd and the National Baptist Publishing Board family went into the non-religious newspaper business, by accident. The *Globe* newspaper was housed and printed at the National Baptist Publishing Board's facilities. The Reverend Richard Boyd financed the paper. And Joseph O. Battle and Henry Allen Boyd served as the young editors of the paper. J. Blaine Boyd and Frank Battle also participated in the new publishing venture.

In December 1905 Richard H. Boyd, his son, Henry A. Boyd, and other National Baptist Publishing Board employees organized the *Globe* newspaper. Boyd stated that the *Globe's* objective was to inform blacks about the recent boycott against segregated streetcars. On January 14, 1906, the first issue of the paper appeared. The January 18, 1911, issue said: "The *Globe* came into existence as a much needed weapon of defense, a champion of its people's rights."[45] To separate the business from the publishing board's operations, the men chartered the Globe Publishing Company. The Globe Publishing Company paid the National Baptist Publishing Board for printing the paper. Dock A. Hart managed the company.

Joseph Oliver Battle edited the *Globe* from 1906 until his untimely death in 1910. Battle died unexpectedly at Tullahoma, Tennessee after a brief illness. He was a young man, full of promise. Battle was born to A. T. and Emma Battle in Dalton, Georgia, on November 9, 1878. J. O. Battle was raised in Chattanooga, Tennessee, where the family moved during his early years. He worked as a newspaper boy, joined the Shiloh Baptist Church in 1892, and graduated from Howard Public High School in 1896 with honors. Richard H. Boyd hired the young man in 1897 as an errand boy. Young Battle soon headed the book publishing department at the National Baptist Publishing Board. He joined the First Colored Baptist Church and the Damon Lodge No. 2, Knights of Phythias.[46]

The *Globe* became black Nashville's first regular newspaper in several decades. The *Colored Tennessean* (1865-1866) was the first black newspaper published in Nashville and in Tennessee. First Colored Baptist Church's pastor, the Reverend Nelson G. Merry, published the *Baptist Standard* for the Tennessee Baptists during the 1870s. A black newspaper, *The Tennessee Star* was published in Nashville during the 1880s. The NBPB published several religious newspapers including the *Clarion*, *National Baptist Union*, and later the *National Baptist Union-Review*. Several local religious organizations published papers including the Fireside School's *Hope*. But the *Globe* was the most successful black newspaper ever published in Nashville. The *Globe* continued publication until 1960.

Boyd's son, Henry Allen Boyd, succeeded Battle as editor of the *Globe*. The *Globe* reflected the philosophy and principles of the Boyds, the black church's leadership, and the black community in general. The *Globe* served as the community's historian, carrying stories on the histories of local churches, fraternal groups, schools and colleges, and promoting the Association for the Study of Negro Life and History's Negro History Week. The *Globe* became the political spokesman for the black community, informing whites about black positions and issues. The newspaper promoted social reform and cultural development in Middle Tennessee's black communities. The paper served as an important vehicle to promote black businesses, and the paper carried reports for the One-Cent Savings Bank and the People's Savings Bank. The *Globe* boasted about black Nashville's progress, and it carried stories on new black businesses.

The Boyds and the *Globe* promoted the "buy black" campaign and encouraged the development of black businesses through the local Negro Business League in which the Reverend Boyd served as vice-president. Several of the National Baptist Publishing Board's employees became involved in some of the new businesses started in Nashville between 1905 and 1912. George O. Boyd, originally from San Antonio, and Frank Battle opened a livery company in September 1908. G. O. Boyd also tried to establish a photograph gallery and a restaurant without success.[47]

Boyd and others organized the National Baptist Church Supply Company. Since the turn of the century, the National Baptist Publishing Board had sold and shipped church furniture and supplies. Generally Boyd and other officers of the board acted as agents for other manufacturing companies to gain items needed by black churches. By 1902, the publishing board had begun to install huge built-in pipe organs in churches. The board advertised bells, benches, bookcases, banners, and all kinds of church supplies.

When the extra business activity drew criticism against the board, the lawyers advised Boyd that this could be a conflict of the National Baptist Publishing Board's charter. Besides, why not have blacks manufacture the products? Boyd and some directors of the publishing board formed a private company, the National Baptist Church Supply Company. Boyd used his personal funds to purchase a bankrupt company in another city, and he shipped the machinery and tools to Nashville. the Church Supply Company used a vacant lot owned by the National Baptist Publishing Board to erect a building. The Church Supply Company used the lot for free in return for agreeing to turn the building over to the National Baptist Publishing Board at the end of the ten-year contract. The company hired black cabinet makers and mechanics to make all kinds of church furniture. The *Globe* and the *Union-Review*, as well as other newspapers, carried advertisements and pictures of the furniture for sale. The company sold church pews, pianos, organs, pulpit podiums, utensils for communion, banners, and almost everything a church needed for its services and building.

The National Baptist Publishing Board became a multi-purpose American corporation, catering to black Baptists. Boyd wanted the National Baptist Publishing Board to give an array of services to the black Baptists. He envisioned that the customers could buy Sunday school literature, books, tracts, organs, pianos, church furniture and supplies, banners, buttons, other paraphernalia, Negro dolls, Christmas ornaments, and Easter supplies and decorations from the publishing board. When these operations became too costly after Boyd's death, the National Baptist Church Supply Company was gradually phased out and the company's facilities were converted to other operations for the NBPB.

Civic Leader

Almost everyone considered the Reverend Richard H. Boyd as a leader in the community. He served as secretary-treasurer of the National Baptist Publishing Board, corresponding secretary of the National Baptist Convention's Home Mission Board, and president of the One-Cent Savings and Trust Company Bank. Boyd became an outspoken political critic, a promoter of education, and a recognized national black leader.

Churches and organizations across the nation constantly demanded Boyd as a speaker and a lecturer. He lectured at local churches, including the Tabernacle Baptist Church in Nashville (February 8, 1907). In November 1909, he traveled to Hopkinsville, Kentucky to dedicate a new building and speak at the Virginia Street Baptist Church. Boyd said: "For I am not ashamed of the gospel of Christ,"[48] when he incited the audience. J. D. Crenshaw, superintendent of First Colored Baptist Church's Sunday school, accompanied Boyd on the trip. In spite of his heavy schedule, Boyd was never too busy to attend to his friends and neighbors in Nashville. The Reverend Boyd served as a pallbearer at the funeral of Mrs. William Carroll Napier (1825-1909), James C. Napier's mother.[49]

Because of his position of corresponding secretary of the Home Mission Board, the Reverend Boyd frequently traveled to meetings and churches. Boyd attended the Layman's Missionary Movement of the World in Philadelphia and stopped in Columbus, Ohio, to speak at a meeting of local black Baptist churches at Bethany Baptist Church in March, 1908. In March, 1913, Boyd was appointed a member of the Federal Council of Churches of Christ in America's Special Committee on the Peace and Arbitration related to the 100th anniversary celebration of the Treaty of Ghent. In July, 1913, Boyd made an extensive tour of Texas, speaking at the St. John Baptist Association of Texas in Palestine, Marin, Austin, San Antonio, and Beaumont. It was homecoming for Boyd, a successful Texas son. Boyd ended the year by speaking at the Emancipation Proclamation Celebration in Toledo, Ohio on November 27, 1913. He said: 'We [black Americans] are going through the fiery furnace, as it were, and all the impurities are being burned away, but we will come out, pure gold, well tried."[50]

In 1910, the Reverend Boyd joined the crusade to promote land and home ownership among blacks. He spoke at a black farmers' conference at Lane College in Jackson, Tennessee, and made a plea for cooperative and collective efforts among Tennessee's black farmers. By 1910, only twenty-five percent of Tennessee's black farmers held title to their own land. Rural blacks became oppressed through the extensive system of sharecropping which replaced the slave system. Boyd urged the blacks to extend the cooperative arrangement to buy capital-intensive machinery including tractors to increase production and profits.[51]

In Nashville, Boyd and the *Globe* promoted land and home ownership among blacks. The *Globe* carried extensive news about new black housing units in 1912. When the first lots near the new Tennessee State Normal School for Negroes went on sale in 1912, the Reverend Boyd, Preston Taylor, and other black leaders set examples by purchasing lots. By now, many black middle class persons, including the Reverend R. H. Boyd and H. A. Boyd, began moving into the North Nashville suburbs on streets within sight of Fisk University's Jubilee Hall.

Boyd and his son, Henry Allen, helped black Nashville to establish a facility for the local Colored Young Men's Christian Association (YMCA). The effort to raise funds to revitalize the local chapter and build a home for it began in 1912 when Henry Allen Boyd, William N. Sanders, and others provided the leadership. In 1917, the blacks bought the Duncan Hotel for seventy thousand dollars. They cleaned and opened the building with two thousand boys and men in attendance at a mass meeting where the leaders collected one thousand dollars in donations. The Reverend R. H. Boyd gave another $1,000 to raise the total subscriptions to $25,000. In February, 1917, a women's auxiliary was formed with Clemmie White serving as president. Katie A. Boyd was elected pianist for the women's meetings which were organized to help support the financial needs of the Duncan Building. Henry Allen Boyd, chairman of the Colored YMCA committee, led the mass rallies to raise more funds for the building. The blacks held a mass at the Ryman Auditorium where white leaders pledged their support. Mayor Robert Ewing said, "I want you to remember that we are your friends—we understand you and you understand us...."[52]

In 1917, Boyd, his family, and the NBPB family displayed their greatest civic loyalty through support for America's first World War efforts. On April 6, 1917, just months before the National Baptist Convention of America convened its annual session, America entered World War I on Great Britain's side to defeat the German army. The entire country, including the black communities, became mobilized. The National Baptist Publishing Board's staff and employees became hearty patriots, supporting the war and promoting and servicing black American troops.

Black Nashvillians eagerly participated in this war because they saw the war effort as an opportunity to gain black respectability through expressions of black loyalty and citizenship. Maybe black participation would convince white Americans to respect the creeds of justice, equality, and liberty for all citizens including colored people. A Negro division of the National Council of Defense operated in the Fireside School's facilities on Gay Street. Preston Taylor, Boyd, and other black leaders sponsored a huge patriotic Fourth of July picnic at Greenwood Park.

When the first consignment of black recruits paraded down Capitol Boulevard and up Broad Street to the Union Station to board the trains to Camp Meade, black Nashvillians, as well as whites, lined the sidewalks. The City Federation of Colored Women's Clubs prepared lunches for the men, and the National Baptist Publishing Board furnished the truck to transport the lunches to the railroad station. The Nashville Colored Women's Chapter of the Red Cross furnished 585 flags, packs of cigarettes, and boxes of matches for the men.[53]

When the men reached the training camp, Richard H. Boyd, the leader of the local black patriotic movement, sent Henry Allen Boyd to visit them. Henry Allen spoke to the men, collected letters to take back to Nashville, took pictures, and reported his visit in the Nashville *Globe.*[54]

The Boyds maintained high visibility with other local black leaders in promoting black support for the nation's war effort. Henry Allen Boyd and John Watson presided over the Negro Committee for the Fourth Liberty Bond Campaign. By October, 1918, local blacks, under the leadership of R. H. Boyd and Henry A. Boyd, had subscribed $200,000 in Liberty Bonds. Henry Allen Boyd held a meeting in the Colored YMCA to culminate the successful Liberty Bond campaign. Richard H. Boyd persuaded the board of directors for the National Baptist Publishing Board to buy over $5,000 in war bonds. Also under R. H. Boyd's presidency, the One-Cent Savings Bank invested in the bonds. The National Baptist Publishing Board donated hundreds of Bibles to the Negro soldiers. Employees of the publishing board formed a War Savings Society and named it in honor of Richard Henry Boyd. Mrs. Henry Allen Boyd and Nettie Langston Napier joined other elite black women to organize a state-wide war conference for the Colored Women's National Council of Defense. Henry Allen, editor of the *Globe*, published huge one page spreads to advertise the war effort. The *Globe* (September 26, 1917) carried photographs of the Meharry Medical Reserve Corps after students at Meharry Medical College were inducted into the Medical Reserve Corps and placed in uniform.[55]

The effort by the Boyds, the National Baptist Publishing Board, and other black Nashvillians insured active participation of the local community in America's World War I effort. This active participation was publicized widely by the *Globe*, especially in the late 1918 issues. Company K (formerly

Company G of the Tennessee National Guard) joined the 387th Infantry and served in France. Members of this black Nashville company shot down a German airplane and sent some pieces to Nashville. Blacks comprised about twenty percent of Nashville-Davidson County's World War I casualties. The *Globe* (December 27, 1918) listed ninety-five deceased black soldiers. The most notable death was that of Lieutenant H. Alvin Cameron, a popular teacher at Pearl High School, who was killed at Flanders Field, France on October 13, 1918. Later, the Cameron Junior High School was named in his honor. [56]

Boyd's enthusiasm for America's war effort influenced the next national Baptist convention's annual session. The September 1917 National Baptist Convention of America, Unincorporated, session passed a resolution to support America's effort in World War I. Because of World War I and the need for cheap labor in northern factories and war factories, thousands of southern Negroes migrated into northern towns between 1914 and 1919. The convention neither opposed nor supported the black migration to the North, but one of its resolutions urged the Negro migrants to find a church home when they arrived in the North. To further support improvement of conditions for blacks in urban America, the convention resolved to support the temperance and prohibition movements. The Woman's Auxiliary supported similar resolutions and issued a special resolution to support the National Baptist Publishing Board. [57]

Boyd: Racial Pride, Injustice

To promote racial pride among black people, the Reverend Boyd established the National Negro Doll company with headquarters at the National Baptist Publishing Board. Henry Allen became the manager of the company, and Richard Boyd controlled the company's treasury. When white newspaper editors and merchants claimed that Boyd's Negro doll movement was a failure, Boyd directed Henry Allen to display hands full of orders at a news conference. Orders came from across the nation. The *Globe* extensively advertised the dolls in various sizes. The *Globe*'s advertisement said:

> These dolls are not made of that disgraceful and humiliating type that we have grown accustomed to seeing Negro dolls made of. They represent the intelligent and refined Negro of the day, rather than the type of toy that is usually given to the children and, as a rule, used as a scarecrow.[58]

Boyd ordered the first batch of dolls from a manufacturer in Europe. The National Baptist Convention endorsed the Negro dolls at its 1908 session at Lexington, Kentucky. Boyd exhibited and sold the dolls at the conventions. Whites bought as many of the dolls as the blacks did in some places. [59]

Within the National Baptist Convention, however, detractors of the National Baptist Publishing Board criticized the operation of the National Negro Doll Company in the publishing board's facilities. Boyd claimed that he had used his private funds and bought the dolls wholesale from a European supplier. Once the orders arrived from customers, Henry Allen Boyd shipped the dolls through the publishing board's mail room. The Reverend Boyd's effort was part of the "buy black campaign" being directed by black leaders in America. But also he said that the purpose was "to instill race pride in their [Negro] children." [60] The doll manufacturing venture did not prove profitable, but it became an important part of Richard H. Boyd's crusade against the negative and psychological effects of American racial oppression. Even though Napier and Boyd represented pro-Booker T. Washington men and racial accommodationists, they, like many elite black men and women, argued that men of the same class, wealth, and social status, regardless of race, should not suffer discrimination in public facilities.

Even though they had wealth, education, and social status in their communities, the black elite members suffered denial of first-class accommodations and had to ride smoking cars with poor whites and poor blacks. The black members of the elite class deeply resented being treated unfairly and like inferiors by the white elite. Black accommodationists agreed to separate schools, churches, colleges, and other institutions, but they disagreed with white leaders about denying black citizens equal public accommodations in transportation. The "separate but equal" rule should be respected by whites who wanted segregation of the races, but did not want to treat blacks as equal citizens.

Richard H. Boyd and his colleagues opposed the unfair segregation (Jim Crow) laws passed by southern states after 1890. These Jim Crow laws denied black-Americans' constitutional rights to free speech, right to assembly, due process of law, equal protection of the laws, and equal access to public facilities and opportunities. Tennessee had passed the first Jim Crow law in 1881 to segregate black and white passengers on railroad cars. In the summer of 1881, the pastor of Nashville's St. John's African Methodist Episcopal Church led a demonstration to the local train depot where the blacks purchased first-class tickets and demanded that they be honored on first-class, non-segregated cars. This freedom-ride was unsuccessful. When Boyd arrived in Nashville in 1896, the town had established racial segregation by custom. Moreover, in 1905, Tennessee's General Assembly passed legislation to force blacks, regardless of class and wealth, to ride on the back of city streetcars.

Members of Nashville's Negro Business League, including James C. Napier and Richard H. Boyd, discussed the debilitating effects of Jim Crow and the racial violence that whites perpetuated to enforce Jim Crow rules. Blacks became the victims of the Jim Crow system, and whites reaped benefits from this racial injustice. By holding blacks back, the whites allowed their children and grandchildren to stay a generation ahead of the blacks. For instance, an all-white Nashville Board of Education spent less money for black public schools than for the white public schools even though black Nashvillians comprised nearly forty percent of the city's school-age population. What could black leaders do about it?

In 1903, Napier wrote to his friend, Booker T. Washington, the head of the National Negro Business League and president of Tuskegee Institute, to urge Washington to support a protest against segregation in the South. Napier said "I think that the time has come when we should take a bold stand in favor of law and order and insist on their rigid execution as applied to the Negro whether in his favor or against him.[61] Napier told Washington that it was time for a test-civil-rights case against the Jim Crow transportation laws. Boyd and other members of the local Negro Business League knew about Napier's letters and agreed to support him.[62]

To fight the Jim Crow streetcar law, the black leaders involved the most powerful black institution, the church. Napier, for example, was not a church leader; he was an attorney. However, his business associate and friend, Richard H. Boyd, was a powerful churchman. And Elder Preston Taylor, another business associate, had great influence in the black community.

The local black leadership, including Boyd and Napier, became angry on March 30, 1905, when the Tennessee General Assembly passed the Jim Crow streetcar law. The all-white legislature passed the law to segregate blacks and whites on city streetcars. When he learned about the new Jim Crow streetcar law, one local black man said "Intelligent [elite] colored citizens of Nashville will not stand for Jim Crowism in the streetcar lines of this city." [63] The black community became angry because of the whites' arrogance and the obvious neglect of white government officials to protect black citizens. By the early twentieth century, many white Americans had become so racially conservative that they publicly proclaimed that mingling with people of color would "destroy white purity and white superiority."

Black leaders called for a boycott of the city's streetcar companies. The boycott began on July 5, 1905. Black preachers promoted the boycott in church services. But the protest seemed weak, because blacks depended on public transportation to get to work and from one part of the city to other sections of town. Some blacks feared being fired by white employers.

On July 31, 1905, members of the Nashville Negro Business League met to discuss the state's Jim Crow streetcar law and the effects of the boycott. Boyd, Napier, and the Reverend Preston Taylor argued for developing a black streetcar company to extend effectively the boycott. This became a great opportunity to create a self-help project, another Negro business enterprise.

Boyd's colleagues in the National Baptist Convention and local leaders, the Reverends Sutton E. Griggs and E. D. W. Isaac, also participated in forming the black streetcar company. The Reverend Luke Mason said that "These discriminations are only blessings in disguise. They stimulate and encourage rather than cower and humiliate the true, ambitious, self-determined Negro."[64] The leaders promoted the boycott through church services and meetings.

On August 28, 1905, Boyd, Napier, and Taylor jointly chaired a meeting at the National Baptist Publishing Board's headquarters. They formed the Union Transportation Company, the city's first black owned streetcar company. A total of fourteen men chartered the Union Transportation Company on August 29, 1905. They elected Taylor president and Richard H. Boyd as secretary-treasurer. The company's first business meeting took place in the National Baptist Publishing Board's offices.[65]

Richard H. Boyd, vice-president of the Negro Business League, and now secretary-treasurer of the Union Transportation Company, began putting the company in business. Boyd traveled to Tarrytown, New York, where he ordered five steam automobiles capable of carrying fifteen passengers. Taylor held rallies to sell stock and finance the purchases. The blacks began wearing buttons with pictures of the cars inscribed.[66]

The cars arrived on September 29 and began operations. The fare was five cents. The lines operated on three routes: Summer to Jefferson with a turn-a-round on 12th Avenue North near Fisk University; Summer to Union to Spruce to Kayne Avenue in South Nashville; Summer to Ash to Market Street, down Lafayette to Wharf to Green and Fairfield, then to Filmore Street in Southeast Nashville.[67]

The steam cars performed too poorly and ran too slowly to take the hilly terrain of Nashville. The Secretary-treasurer of the Union Transportation Company, the Reverend Boyd, traded the steam cars for fourteen electric cars. These cars began operations in July 1906. Boyd installed generators in the facilities of the National Baptist Publishing Board and charged the cars' batteries each night. On April 27, 1906, the city council passed a law requiring a $42 per car tax on private streetcars. The tax plus the poor subscription of the stock caused the Union Transportation Company to falter.[68]

The stockholders and the officers of the Union Transportation met at the offices of the National Baptist Publishing Board. Boyd, Taylor, and the other officers decided to sell the cars to a company that wanted to use the cars in the Norfolk and Jamestown Exposition. The Union Transportation Company closed for good. A debt of $735 remained to be paid. The Reverend Boyd and Elder Preston Taylor absorbed the loss through their personal funds.[69]

Like the black protest against the 1881 railroad Jim Crow law, the black community lost the battle. But the war against racial discrimination continued in Nashville, and the Reverend Richard H. Boyd continued to be involved in the fight against Jim Crow.

Boyd and his fellow preachers helped to campaign against Jim Crowism. They sent petitions to the government of the United States through the National Baptist Convention. In 1909, Boyd published *The Separate or "Jim Crow" Car Laws, or, Legislative Enactments of Fourteen Southern States: A Reply in Compliance with a 1907 Resolution of the National Baptist Convention.* Boyd had influenced the convention to pass the resolution in support of the streetcar boycotts being carried out by blacks in Nashville and throughout the South. Boyd's clever compendium showed how comprehensive, institutionalized, and ridiculous white Southerners had become in their racism against black people.[70] The introduction read partly:

> The purpose of this little book is to be a constant companion in the pocket or hand of every self-respecting, law-abiding Negro who is compelled to travel by rail in any of the fourteen states of the Union that have passed separate or "Jim Crow" car laws for the purpose of humiliating and degrading the Negro race in the eye of all the civilized world. It may be surprising to the reader if he or she will peruse and study carefully these so-called "Jim Crow" laws or legislative enactments to learn that according to the letter of the law there is no "Jim Crowism" in these laws if properly and justly enforced or executed. One of the peculiar features of these enactments is that they have a sameness in each state and if they were properly enforced or executed by the courts, or obeyed by the railroad companies, they would truly promote the comfort in travel of all colored passengers, for each one of these legislative enactments requires the railroad companies to furnish separate but *equal accommodations.* [71]

Boyd argued that the Jim Crow laws were not enforced to guarantee equal accommodations for black citizens. Therefore, black travelers should use the book to know and demand their rights when traveling on the railroads. Boyd's book cited the recent Interstate Commerce Commission ruling which allowed racial segregation on interstate carriers but ordered equal accommodations for black and white passengers.[72] The passage of Jim Crow legislation had reached a crescendo in America some four years before Boyd's Jim Crow compendium appeared.

Conclusion: Boyd and the NBPB in Retrospect

In reflection, Boyd's clever approach to publishing the compendium and instructing blacks to demand equal facilities according to law became a successful strategy some two generations later. A generation after Boyd's death (1922), the idea that whites were violating their own doctrine of "separate but equal" became the foundation of court suits by black civil rights activists during the period 1940 through 1954. Based on this argument, black attorneys for the National Association for the Advancement for Colored People (NAACP) forced several southern states to create law, medical, and graduate schools for blacks. The idea of the strategy by NAACP lawyers during the 1940s was to force the poor, southern states to create two expensive institutions of a kind, causing them to go broke trying to fund segregation. Thus the whites would soon see that segregation was too expensive to maintain. By 1954, the all-white federal Supreme Court ended the "separate but equal" doctrine and ordered public institutions to be integrated. Few students of history recognized that Richard H. Boyd and other black leaders had pursued this general strategy around 1909. Also few young blacks realized that Boyd and other black Nashville leaders, as well as black leaders in some other southern towns, had organized extensive streetcar boycotts long before the 1955 Montgomery Bus Boycott.

Not only did Boyd and the members of the NBPB help to form the Union Transportation Company, Tennessee's first black owned and operated streetcar line, but the National Baptist Publishing Board became an active citizen of the Nashville community. The publishing board distributed Nashville's largest and most successful black newspaper, took a leadership role in black Nashville's fight for civil rights, and fought to secure and retain black participation in the political process. The National Baptist Publishing Board published a weekly newspaper for the nation's black Baptists. The NBPB's officers, including Boyd, and other local black leaders organized a bank to improve black Nashville's economy. The Reverend Boyd was a renaissance man far ahead of his contemporaries.

Cabinet Department (NBPBLA)

Congress Visits NBPB

Chapter 6

After R. H. Boyd: The NBPB, 1922-1992

Chapter 6
After R. H. Boyd: The NBPB,
1922-1992

Your father made great contributions to the progress of his race, and his life reflects very great accomplishments. Your mother did her part in the accomplishment of all this. - John B. Keeble [1]

Keeble served as one of the NBPB's attorneys. Keeble's letter to Henry Allen Boyd showed appreciation for the genius of Boyd and his untiring efforts to make the publishing board a success.

Secretary - Treasurer Henry Allen Boyd, 1922 - 1959

Upon the death of Richard Henry Boyd, the National Baptist Publishing Board's board of directors elected the Reverend Henry Allen Boyd as the Secretary-Treasurer. Henry Allen Boyd would give leadership to the publishing board for the next thirty-seven years.

Henry Allen Boyd (1876-1959) was born on April 15 in Grimes County, Texas. He grew up and attended public schools in Palestine, Texas where he joined the West Union Baptist Church, headed by his father. Henry Allen professed to be a minister at an early age. His young adult life was spent in San Antonio where the family moved. He became the first black American postal clerk in San Antonio. Henry Allen married Lula M. Smith and had one child, Katherine. Lula soon passed away. In 1908, Henry Allen married Georgia A. Bradford, who died on March 24, 1952.[2]

Henry Allen Boyd became a director for the Supreme Life Insurance Company in Chicago and the Atlanta Life Insurance Company, and he served as president of the Globe Publishing Company, secretary of the Sunday School Congress, life member of the National Association for the Advancement of Colored People, member of the National Council of Churches of Christ in the United States of America, and a member of the board of trustees for Meharry Medical College and Fisk University. Henry Allen gave leadership to organize Tennessee Agricultural and Industrial State Normal School for Negroes (Tennessee State University). And he presided over the Citizens Savings and Trust Company Bank from 1922 until 1959.

Henry Allen continued most of the Boyd enterprises, although the National Baptist Church Supply Company and the National Negro Doll Company closed eventually (by the 1950s). He built the National Baptist Publishing Board into a large company that completely recovered from the 1915 setback. Also he cultivated good relations with the National Baptist Convention of America (Unincorporated) and helped to rebuild this national black Baptist association.

Like his father before him, Henry Allen Boyd continued to emphasize traditions, family, and group activities at the NBPB. He continued the daily morning prayer services and the annual New Year's Day Dinner in the chapel. To celebrate the coming of summer, the publishing board continued the annual picnic at Greenwood Park. The twenty-fifth National Baptist Publishing Board Picnic took place on Tuesday, July 22, 1930, when the employees boarded chartered streetcars at the publishing board and rode to the park where the National Baptist Publishing Board Giants played a baseball game. Many other activities took place. The National Baptist Sunday School Congress Brass Band furnished the music at Greenwood Park's beautiful bandstand. For the picnic, the publishing board furnished the refreshments and a day's pay for employees. Henry Allen Boyd and the directors joined the festivities at Greenwood Park. To close the calendar year, Henry Allen organized the annual Christmas party. The employees decorated the chapel with a tree full of presents and presented a play. Employees received a half day off for Christmas Eve and a full day on Christmas.

Like his father, Henry Allen continued to hammer away at the nation's Jim Crow laws and racial discrimination. During the 1920s, racial violence and the growth of the Ku Klux Klan openly pervaded American society. Henry Allen so severely criticized the lynching of blacks in Texas and Alabama until the governors of both states wrote personal letters to promise Boyd that they were doing all in their power to remedy the situation and promote better race relations.

Henry Allen and Citizens Bank

Henry Allen - as he was called affectionately by friends - continued to preside over Citizens Bank, just as his father had done. The *Pittsburgh Courier* paid tribute to Citizens Bank because of its $50,000 in capital and $300,000 plus in resources. The bank had paid a six percent dividend to stockholders some twenty-four of its twenty-six years of existence.[3] Such confidence existed in the management of the bank that stockholders represented twenty-eight states and four countries.

The bank suffered only slight decline because of the Great Depression which closed many local banks in 1929-30. Some devious characters attempted to spread rumors that the black bank, Citizens Bank, was insolvent. But before the depositors could make a run on Citizens Bank, Henry Allen Boyd appeared and displayed stacks of money to prove that the bank could meet depositors' demands. The *Globe* newspaper featured the following headline: "ATTEMPT TO DESTROY THE OLDEST NEGRO BANK" blocked by stockholders and officials.[4] Apparently the conspirators made their move when they thought Henry Allen and J. C. Napier, the cashier, had left town.

Citizens Savings Bank survived the Great Depression. By 1934, the bank included the following departments: regular checking, Christmas savings, home savings, banking by mail, regular savings, and safety deposit boxes. Located in the Colored YMCA building at 4th and Cedar, the Citizens Bank increased its deposits by instituting banking-by-mail to tap the rural Middle Tennessee area. After Congress and the federal New Deal program created the Federal Deposit Insurance Corporation to insure deposits and better regulate banks in America, Citizens Savings Bank became a member of the Federal Deposit Insurance Corporation which insured deposits up to $5,000. By 1940, Citizens Bank had hired its first female assistant cashier, Ms. H. L. Jordan who became the cashier when the bank reorganized its structure with Meredith G. Ferguson as the executive vice president (manager). The bank's books balanced at $303,782.71 in 1940, causing local leaders like W. J. Hale to send letters of praise about Henry Allen's management and leadership skills. Now residing in Richard H. Boyd's former home, Henry Allen continued the tradition of the dinner for the bank's directors.[5]

Changes in the bank's structure began in April 1940 when James Carroll Napier passed away. A. G. Price, formerly assistant cashier, succeeded Napier who had been sick for three months. Napier's services were held in the Fisk University Chapel. The publishing board closed for the afternoon. Tennessee A & I State College and the city public schools closed for the day; the mayor sent a police escort for Napier's funeral processional. Napier (1845-1940) had influenced more than three generations of black Nashville's life and politics.[6] He had been a close friend to the Boyds for forty-five years.

In 1944, with a booming local economy caused by World War II, Citizens Savings Bank announced a campaign to reach one million dollars in deposits. President Henry A. Boyd assured the public that the campaign would be successful. The bank held "Deposit Showers" to attract new customers and show the bank's services, and the *Globe* carried huge one-page advertisements to promote the showers and the one million dollar campaign. Within six months, Citizens Bank announced $1,000,000. Moreover, in December, 1944, the bank announced $33,000 to be paid to Christmas Club account holders whom Henry A. Boyd urged to use the money to buy war bonds. Boyd became a leading supporter of America's Second World War effort just as he and his father had done during World War I.[7]

Henry Allen Boyd instituted the President's Dinner, inviting hundreds of teachers, ministers, depositors, and other guests to the gymnasium of the Colored YMCA to have dinner with him and the Citizens Bank's officers and employees. By the 1950s, black Nashvillians had a strong attachment to the bank, and they held the National Baptist Publishing Board, also under Boyd's guidance, in high respect.

Continued Growth for NBPB

The viability of the publishing board could be seen by the large number of music publications and other supplies offered during the 1930s. For example, the National Baptist Publishing Board offered the following song books:

National Baptist Hymnal
National Baptist Hymn Book - World Edition
National Gospel Voices, No. 1
National Gospel Voices, No. 2
National G. B. Hymnal
National Hymnal of Victory
Celestial Showers, No. 1
Celestial Showers, No. 2
National Tidings of Joy
National Harp of Zion and B.Y.P.U. Hymnal
Choice Songs, No. 1
Choice Songs, No. 2
Pearls of Paradise, Part I
Short Talks on Music
National Temperance Songs
Lasting Hymns
Victory Song Book
National Anthem Series
Hail the Baptist Congress and Beatitudes
Steal Away to Jesus - Anthem
Metoka and Galeda Class Anthem[8]

The National Baptist Publishing Board carried a large stock of mission supplies, Bibles, collection plates, communion ware, marriage certificates, other certificates, banners, Sunday school helps, Baptist Young People's Union supplies, records, and roll books.

Henry A. Boyd continued to seek new business for the publishing board. He traveled widely, delivering speeches and sermons, and researching the market for religious publications and services. He sensed the changes in the churches when younger ministers began to replace the old guard. In January, 1930, the publishing board began correspondence courses to attract young ministers and new religious workers. The four courses follow:

Biblical Introduction
Exegesis
Homiletics
Systematic Theology

These courses were advertised in the *National Baptist Union-Review.*[9]

Into the third generation after slavery, Henry A. Boyd found it necessary to introduce the younger blacks to the purpose of the National Baptist Publishing Board. Boyd explained the purpose of the National Baptist Publishing Board:

> Because the National Baptist Publishing Board is operating for the sole purpose of giving service to the race and denomination, every phase of religious life has been considered. The interest of the institution is naturally centered on the things pertaining to religion and spirituality, and that interest is deep and abiding. 'Service' is the keynote of the institution.[10]

The publishing board's printing and publication business remained its main focus. By this time, the publishing board produced fifteen periodicals, the Baptist Young People's Union materials, twenty-three song books, two anthem books, letter-heads for churches and organizations, fraternal and church order cards, minute books, record books, and other materials worth over $300,000 per year in business.[11]

In spite of the economic depression, the publishing board's business increased by $24,779.09 over that of 1929. The excess revenues supported the National Baptist Convention of America's Foreign Mission Board, the mission in Panama, and the Sunday School Congress. For now, the publishing board left vacant the positions of editorial secretary and superintendent of teacher training. The Brass Band became a pet project for Henry Allen who often took photographs and marched with the band in various cities. By 1930, the publishing board's Sunday School Congress Brass Band numbered eighteen persons and instruments. The band, like brass bands of that day, attracted crowds (and publicity for the NBPB).[12]

By 1934, the publishing board serviced 20,000 Sunday schools and 8,000 churches. The memory of Richard Henry Boyd helped to persuade many Baptists to continue to patronize the National Baptist Publishing Board. To commemorate Richard H. Boyd Month (March) the National Baptist Publishing Board gave thousands of NBPB stick pens and other gifts to Baptists across the country. Henry Allen Boyd said that he had received many letters from returning customers who said: "We are coming back home; we are returning to our first love." He assured the customers that the National Baptist Publishing Board was managed efficiently. Boyd emphasized that : "It is our plan to send the orders out the very day that they are received here by mail, and thus cut down delays, increase the dispatch orders and save the time."[13] The publishing board's customer base steadily increased.

Incidentally, the National Baptist Convention of America created the Richard Henry Boyd Commemorative Commission to honor his memory. By the mid-1940s, a life-size statue of Richard H. Boyd was completed and erected on the east side of the NBPB's administration building. The NBPB completely renovated the administration building and named it the Richard Henry Boyd Memorial Building. The publishing board paid all but $7,000 of the $72,000 cost for the statue and the construction work.

In the meantime, beginning with the opening of the Sunday School Publishing Board's new Morris Memorial Building in 1924, Henry Allen Boyd had to contend with increased competition in the business of black publishing and Sunday School education. Now two black Baptist publishing boards operated in Nashville, and some 3.5 million black Baptists now belonged to three national conventions: National Baptist Convention of America (NBCA), Lott Carey Baptist Foreign Mission Convention (LCBFMC), and National Baptist Convention, U. S. A., Incorporated (NBCI). In 1922, the NBCI and the Lott Carey people fell further out of favor with one another because of a dispute between the NBCI's Foreign Mission Board and the Lott Carey leadership. The arguments became vicious and petty, as illustrated in the *Baptist Voice*.[14] In 1925, the NBCA and the LCBFMC signed a joint agreement for foreign mission work. This agreement intended to help the unincorporated convention to attract more churches in the eastern United States and help the NBCA and the LCBFMC to pool their resources to finance more extensive foreign mission operations. Because of their denominational fragmentation, it became difficult by the 1920s for any one of the black American Baptist conventions to conduct extensive missionary activities abroad.

The NBPB's Sunday School Congress remained a bright star although it had to compete with the NBCI's annual Sunday School Congress. But after nearly forty years of organizing Sunday School Congress sessions, Henry Allen Boyd became an expert statesman for this affair. The NBPB's 1937 Congress met in Cincinnati, Ohio. "It was the best one ever," said Boyd. Enormous crowds attended the workshops and mass meetings. The spirit rose so high that Boyd invited delegates from a half dozen states to detour to Nashville on their return trip home.[16]

Some 120 delegates accepted the invitation and stopped at Nashville. The Reverend J. A. Turner, pastor of Nashville's Greater St. John Baptist Church, and the late J. Blaine Boyd's son coordinated the visit. Four chartered city buses transported the delegates. The day began with picture-taking sessions for the *Review* and breakfast at the Colored YMCA's gymnasium where the delegates ate fruit cocktail, broiled chicken, hot rolls, hominy, croquets, rice, bacon, eggs, apple rings, and coffee. Then the delegates toured the National Baptist Publishing Board's offices, the campus of the National Baptist Theological and Training Seminary on Sevier Street, the 20-acre Greenwood Park on Lebanon Road, R. H. Boyd's grave at Greenwood Cemetery on Elm Hill Pike, Tennessee Agricultural and Industrial State College, Hadley Park, Meharry Medical

Citizens Bank Dinner, Employees' Table, 1949 (NBR)

Colored YMCA, 1925 (NBR)

H. A. Boyd Entertains Congress Guests in Nashville (NBR)

All aboard for Little Rock, Ark., to attend the National Baptist Convention Sept. 3rd to 9th.

"Congress Special"

College, Fisk University, Henry Allen Boyd's home, and lastly to Mrs. Richard H. Boyd's home for lemonade. Boyd's hospitality, especially in the midst of economic depression, impressed the black Baptists to no end and gained valuable publicity for the publishing board.[17]

Henry Allen became a master at using public relations and the personal touch with his employees and associates. Near Christmas time, he allowed the employees extra lunch time to cash their checks at local banks. Henry Boyd personally passed the pay checks to each employee. Each employee was directed to stop by the Secretary's office before the day ended and pick up a Christmas card with a personal message and a small cash bonus, a new greenback bill. Henry Boyd sent the Panama missionary, R. H. Thorbourne, and his family a Christmas gift of $75.[18]

In addition to managing the company and effectively directing its public relations, Henry Allen Boyd headed the large Boyd family. Only two of Richard H. Boyd's sons remained alive by 1934. J. Blaine Boyd had passed away in 1922. Henry A. Boyd and Theophilus B. Boyd, R. H. Boyd's surviving sons, continued to work at the publishing board, with Henry Allen directing the show. Two of R. H. Boyd's three daughters, Lula Boyd-Landers and Mattie Boyd-Johnson, continued to reside in Nashville. The third daughter, Mrs. Thomas E. Hall lived in Galveston, Texas. When Mrs. Hall needed a medical operation, Henry Allen arranged through a local and notable doctor, John Henry Hale, to have her transported to Nashville. Many persons considered Dr. Hale to be among the best surgeons in the country. A Galveston doctor escorted Mrs. Boyd-Hall to Nashville, where she was successfully operated on by Dr. Hale in the Millie Hale Hospital and comforted by sisters and brothers, including Henry Allen.

Henry Allen Boyd traveled often. He visited Chicago and Texas like they were his second and third homes. Boyd visited nearly a dozen states each year. But he often avoided invitations to visit the West Coast because Henry Allen refused to fly airplanes. Because of his frequent travel by railway, throughout the eastern railroad lines, members of the Brotherhood of Sleeping Car Porters knew Henry Allen on a personal basis; and these black porters went out of their way to give "Brother Boyd" better service than they gave to the white travelers who humiliated the porters, calling them all "George."

Particularly because of his vast experience and propensity to work hard, Henry Allen Boyd left his brothers in his shadows when directing the publishing board with his father. For sure the work was demanding, and Henry A. Boyd, for one, sacrificed and devoted exclusively his time and energy to the business of his father and the National Baptist Publishing Board. Henry Allen Boyd liked his nephews, possibly because he and his wife had no sons of their own. He nurtured the son of the late J. Blaine Boyd, involving him in the Sunday School Congress' work. Henry Allen also maintained close relations with

Theophilus B. Boyd, Jr., brother T. B., Sr.'s son. The latter young nephew, T. B. Boyd, Jr., stayed close to Uncle Boyd. After returning from military service in the mid-1940s, T. B. Boyd, Jr. worked faithfully at his uncle's side, learning every aspect of the National Baptist Publishing Board's business and putting his heart, soul, energy into the purpose and the mission of the company.

Henry Allen, the NBPB, and Black Movements

Not only did Henry Allen Boyd dominate the leadership at the publishing board, he headed black politics in Nashville. Boyd was president of the Lincoln-Douglass Voters' League of Nashville and Davidson County. By the 1930s, he had established a goal to recruit ten thousand black voters. Negroes continued to vote Republican on the state and national levels but often preferred the powerful local Democratic machine in city and county elections. Possibly because of his frequent trips to Chicago, Henry Allen Boyd became a close friend to Oscar DePriest, the first black to be elected (1928) to the Congress since the turn of the century. DePriest represented black Chicago, Illinois, and the Republican party. In late April 1931, DePriest visited Nashville where Henry Allen met him at the train station and escorted DePriest overland to speak in Kentucky.[19]

Because of his presidency and other positions in the Negro Press Association as well as his editorship of the Nashville *Globe,* the politicians respected Henry Allen Boyd. Since R. H. Boyd's time, the *Globe* had been selected by the Davidson County Republican Party as the official organ for the organization, and the *Globe* reached all Middle Tennessee's black communities with an influential message for the black voters. Boyd and others instituted annual banquets for the Lincoln-Douglass Voters' League. After being mobilized by black Republican and Democratic leaders and the repeal of Tennessee's poll tax in 1951, black Nashvillians elected the first two Negro city councilmen (Democrats) since 1911. Henry Allen Boyd continued to head the Lincoln-Douglass Voters' League until the early 1950s when the black Democratic Voters League of Davidson County became dominant. Black voters abandoned the Republican party and shifted their loyalties to the Democratic party even on the national level by the mid 1950s. By now, Henry Allen's health had begun to fail, and his traveling and political activities had been curtailed severely.

The main characteristic of the Boyds and the NBPB's leadership was the ability of its leaders to sense the changing sentiments in black American society. By 1940, free black society celebrated three generations since slavery, and the third and fourth generations of freedmen assumed new aspirations for equality and justice. Hundreds of thousands of young black men served in America's military. Many of the black soldiers went abroad to foreign lands, and they returned home to inspire their children (the fourth generation since slavery) to fight for their rights as Americans. The black American population increased drastically, and members of America's black Baptist churches also grew rapidly. Boyd and the leaders of the National Baptist Publishing Board adapted quickly the publishing board's attitude and operations to accommodate the changes.

For example, Henry Allen and the *Globe* moved with the flow of the times. The paper continued to feature political news, information about Citizens Bank, the activities of the Boyds and their travels, and a wealth of information on local schools, colleges, churches, sports, the National Baptist Publishing Board, and the National Baptist Convention of America. The newspaper began carrying a "*Globe's* Weekly Round-Up" about civil rights happenings across the nation and news on the National Association for the Advancement of Colored People (NAACP). Henry Allen became a life member of the NAACP. In March 1960, the *Globe* and the National Baptist Publishing Board would support a citizens' rally after nearly eighty black college students were arrested and abused for sit-in demonstrations in Nashville's downtown stores.[20] The protest by the young blacks (the fourth generation of blacks since slavery) forced Nashville's white authorities to desegregate the city.

The Civil Rights Movement brought a new surge of black pride and made many blacks feel more positive about doing business with black companies. Henry Allen Boyd sensed this new attitude when he said:

> Your board has continued to operate every work day in the year, except Sunday, which is the Lord's day, on which we endeavor not to desecrate the Sabbath. The employees of the institution, normally under the Wage Hour Law, cannot put in but forty hours a week, regular time, but the work has increased to such proportion that we have been compelled to put in more than forty hours, thus we have had to struggle with the over-time pay which according to the government rules and regulations, must be at the rate of time and a half for overtime.
>
> ...It is in the nature of a labor of love, because we are all committed to the task of carrying on every phase of this activity so that it will reflect credit upon the denomination, because the institution known as the National Baptist Publishing Board's plant, is a part of our great denominational structure. I am conscious of the fact that it is, so to speak, the apple of the eye of millions of religious workers who make up the constituency of this body of Missionary Baptists. It is also the pride of people who are not Baptists, because they look upon it as a race institution. Its founder and builder, the late Richard H. Boyd, saw it in this way, because he too had but one aim in view, and that was to do something worthwhile, something that would stand, something that

Dr. R. H. Boyd (NBR)

would be monumental not only in its effort to do good, but that would be lasting, so that this as well as unborn generations might look upon it as an institution, a business concern, a religious plant as an expression of what we can do in our day and generations as constructive builders, organizers and operators of a plant that is known throughout the world today....[21]

Meanwhile, the NBPB had to make adjustments in response to changes in the World War II and post-World War II society. The Reverend J. B. Ridley, pastor of Nashville's Mt. Olive Missionary Baptist Church, became chairman of the company's board of directors. The board began to hire World War II veterans and train them to be cabinet makers, art preservationists, and printers. The National Baptist Publishing Board shipped religious materials across the world to military personnel, Lott Carey Baptist Foreign Mission Convention workers, Foreign Mission Board field workers, and others. The mission work in Panama continued, although R. H. Thorbourne had passed away and Mrs. Bessie Thorbourne directed the Panama work. Boyd asked the National Baptist Convention of America to establish a Panama Board and direct the work there. The board installed some twenty thousand dollars in new machinery. The publishing board realized receipts and disbursements of $446,678.89, according to the NBPB's 1946 annual report.[22]

Near the End of an Era

Like in past decades, the NBPB symbolized a large family, and the family experienced a sad time when it received news that a longtime friend of the publishing board, Grace M. Eaton, had passed on August 13, 1946. This white missionary, a member of the Women's American Baptist Home Mission Society, had supported Richard H. Boyd, Henry Allen Boyd, and generally the National Baptist Publishing Board since her arrival in Nashville. Grace M. Eaton was born in Massachusetts on May 6, 1866. She came to Nashville with another white missionary, Joanna P. Moore, to operate the Fireside School. When Moore died in 1916, Eaton directed the Fireside School until 1923 and worked closely with the NBPB to publish the *Hope* magazine. In 1923, she established the Grace M. Eaton Day Home on Gay Street. A second home was established at 1402 Jo Johnston Street and operated there until 1940 when a replacement home was secured at 505 17th Avenue North. The Eaton homes cared for children, up to age seven, for mothers who had to work and could not afford expensive child care services. Grace M. Eaton organized the Joanna P. Moore Women's Christian Temperance Union in 1933 and devoted her entire life to improving social conditions in black Nashville.[23]

The publishing board and Henry A. Boyd were so moved by Ms. Eaton's death that the *Union-Review* devoted almost a page to memorialize her life and death. Like Joanna P. Moore, although she was of white ancestry, Grace Eaton chose to be funeralized in a black church, Mt. Olive Missionary Baptist Church, and to be buried in a black cemetery, Greenwood Cemetery. Henry Allen Boyd, Secretary-Treasurer of the National Baptist Publishing Board, attended Grace M. Eaton's funeral just as R. H. Boyd had attended the funeral of Joanna P. Moore in 1915. Both women had been loyal friends and supporters of the National Baptist Publishing Board. Grace Eaton's passing marked the end of one era and the beginning of another one because she was among the last of the white missionaries who had journeyed to Nashville during the Civil War and post-Civil War years to bring education, religion, medical, and social services to the freedmen. During the next twenty years, the last of some 45,000 former American slaves and blacks born soon after slavery passed away.

Henry Allen's life bridged these generations, and his experiences helped to give wisdom and intelligence to his decisions at the publishing board and in the NBCA. By the 1950s, the National Baptist Publishing Board and the National Baptist Convention of America became huge, successful operations.

However, by the middle of the 1950s, Henry Allen Boyd became less able to lead the company during his old age. In 1952, Henry Allen lost his beloved wife, Georgia. The 77-year old Henry A. Boyd began to tire after working at the publishing board since his twenties. He had no sons to follow him, but Henry Allen Boyd had trained and nurtured his nephews.

Henry Allen Boyd's nephew, Theophilus Bartholomew Boyd, Jr., became his "understudy." A World War II veteran, T. B. Boyd, Jr., acted as assistant secretary-treasurer when Uncle Allen's energy began to decline. T. B. Boyd, Jr. was reliable, steady, loyal, and dedicated to the work of his uncle Henry Allen.

The NBPB became a complex organization with many programs, problems, and achievements. In 1952, the publishing board bought $6,950 in machinery. The books balanced at $584,997.95 in 1953.[24] The 1946 renovation of the turn-of-the-century building on Second Avenue North had begun to deteriorate, and the NBPB's business demanded modern facilities. Even the NBCI's Sunday School Publishing Board's Morris Memorial Building was nearly twenty-five years old by now. Inflation rocked the NBPB's operations by 1953 when the price of paper skyrocketed, causing the publishing board to affiliate closer with the Protestant Church-Owned Publishers Association to gain lower prices. Henry Allen Boyd continued to say that the poor educational background of blacks made it difficult for the NBPB to find, train, and keep qualified workers. "This is no criticism against the race, but a mere statement of facts," said Boyd.[25] The board paid the required minimum wage of seventy-five cents per hour and more. The NBPB continued to publish the *Hope* magazine for the Fireside School and women's missionary societies, study groups, and others. The *Union-Review* continued to lose money, costing about $550 per week to produce. Henry Allen Boyd asked the convention to require all members to subscribe to the paper and pay their subscription fees during the annual session of the National Baptist Convention of America. The National Baptist Publishing Board published three quarterlies for the Baptist Young People's Union, including the *Senior B.P.Y.U.* and *Junior B.Y.P.U.* magazines. The board continued to publish annually the *National Baptist Sunday School Lesson Commentary* even though the editor, E. H. Borden, had died. The board finally hired a "well-trained writer" to prepare the 1954 manuscript to interpret and explain every lesson. The National Baptist Publishing Board supplied over seventy churches in the Bahama Islands. Plans were made to replace the old church building established in Panama by the late R. H. Boyd. Three missionaries continued to receive support from the publishing board.[26]

The work at the plant staggered Henry Allen Boyd, whose health increasingly began to fail him. He said:

> I must pay tribute and give thanks to the executive secretary of the National Baptist Publishing Board, Mrs. Sadie B. Wilson, to the head bookkeeper, Mrs. Zula B. Campfield and her two assistants, Mrs. Lula Baker, granddaughter of the late R. H. Boyd, and Mrs. Addie Taylor; to the chief of the stenographer department, Mrs. M. W. Tittle, and to my understudy, T. B. Boyd, Jr., and the other office force and Publishing House employees for the loyal service they gave to the plant during my period of hospitalization in New York.[27]

Henry Allen had lingered between life and death when his daughter, Mrs. Katherine Boyd-Roach, and Sadie B. Wilson (executive assistant), stayed by his bedside. After being released from the hospital, Henry Allen was taken to the Clinton Hotel and then transported to Nashville by October 1952. From this point, his travels became limited.[28]

The Assistant Secretary-Treasurer, Theophilus B. Boyd, Jr., was thrust into the leadership position at an early age. Young T. B. Boyd, Jr. had to hit the road, speaking at churches, Sunday school meetings, and state association meetings when invitations became piled on the Secretary Treasurer's desk. He read the publishing board's report at the 1952 annual session of the National Baptist Convention of America. By 1954-55, T. B. Boyd, Jr. had joined the board of directors for the National Baptist Publishing Board.

The National Baptist Publishing Board continued to experience success and problems. The board added group and hospitalization insurance for its workers. But the assistant Secretary-Treasurer, T. B. Boyd, Jr. had trouble getting competent editors. Mae E. Hunter, editor of the *Hope* magazine, became ill, forcing others to keep the monthly magazine going. The publishing board had not missed an issue of the *Hope* magazine since assuming control of the publication. The *Union-Review* was edited by the president of Virginia Theological Seminary and College, Dr. M. C. Allen, who was selected by the convention. Zula B. Campfield, the bookkeeper, continued to have problems with bad checks and outstanding accounts. The board responded by refusing to accept C. O. D. orders instead of cash and money orders.[29]

The National Baptist Publishing Board's operations were large in 1955. The publishing board handled more than 4,325,650 letters and circulars and printed some publications by the millions:

Primary Quarterly	2,532,325
Intermediate Quarterly	2,350,275
Beginner Quarterly	1,183,750
The Teacher	1,230,715
Senior Quarterly	2,552,450
Junior Quarterly	2,150,475
Advanced Quarterly	2,625,420
Easy Lesson Primer	1,852,000

Millions of copies of the *Union-Review* were published in 1955 when the publishing board balanced its books at $670,809.33. The Fifty-first Session of the Sunday School Congress met in Kansas City, Missouri, where T. B. Boyd, Jr. led the various bands into the auditorium.[30]

When the National Baptist Convention of America convened at Chicago, Illinois, in September, 1955, T. B. Boyd, Jr. presented the National Baptist Publishing Board's annual report. The publishing board continued its mission work despite the work of the convention's Home Mission Board and Foreign Mission Board. The publishing board's mission work centered mainly in Panama and the West Indies. The NBCA's president said: "During these years of progress [1933-1955], we have had the great hand of support at every turn of distress...; we must feel as one family should feel towards another family that has given unselfish support in helping to maintain and lead us to success, as has been the conduct of the National Baptist Publishing Board, and its Secretary, Dr. Henry Allen Boyd, to the great Baptist family of the National Baptist Convention of America."[31]

The 1958 Sunday School Congress convened in the Greater St. James Baptist Church in Fort Worth, Texas, during June 11-15. Like Henry Allen had taken charge of the Sunday School Congress during the days of R. H. Boyd, young T. B. Boyd, Jr. headed the Congress and led the Congress' parade into the meeting hall. Now the Congress included the following departments: Home and Extension Work, Intermediate Juniors, Metoka and Galeda, Music,

Wedding Photo, H. A. and Georgia B. Boyd (NBR)

Rev. and Mrs. H. A. Boyd (NBR)

Negro Soldiers' Band, World War I (NBR)

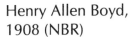

Henry Allen Boyd,
1908 (NBR)

H. A. Boyd with NBPB Brass Band (NBR)

H. A. Boyd and
NBPB Brass Band (NBR)

H. A. Boyd Entertain
Young Boys at the Congress (NBR)

H. A. Boyd Parades
with Boy Cadets (NBR)

A. G. Cadet Drill and Exhibition, Sunday School Superintendents, Teacher Training, and Ushers. The Sunday School Congress sessions included other workshop topics and allowed independent vendors to exhibit and sell products at the sessions.

Under his uncle's guidance, T. B. Boyd, Jr. continued to lead the publishing company forward. In 1957, the National Baptist Publishing Board had assets of $868,711.13. For the following year, 1958, the publishing board company's liabilities and assets were $863,713.70. Assets declined because many machines and facilities had depreciated, and the board had disposed of many of its band instruments. The younger Boyd seemed reluctant to invest in too many new machines when contemplating building a new plant. But to remain competitive, T. B. Boyd, Jr. had to continue to modernize the company and its operations.[32]

NBCA, NBPB, and Civil Rights

Again, it was three generations since slavery, and the last of the slave persons born during the 1860s began to pass away. A fourth generation of post-emancipation black-Americans entered the schools and prepared to lead a momentous Civil Rights Movement against Jim Crow practices.

The National Baptist Publishing Board and the National Baptist Convention of America would not and could not be disinterested in the Civil Rights Movement. The Civil Rights Movement bitterly divided the other black Baptist group, the National Baptist Convention U.S.A., Inc. But, the National Baptist Convention of America and the National Baptist Publishing Board supported King's tactics and the militancy of the Civil Rights Movement. The Reverend G. L. Prince, President of the NBCA, said to the 1956 Convention: "The Negro has demonstrated to the world that he has physical and mental ability equal to any other race with the same opportunity. The present condition through which we as a race are passing should encourage us as a group to take every advantage to assert our claim and right to full status of first class citizens in this country for which our sons have bled and died. The day of 'Uncle Tom' is gone forever."[33] In 1959, the NBCA's Baptist youth attended a workshop at the Highland Folk School in Monteagle, Tennessee, where many civil rights leaders, including M. L. King, Jr. and Rosa Parks, had received training in non-violent tactics and philosophy. The Tennessee state troopers broke into the meeting, turned off the lights, and arrested Septima Clark and three other Highlander officials. The group sang "We are not afraid, and we shall overcome" in the dark. The troopers claimed they were looking for "illegal whiskey."[34]

The Reverend Martin Luther King, Jr. was allowed to speak and raise funds at the September 1959 National Baptist Convention of America's annual session at Detroit, Michigan. The NBCA's 1959 session resolved to support the civil rights movement and King's Montgomery Improvement Association. Black Baptists, including the Boyds, criticized the white churches for remaining silent, for criticizing black leaders like Dr. Martin Luther King, Jr., and failing to help the blacks fight against injustice, violence, and human oppression.

Some black Baptist leaders attacked the Southern Baptist Convention for its silence about white racial violence in the South, its preachers' criticism of King and the SBC's refusal to help promote civil rights. But, the SBC's leaders, too, struggled to properly position the Convention to support the Civil Rights Movement. The SBC recognized the Brown v. Board of Education (1954) federal schools desegregation case as being in harmony with the constitutional guarantee of equality. The SBC refused to support southern extremists and fundamentalists in their movement to erect "Christian Academies" and religious schools with public funds to circumvent the desegregated schools. In 1958, the SBC's president said to the Convention's delegates: "I realize that we cannot have complete unanimity in these matters, but it would be tragic for us to assume that we can function as a Christian body without assigning to trusted representatives of the convention the task of pointing out our Christian duty with respect to social evils and current conflicts." "Discontent of the minority is the symptom of an illness which affects the nation and the world," said the president.[35] A joint committee on Baptist Work Among Negroes held a meeting in Nashville in February 1959 and agreed that the leaders of the SBC, the NBCI, and the NBCA should meet to discuss the civil rights conflicts.

The civil rights movement influenced harmony within the NBCA and motivated its leaders toward activist rhetoric. During the 1960 convention at New Orleans, T. B. Boyd, Jr. said that the NBPB stood ready and willing to do its best in supporting the NBCA. At the 1961 NBCA session, the president said: "Men and women of the National Baptist Convention of America take courage, do not despair, lift up your heads, our dawn is breaking . . . . I want the rights, the privileges that the Constitution of the United States grants me." At the Oklahoma City convention in September 1962, Boyd, Jr. reported that the NBPB received $820,766.99 and disbursed $797,464.09 including contributions to the convention's boards and programs; Boyd said: "Since faith has brought us thus far, let us continue in this faith, and march steadily up the King's highway." The Reverend E. M. Elmore responded to the 1962 convention's theme, "Appreciate the Past, Take Advantage of the Present and Prepare for the Future," by saying: "Our convention marches on without lawsuits, without fighting, and without accidental deaths by useless frustration; that's why the past should inspire us." The convention's 1962 Commission on Social Justice reported: "Militant leadership in the Negro church is mandatory, if the problems of injustice confronting the Negro community are to be met with any degrees of success."[36]

The Reverend Henry Allen Boyd, Secretary - Treasurer, NBPB

End of an Era

The illustrious Henry Allen Boyd died on May 28, 1959.[37] At the invitation of President Walter S. Davis, the community held Boyd's funeral services in the auditorium of Tennessee State University, the institution Henry Allen Boyd had helped to bring to reality. Henry Allen had been a member of the elite board of advisors for the past two presidents of the University. For more than half a century, Henry A. Boyd had been a force in local politics, a business leader, and a nationally renowned religious leader. He had taken the publishing board out of controversy in 1922 and expanded the company into a modern American corporation. His death became a great loss to America's society.

T. B. Boyd, Jr., Secretary -Treasurer, 1959-1979

Secretary-Treasurer, T. B. Boyd, Jr. directed the next Sunday School Congress. During the June 17-21, 1959, Sunday School Congress at the Union Baptist Church in Denver, Colorado, some forty-six states were represented by delegates. A pre-Congress musical involved 250 voices under Edna H. Porter of Los Angeles, California. Seven bands and musical groups performed at the Congress. Houston, Texas' "Henry Allen Boyd Brass Band" led the traditional parade. The Congress included a department for Band and Orchestra. The delegates dedicated the entire Congress to the memory of the late Henry Allen Boyd.[38]

In September 1959, T. B. Boyd, Jr. addressed the annual session of the National Baptist Convention of America. He said:

> It is with deep humility and with great appreciation that, I, your secretary, stand before you to make this report in place of my illustrious Uncle, Dr. Henry Allen Boyd, who departed this life on May 28, 1959, and who left a mark that time nor tide can ever erase. We lost one of the greatest leaders the world has ever produced.[39]

Boyd reported that the publishing board balanced its books with $758,642.37. The National Baptist Publishing Board's assets totaled $813,069.53. The publishing company's assets seemed to be on a decline:

1957 Assets	$868,711.13
1958 Assets	$863,713.70
1959 Assets	$813,069.53

But the company remained sound.[40]

Theophilus Bartholomew Boyd, Jr. was born in 1917. He attended Fisk University but graduated from Tennessee Agricultural and Industrial State College in 1940. T. B., Jr. became a linotypist in the composing room. Between 1941 and 1945, he served in the United States Army. After World War II, he and his wife, Mable, had four children: T. B. III, Brenda, Gerrylyn, and William Allen. Faithful to their father's alma mater, his children also attended Tennessee State University. In 1956, T. B. Boyd, Jr. became a minister, and ten years later he was elected pastor of the Greater Salem Baptist Church in Louisville, Kentucky, commuting to and from the church and Nashville. He became the first head of the publishing board to continue to pastor a church.[41]

Dr. T. B. Boyd, Jr. became a member of the Metropolitan Human Rights Commission, chairman of Citizens Bank's board of directors, and president of Citizens Realty and Development Company. He became a member of Tau Lambda Chapter of Alpha Phi Alpha Fraternity. Boyd was listed in personality magazines for important leaders of the South. Under T. B. Boyd, Jr.'s leadership, the National Baptist Publishing Board completed a million dollar plant at 7145 Centennial Boulevard and served thousands of churches. In spite of his age, and youthful appearance, T. B. Boyd, Jr. maintained excellent relations with the National Baptist Convention of America.[42]

By 1960, the National Baptist Convention of America had a complex organization with sixteen elected officers, including a historian and a musical director. The NBCA included a Junior Woman's Auxiliary, a National Baptist Brotherhood Union, and a Youth Convention.[43] The Reverend C. D. Pettaway became convention president. He was preceded by the following convention presidents:

> G. L. Prince (1933-1957),
> J. W. Hurse (1930-1933),
> J. E. Woods (1923-1933),
> E. P. Jones (1915-1923).[44]

By maintaining excellent relations with the Convention and its officers, T. B., Jr. was able to devote a considerable amount of his time and energy to the management and the expansion of the publishing board and its programs.

In 1960, T. B. Boyd, Jr. began to change the procedures at the publishing board company. He instituted changes to improve the quality of the products. He allowed no more commercial advertisements in the National Baptist Publishing Board's publications. He modernized the *Teacher Quarterly*. Boyd bought three new printing machines and planned to buy a two-color press to add color and compete better with other publishing houses. With humility, he credited Sadie B. Wilson for his smooth transition after Henry Allen's death. Boyd said: "Without her advice, help and support, my job would be of small consequence."[45]

In 1960, the board balanced its books with $756,766.43. The NBPB's assets totaled $851,655.35. The latter figure signaled an increase after a slight three-year decline. Boyd said to the convention's delegates:

We want you to know that we cannot operate this Publishing Board without your cooperation and support, and we appreciate very much the patronage you have given us in the past, and ask for a continuance of the same in the future. We also ask an interest in your prayers in our behalf in order that we may do the things that are right and pleasing in the sight of God.[46]

Boyd quickly modernized the plant and increased its business. By 1961, the National Baptist Publishing Board had assets of $950,006.62 including $300 in "band instruments." Boyd said: "...if we would be emancipated, Christian education is the process, basically by which it is done."[47] By 1962, the NBPB had installed new machinery. The board remodeled the former church furniture factory so that the composing room, the bindery, and the proof reading rooms could be located in better facilities. The NBPB dedicated the remodeled building to the late Henry Allen Boyd. During the Sunday School Congress session, Boyd implemented the Department of Christian Education. He instituted a pension plan for the publishing board's employees.

Although the company's assets declined during the late 1950s because of depreciated old machinery, outdated facilities, and recurring American economic recessions, however, within a ten year period, T. B. Boyd, Jr. had brought the company's declining assets to over a million dollars. The company's assets had grown to $868,711.13 in 1957 from a worth of over $300,000 during R. H. Boyd's administration. In 1962-63, T. B. Boyd, Jr. balanced the books at $901,974.96 with assets and liabilities balancing at $1,128,814.20.[48] By 1969, the publishing board company had a net worth of $1,667,680.05, and the books balanced with $1,222,925.88.[49]

Like his predecessors, Boyd, Jr. managed not only the large publishing board, also he headed Citizens Bank, served as a religious leader in the National Baptist Convention of America, became pastor of a church, and became involved in national and local issues and movements. All these things he did energetically.

Civil Rights Movement Divides the Baptists

Meanwhile, 1961, the Civil Rights Movement generated great controversy in the National Baptist Convention, U.S.A. Inc. The NBCI's president would not publicly back Martin L. King, Jr. and his civil rights protests and demonstrations. At a time when the director of the Federal Bureau of Investigation had begun a smear campaign against King, the NBCI's president, Joseph H. Jackson said: "All protest being directed according to the Constitution of the United States will be of such caliber that hostile forces of the nation and enemies of a democratic society will not join with us and use our methods and techniques for the purpose of weakening and destroying the nation." Jackson wanted the black Baptists to "emphasize the use of economic tools . . . to gain equality." The convention's leadership had remained committed to the old accommodationist approach and nonconfrontational relations with whites, and the NBCI had remained closer to the Southern Baptist Convention than the NBCA. Jackson supported a movement for black rights but opposed black militancy. The president persuaded the NBCI to support black progress by buying and operating land and Freedom Farms in West Tennessee and West Africa. The dispute about supporting King's Southern Christian Leadership Conference's (SCLC) civil rights movement became bitter when Jackson's opponents disrupted the 1960 NBCA annual session with a sit-in demonstration, causing the Convention to close with a financial loss and without electing a president. THE NBCI's board of directors met later and re-elected Jackson by 70 votes to 0. A summer 1961 meeting between King and Jackson failed to resolve the dispute; Jackson refused to permit any of King's supporters to hold offices in the NBCI. At the September 1961 annual session in Kansas City, Jackson was re-elected although he had served as president since 1953. He removed King from the vice president at-large position in the NBCI's Congress of Christian Education "because of the type of militant campaign carried on against his own denomination and his own race." Jackson said: "The Convention by it s actions rejected non-violent civil disobedience as the best tool to use in the struggle for first-class citizenship. In a democratic social order, one cannot harmonize disobedience with non-violence . . . ." The controversy caused the NBCI to split once more since 1915. The pro-King faction formed the Progressive National Baptist Convention of the United States of America in Cincinnati's Zion Baptist Church on November 15, 1961, and incorporated it on May 10, 1962.[50]

T. B. Boyd, Jr. and the NBPB admired and supported Dr. King's movement. Contrary to what conservative whites and the federal intelligence agencies tried to portray, King's SCLC represented a coalition of preachers and churches. After the unexpected murder of Martin Luther King, Jr. in 1968, Boyd published King's picture and speeches in issues of the *Union-Review*. After being contacted by the National Council of Churches of Christ's officials, Boyd, Jr. sent a letter to black Baptist pastors, asking them to help prevent the racial riots from recurring. He said: "There is one good thing that has happened as a result, however, and that is, the unmasking of white America and the fact that white Americans have been forced to take a good look at themselves, as well as the prevalent social system which has created the climate for these disturbances." Boyd continued:

> In the struggle to find ourselves as a race, our own self-examination is urgently needed. Although it is a well-known fact that men have never

Dr. T. B. Boyd, Jr., Secretary-Treasurer, NBPB (NBR)

gained very much by lying down, yet there is more to be gained by using our energies constructively rather than on destructive measures. It is gratifying to know that in many instances we as black Americans are finding ways to use our talents and resources, but we have not yet reached our full potential - we have fallen short. As Baptists and religious leaders, we need to call for more unity among ourselves, that we may present a united front by pooling our resources and our efforts instead of pulling against each other....[51]

NBPB Expands Under Boyd, Jr.

T. B. Boyd, Jr. put a lot of energy and time in developing the National Baptist Publishing Board as a modern corporation. He plunged into completing plans for a new plant to be built on 4.5 acres of land on Centennial Boulevard in West Nashville, far from the site of the old plant in downtown Nashville. His son, T. B. Boyd, III a recent college graduate with a degree in business administration, headed the building program. The publishing board's business was slightly affected by the mid-70s economic recession. The balance sheet fell to $996,663.56 in 1974.[52]

The National Baptist Publishing Board bounced back. The Sunday School Congress' attendance exceeded eight thousand participants. In 1975, the National Baptist Publishing Board relocated to an ultra-modern facility at 7145 Centennial Boulevard (later changed to 6717 Centennial Boulevard). The books were balanced at $1,032,135.37 in 1975.[53]

By now, T. B. Boyd, Jr.'s ultimate successor had climbed aboard. This young man, T. B. Boyd, III would be taking the helm of the company in a few years. He was among the third generation of Boyds who had attended local Tennessee State University where his great Uncle, Henry Allen Boyd, had spearheaded the effort to build this great University in Nashville-Davidson County. Even one of the boy's dormitories at the University was named Boyd Hall.

In 1975, the National Baptist Sunday School and Baptist Training Union Congress met in Wichita, Kansas, June 11-16. Whereas the older Congresses had relied on private homes and churches to host the annual meeting, the Congresses of the 1970s used hotels and city auditoriums to house over ten thousand delegates. The 70th Annual Sunday School Congress attracted 11,000 delegates. The local Macedonia Missionary Baptist Church held the meeting.[54] Because of the difficulty and expense of scheduling parades in large, urban centers with traffic problems, the board phased out the parades, and the Congress Brass Band was disbanded.

After being hospitalized, Dr. T. B. Boyd, Jr. passed away on April 1, 1979, leaving a wife and four children, his father, and sister Rose Evelyn

Morgan and brothers Edward and James Boyd of Washington, D. C. and St. Louis, respectively. The *National Baptist Union-Review* said that "Dr. T. B. Boyd, Jr. was one energetic community leader, a kind and personable man."[55] During her September 5, 1979, message at the 99th Annual Session of the National Baptist Convention of America, Mrs. Ruby G. Lockridge, president of the National Baptist Nurses Corps Auxiliary, said: "The passing of a very dear friend and brother, Dr. T. B. Boyd, Jr., a great National figure, and a nobleman to the Nurses Corps, Wednesday, April 4, 1979, is an epoch marking day in National Baptist history."[56]

T. B. Boyd, III, 1979 - Present

In April, 1979, the board of directors elected Theophilus Bartholomew Boyd, III president and chief executive officer of the National Baptist Publishing Board. He had begun working at the publishing house in 1963 when a student at Pearl High School. He completed Tennessee State University in 1969 and became personnel director at the National Baptist Publishing Board in 1974. T. B. Boyd, III received college training in business administration, eco-nomics, and accounting. Under his father's guidance, he designed and took charge of the new building project worth $1,000,000. On November 3, 1976, he won election to the board of directors for the National Baptist Publishing Board. He became a member of the Tennessee Commission on Human Development and a board member of Citizens Realty and Development Corporation. The NBPB balanced the books with $2,420,885.44 in 1979.[57]

The June 12-17, 1979, Sunday School Congress met in the aftermath of T. B. Boyd, Jr.'s death. The Reverend W. N. Daniel and the Antioch Missionary Baptist Church on 415 West Englewood Avenue in Chicago served as host church for the Congress. By now the Congress had expanded its departments to reflect the evolution of the Congress' workshops and the changes in the services of the publishing board and the needs of the convention and churches. The expanded list of Congress departments read as follows:

Older Children's Teachers
Young People's Teachers
Adults' Teachers
Superintendents
Home and Extension
Metoka and Galeda
Daily Vacation Bible School
Baptist Training Union
Woman's Missionary Auxiliary
Junior Women's Missionary
Music

Church Ushers
Church Nurse Corps
Brotherhood Union
Ministers

T. B. Boyd, III addressed the Sunday School Congress session. He said: "It is a day of peace, a day of tranquility, a day of progress, and a day of recommitment to the very principles that our forefathers laid down before us. Although the mantle has fallen on my shoulders I will not let it hit the ground."[58] Young Theophilus B. Boyd, III's speech denoted his intent to assert himself as the new leader of the publishing board and the Congress.

Already under his father, some elements, including the Foreign Mission Board, had grumbled when T. B. Boyd, Jr. denied them permission to collect money at the annual Sunday School Congress. Boyd, Jr. stopped the process because he feared that each board and every Baptist agency would use the huge annual Congress like a collection plate.

Some of the black preachers had forgotten the history, origins, and purpose of the Sunday School Congress; or they had chosen to ignore that history. In 1906, the NBPB and Richard H. Boyd had designed the publishing board to train and educate church workers and help attract young Christians to this work. In R. H. Boyd's day, the convention's president had used the annual June Congress to meet with the boards and secretaries prior to the September convention session. But, during the period 1910-1914, some elements in the National Baptist Convention had argued that the Congress competed with the annual convention, and either it should be discontinued or attached to the convention. The NBPB and T. B. Boyd, Jr. did not intend to allow the preachers to change the Congress' historical mission and turn the Congress into a mere extension of the annual Baptist convention; such action would defeat the original intent of the Sunday School Congress. Still nearly two generations later (the 1970s), some of the preachers viewed the Congress as controlled by the publishing board, not the convention.

T. B. Boyd, III, the capable graduate of Tennessee State University, answered the challenges presented by a few of the older leaders and some jealous persons within the Convention. His aforementioned speech served notice that he would not be bullied because of his age and youthful appearance. Like the turmoil in 1912, the anti-NBPB faction would not quit, and the controversy about the relationship between the Congress and the NBCA and the convention's election of directors to the NBPB's board would continue and result in a denominational split in 1988.

Under T. B. Boyd, III, the Sunday School Congress continued to expand and undergo organizational changes to reach higher levels of efficiency and sophistication. The board installed new major machinery in the bindery department and bought a new computer system including computer typeset-ting equipment. Just as his father had assumed major responsibilities and management for the incapacitated Henry Allen Boyd years before, the young Theophilus B. Boyd, III stepped quickly into his father's shoes, directing the Congress and the board's other operations.

A young, energetic and charismatic person, T. B. Boyd, III had begun to make his mark under the supervision of his father, T. B. Boyd, Jr. In 1975, Boyd III began research on developing a new *National Baptist Hymnal.* The publication appeared in 1977, and it eventually sold millions of copies. In 1978, T. B., III was elected to the board of directors of the Citizens Savings and Trust Company Bank. He became chairman of the bank's board in 1982. Having matriculated in college during the turbulent 1960s, T. B., III naturally involved himself in community and social issues, becoming a member of Kappa Alpha Psi Fraternity, Chi Boule of Sigma Pi Phi Fraternity, and chairman of the United Negro College Fund Telethon for Middle Tennessee. He became vice chairman of the board of trustees for Meharry Medical College, member of the Richland and Maryland Farms Country Clubs, and president of The 100 Black Men of Middle Tennessee organization. Dr. T. B. Boyd, III earned listings in *Who's Who, in Black America, Personalities in the South,* and other notable publications because of his active involvement in various organizations and movements.[59]

T. B. Boyd, III expanded the publishing board's contributions to benevolent, community, and philanthropic programs. By 1981, the NBPB balanced the books with $3,453,972.63. The National Baptist Publishing Board established the T. B. Boyd, Jr. Endowment Fund to "...put back into the community in a creative, positive, and helpful way," said T. B. Boyd, III. He said: "Because we care, we get involved."[60] The Endowment Fund had a fund of $300,000 with the first grants scheduled for January, 1981. The annual Sunday School Congress continued the T. B. Boyd, Jr. Essay Contest, and it reserved $1,500 to reward high school students who read the best papers at the Congress. In 1981, the 12th Annual Scholarship Contest's awards increased to $1,750. In another benevolent project, Boyd, III supported the feed-the-children movement in 1985 when he said: "This great effort can serve not only for the strengthening of under-nourished bodies, but also the strengthening of the spirit of unity in the body of Christ among the nations of the world."[61]

In the area of politics, the influence of the publishing board and the National Baptist Convention of America went beyond local boundaries. T. B. Boyd, III and the NBCA leadership supported Jessie Jackson, a black man and a Democrat, in his bid for the American presidency in 1984. Boyd, III said: "What is important is that we had a black man who stood and defied the thinking of America as a whole . . . and emerged with much the same pride for his people as David did with Goliath."[62]

Four years after his election to head the publishing board, T. B. Boyd, III addressed the "biggest and best" of the Sunday School Congresses ever held at Chicago during the week of June 14-19. Some sixteen to eighteen thousand messengers and visitors shared in study, fellowship, and learning about Sunday school education and methods. The theme of the Congress was "The Church: Reaching, Teaching, and Keeping." Boyd delivered the Wednesday morning address, challenging the messengers to live a life of commitment to God, to stand tall, walk upright, talk right, and live right. "An upright man can never be a downright failure," said Boyd, III.[63] Boyd's mother, Mrs. Mable Boyd, the highly respected matriarch of the Boyd family, received a dozen long-stem roses from the host pastor, the Reverend Wilbur N. Daniel.

Mable Landrum Boyd was born in Nashville, Davidson County, Tennessee. She was the daughter of Margaret Jenkins Landrum (born in Kentucky) and Jessie Landrum (born in Rutherford County, Tennessee). Mable attended Pearl High School and Tennessee A & I State College in Nashville. In 1941, she married T. B. Boyd, Jr. During T. B., Jr.'s five-year service in the African theater of World War II, Mable worked in a factory like so many other patriotic women who contributed to the war on the homefront. After her husband's return, the couple began raising their four children. When her husband became pastor of a Louisville, Kentucky church, Mable L. Boyd accompanied him to the services, either flying or driving by car. Sometimes she drove the car to Louisville, supporting and helping her husband at the 1,000 member church.[64]

After T. B. Boyd, Jr. passed in 1979, Mable became a member of the board of directors of the National Baptist Publishing Board, a member of the board of directors of Citizens Savings Bank, and chairperson of the T. B. Boyd, Jr. Endowment Fund of the National Baptist Publishing Board. Mrs. T. B. Boyd, Jr. also became a member of the board for the Grace M. Eaton Day Home in Nashville. She viewed her position on the board as fitting and proper for a member of the National Baptist Publishing Board which had been affiliated with the Grace M. Eaton Home since its founding.[65]

Mable Boyd remained a quiet influence in the family, always displaying fortitude, dignity, and wisdom and maintaining an office at the National Baptist Publishing Board. Like her husband, T. B. Boyd, Jr., Mrs. Boyd was well-liked and admired by all who met her. Mrs. Boyd worked closely with her daughter Brenda in planning the annual Sunday School Congress sessions.

Sunday School Congress: Bigger Than Ever

Since Richard H. Boyd had conceived and organized it, the Sunday School Congress had been a major event for black Baptists. During the Congress' sessions, Dr. T. B. Boyd, III exhibited the management sense of his father and great-grandfather. And he displayed the charisma of great Uncle

Henry Allen Boyd, dressing immaculately, impressing the delegates with style, class, good management, and articulation of religious, moral, and social issues.

Reflecting on the importance of the annual sessions of the Sunday School Congress, the late Reverend Henry Allen Boyd had said: "A preacher may preach over the heads of the little children, but it is the teacher in the Sunday School who must go right to the heart of the child and lift it up. He must teach it about God, about Jesus Christ, and must inspire its life for holy and higher things."[66] T. B. Boyd, III's sister, Brenda Boyd-Walker, organized the annual Congress sessions and made the complex travel and logistical arrangements. By the 1980s, the publishing board's operations, the management requirements for the huge Congress sessions, and the number of employees necessitated acquisition of additional offices to be leased in an office building on White Bridge Road where Brenda directed the operations. Later, these operations settled into an office building on Heiman Street. A highly skilled professional, T. B., III's sister, Brenda, became a key person in continuing the Boyd tradition of excellence in religious programming.[67]

At the 1985 National Baptist Sunday Church School and Baptist Training Union Congress, T. B., III said:

> I thank you, Lord, for putting breath in my body so that I might stand before this great Congress today and tell you that the *young people are the future*. These little children running around here today are the ones who are going to have to finish much of what we start. We must invest in our young people and make them a part of what we are about. Our young people of today will be the world of tomorrow and I am proud of them.[68]

Boyd, III also said: "Now, more than ever, there is a need for continued love and brotherhood within our Convention so that we may become what we know we ought to be in order to exemplify what God's children should be."[69] The latter words were spoken in response to the recent death of Dr. James Carl Sams, president of the National Baptist Convention of America. By now the NBCA claimed a membership of some 3 million persons.

The late President Sams and T. B. Boyd, III had worked with the publishing board to form a Congress Commission to decide the program and format for the annual Sunday School Congress. This arrangement quieted the critics who wanted the National Baptist Convention of America to take control of the popular Congress like the National Baptist Convention of the United States of America, Incorporated, had controlled its Sunday School Congress since 1916. Some of the critics believed that the Boyds and the NBPB had too much influence with the churches through the annual Congress. Some of the convention's leadership wanted to place some Convention nominees on the publishing board and control directly the Congress.

When E. Edward Jones succeeded Sams as president of the NBCA, the controversy about the Congress and the NBPB came into the open. Jones, President of Louisiana's Baptist Missionary and Education State Convention and pastor of Shreveport's Galilee Baptist Church, pursued a strong economic theme within the NBCA. He wanted to consolidate the Convention's power because the NBCA seemed to have too many Conventions (independent Boards and auxiliaries) in one Convention. Jones argued that the NBCA represented an umbrella under which every single board must rest. Jones believed that the Boards should operate for the Convention, and not the Convention for the Boards. He argued that the black Baptist churches needed to support economic enterprise in the black community instead of closing their buildings Monday through Saturday.

By now, Boyd, III had expanded the Sunday School Congress, revising its name to the National Baptist Sunday Church School and Baptist Training Union Congress. He added divisions for children, youth, and young adults, ages four to twenty-four. The Congress drew more than twenty thousand delegates to the annual sessions which were held in huge city auditoriums and convention centers. The delegates patronized hotel rooms for miles around the host city. The Congress continued to focus on promoting Christian education training through the National Baptist Publishing Board and the use of its materials and services.

The 83rd Annual Session of the National Baptist Sunday Church School and Baptist Training Union Congress convened in Dallas, Texas' huge convention center during the week of July 16-21, 1987. The one thousand plus Congress Chorus presented a soul-stirring musical on Tuesday night. Following an instrumental ensemble prelude with Doug Baskin as conductor and a processional of colors featuring the Lincoln High School R. O. T. C. Cadets, the official Congress Family members made their entrance with Dr. T. B. Boyd, III and his wife, Yvette Duke Boyd, leading the way. By now, Dr. F. Benjamin Davis was chairman of the National Baptist Publishing Board, the person who formally opened the Congress sessions. The exhibit hall became filled with displays, vendors, and thousands of delegates and visitors. Most impressive was the large number of young people and children who seemed delighted to be present at the Congress. Massive crowds attended the classes and events, and preachers filled a ballroom to hear fellow preachers teach (preach) dynamic lessons (sermons). Attending a Congress became a cherished experience for young and old Baptists.[70]

After the Congress, the publishing board immediately started the plans for the next one. The Congress Commission scheduled the next Sunday School Congress' annual session for Nashville's Stouffer Hotel and Convention Center, 1988.

NBPB and the Technological Age

Meantime, the publishing board continued its usual business. *In-Plant Productions* (1984), a purchasing monthly, listed the National Baptist Publishing Board among the top 100 religious and other non-profit businesses. The facility included black-white and four-color process printing, photocomposition, computers, three sheet-fed presses over 17", two sheet-fed presses 17" and under, computer graphic systems, micrographic equipment, camera and plate-making department, and a bindery.[71] Whereas the older company had used departments and assistant secretaries and field secretaries, now for greater efficiency, the company's structure included five modern divisions:

FINANCE
PUBLICATIONS
BUSINESS DEVELOPMENT
MARKETING
OPERATIONS

The Customer Relations Department directed the continuous improvement of customer relations by using computer technology and modern communication devices. The publishing board instituted church growth and development workshops through intensive one-day workshops which used the latest trends in Christian education. Each year at the International Christian Booksellers Association, the National Baptist Publishing Board company presented prominent displays equipped with video screens and convenient sitting and browsing facilities in the displays. Soon, the company distributed fourteen million publications worldwide, using high speed data processing computers and large printing equipment.[72]

Increasingly, the president and chief executive officer, T. B. Boyd, III used the editorials of the *National Baptist Union-Review* to make commentary on world and societal conditions. In the February 1986 issue, he said: "Bureaucracy is an unnecessary evil in our society brought about by the employment of too many people to do too little work, therefore causing these people to constantly justify their jobs."[73] Like his great-grandfather, Richard H. Boyd, T. B., III became concerned about how black people perceived themselves. He expressed disappointment that black people had "abandoned the Afro haircut for jerri curls, the old process technique and other ointments or chemicals that alter and hide our God-given beauty that we have naturally as black people."[74] In the April 1985 issue, T. B., III criticized the white backlash that had beset civil rights in America. After President Ronald Reagan, a Republican, had appointed an outspoken black conservative, Clarence Pendleton, to head the United States Civil Rights Commission, T. B. Boyd, III said: "Never before has there been such an outright undeniable effort by an administration to use a whip (the whip being the commission) that has been placed in the hands of a black man to be used on the backs of his black brothers and sisters."[75]

One significant change at the publishing board was the transformation of the *Union-Review*. For a time, during the 1960s, the paper took the character of a regular newspaper on standard size newsprint paper. By the 1980s, the newspaper had become a monthly, cutting the board's financial losses for publishing the paper. Under T. B. Boyd, III the paper became more of a commentary on contemporary events, social changes, and important news as well as religious news about the National Baptist Convention's churches, pastors, and programs. The February 1986 issue carried front page news about the explosion and destruction of America's space shuttle. But like in the past, the *National Baptist Union-Review* remained the important organ for the National Baptist Publishing Board, its communication link with its customers, the churches, Sunday schools, pastors, and teachers.

Convention Splits

Meanwhile, the opposition against the successful National Baptist Publishing Board and its lucrative programs never stopped. The death of President Sams signaled another movement to resurrect the issues of control of the Sunday School Congress and election of convention nominees to the NBPB's directors. The Baptist preachers and black religious leaders continued to eye the publishing board as a healthy operation. By 1987, for example, the NBCA had an income of $1,089,856 compared to several millions for the NBPB. And although the NBPB contributed thousands of dollars to the NBCA's boards and programs, like great grandfather Richard Henry Boyd, young T. B., III became destined to experience another split in the National Baptist Convention of America.

In 1987-88, new rumblings surfaced within the National Baptist Convention of America. During the September, 1987, NBCA session at Chicago, President E. Edward Jones wanted to redefine the goals of the convention, and apparently he was not pleased with the publishing board's $17,000 contribution to the convention's programs for 1987. Dr. Jones recommended that the convention publish its own monthly newspaper and consider a contract with a white publishing house that promised to give the convention twenty percent of every dollar the convention spends with them. At the September, 1988, convention session at Fort Worth, Texas, a vocal faction argued for more convention control of the successful Sunday School Congress which had been founded, directed, and controlled by the National Baptist Publishing since 1906. The publishing board refused to yield to the demands of the Jones men who seemed to be moving toward a centralized, authoritative, incorporated convention. Jones had scheduled the Youth Convention to convene in Dallas during the same week of the Sunday School Congress which also met in Dallas and included its traditional Youth Division (Mini Congress), an important part of the Congress organized by R. H. Boyd during the early twentieth century to support the "Save the Children (Boys)" movement. Classes, activities, drill teams, and speech contests had been a part of the NBPB's annual Sunday School Congress for many decades.

Many Baptist leaders who were displeased with Jones' leadership met in Dallas during November 14-15, 1988. This "Restoration Meeting" proclaimed the National Missionary Baptist Convention of America on November 15, 1988. The purpose of the organization was to restore a Convention that was controlled by its affiliated churches and members while "serving the call of Jesus Christ whose divine sacredness the churches are called to respect."[76] The pro-NBPB leaders desired to maintain the unincorporated status of the National Baptist Convention of America and retain the convention's original values and mission. The Reverend S. M. Lockridge became president of the National Missionary Baptist Convention of America which fully supported the NBPB and its independence.

The first session of the NMBCA opened on Wednesday morning, September 6, 1989, in Chicago's Palmer House Hotel's convention facilities. Ruth Saul and Artricia Matthews played organ and piano music as the delegates and visitors filled the meeting hall. Ruth Davis directed the choir in lively songs that signaled "a new beginning" for the national Baptist convention. Two days before the official opening session, the leaders of the NMBCA, the NBPB, and some 400 person had attended a "Unity Banquet" at the Reverend W. N. Daniel's church. According to the *National Baptist Union-Review* (September, 1989), Convention president Lockridge introduced Boyd, III who said:

> When we combine the efforts of the Congress, the Publishing Board, along with the work of the Convention, we are unmatched. . . . We are here and concerned only with our agenda, not to make anybody look bad or criticize others, not to determine who's right, who's wrong, but to do the work before us. God is still in the blessing business. After publishing 12 million pieces of literature last year, we braced ourselves for a slight decrease at the Publishing Board in our literature, but we have experienced an increase in sales . . . . Evidently, you as proud black men and women wanted to show the nation that you would not turn your backs on your own businesses. You refused to preach blackness and buy white.

NBPB and NMBCA

Meanwhile, the Sunday School Congress had reached greater heights during its June 1988 meeting in Nashville—its first meeting there since 1906.

Brenda Boyd-Walker used computers to preregister and register over 20,000 delegates at the Congress and local hotels.

The National Missionary Baptist Convention of America, the National Baptist Publishing Board, and the National Baptist Sunday Church School and Training Union Congress evolved quickly into highly sophisticated and complex organizations and operations. Because of this complexity, the organizations collaborated to modernize the form and frequency of lines of communication. Maintaining effective lines of communication between the publishing board and the convention became important to the officers of both institutions.

The 1989 winter meeting of the National Missionary Baptist Convention met in Tulsa from February 28 to March 3. Theophilus B. Boyd, III addressed the convention, pointing out the atmosphere of love and peace. A 200-voice choir sang "The Lord is My Light" and other soul-stirring songs. It was an exemplary session. And the National Baptist Publishing Board continued to thrive.[77]

In 1989, the National Baptist Publishing Board held the Annual Baptist Training Union Writers' Conference to help stimulate the mind, interact with the better minds in the National Missionary Baptist Convention of America, and bring the writers and planners of the Baptist Training Union curriculum together for the purpose of establishing its future goals and objectives. Among others in attendance were T. B. Boyd, III, Dr. F. Benjamin Davis (chairman of the National Baptist Publishing Board), and Dr. S. M. Lockridge.[78]

The 1989 National Baptist Sunday Church School and Baptist Training Union Congress met in Houston, June 13-18. There was a full program, with standing room only. Some five thousand messengers of the Mini Congress marched through the convention hall carrying placards and banners when singing "Hail, Hail the Baptist Congress" on Wednesday morning, June 14. It was a spectacular sight to behold when T. B. Boyd, III and publishing board and convention officers viewed the processional. The Dr. T. B. Boyd, Jr. Essay Scholarship Contest took place, allowing some of America's most talented young black children to exhibit their academic skills, talents, and competencies. Some forty-six church drill teams marched before the podium. Visitors saw black youngsters and their adult advisers marching, acting and speaking in unison, and exhibiting the real skills, the cohesion, the discipline, and the organizational potential of young black Americans. The church drill team competition became one creative and dramatic sight developed by the publishing board's annual congresses. A progressive development of the old Boy Cadets units, the drill teams included boys and girls dressed in bright-colored uniforms and military caps, marching with precision steps and reciting biblical and Sunday school pieces together. This event usually filled the convention hall, like days of old. Speaking to an audience of fourth, fifth, and

National Missionary Baptist Convention of America, 1988

Dr. T. B. Boyd, III, President/CEO , NBPB (NBPBLA)

sixth generation post-Emancipation blacks, Dr. T. B. Boyd, III proclaimed: "It is a day of peace, a day of tranquility, a day of progress, and a day of recommitment to the very principles that our forefathers laid down before us."[79]

The NBPB, the Sunday School Congress, and the affiliated convention had come over a stony road watered with tears, built on personal sacrifices, and worn by bitter battles, to face success. On Friday night, T. B. Boyd, III presented the 1989 session with a check for $27,000 from the National Baptist Publishing Board. The funds were designated for the National Missionary Baptist Convention and its programs. The publishing board had given the Convention previous checks.[80] Now the NBPB, the Sunday School Congress, and the convention worked together.

The National Missionary Baptist Convention showed strength and vitality. The literature said that the reorganization was necessary to return to basic Baptist principles that...

> they are free and independent of any dictatorial and authoritative powers over their churches and pastors . . . . Without the National Baptist Churches, there can be no National Baptist Convention. The organization [National Missionary Baptist Convention] is a voluntary agreement among churches to work together to do ministries of the Lord which they could not do by themselves.[81]

The official delegates represented more than twenty states. Texas church persons were heavily represented, constituting nearly one-third of the delegates. Visitors from across the land attended the exciting convention session.

The restructured National Missionary Baptist Convention of America illustrated the level of sophistication reached by Baptist leaders by the late 1980s. The organization had a complex structure to service every aspect of the church and address the growing needs of religion for the coming century. The officials of the organization included a large number of men and women, and the governing structure of the National Missionary Baptist Convention of America exhibited, for sure, the democratic decision-making mechanism of the convention. The National Missionary Baptist Convention of America had four major boards. The Evangelical Board sponsored evangelical crusades to gain and baptize converts. The Foreign Mission Board conducted missionary fields across the world including the Caribbean Islands and Africa. The Education Board gave financial help and resources to deserving institutions of higher learning (i. e., historically black colleges and universities). The Home Mission Board undergirded the ministry of local churches with financial difficulty. The structure of the organization insured the inclusion of all classes and constituencies of the denomination.

The National Missionary Baptist Convention of America included several auxiliaries to perform its work and functions. The Senior Woman's

Auxiliary promoted Christian fellowship and involvement of female Baptists in Christian service. The Junior Women's Auxiliary involved energetic young women in addressing social issues related to the world community. The Brotherhood Auxiliary enlisted men in the work of missions and involved them in their communities and churches. The Brotherhood Auxiliary II created a fellowship of young men for Christian work. The Usher's Auxiliary trained doorkeepers to specialize in hospitality and lend spiritual dignity to church services. The Nurses' Auxiliary provided professional health care within the churches. The Ministers' Wives Auxiliary engaged the wives of ministers and developed their positive self-image and understanding of the ministry. The Youth Convention Auxiliary invested in the church's future, the young people and sponsored forums, retreats, workshops, and other character-building experiences. The Ministers' Conference Auxiliary involved the preachers and the pastors in a rich, intimate fellowship for support, discussion of current issues, and information-sharing.

The National Baptist Publishing Board rested comfortably with the National Missionary Baptist Convention of America. The publishing board company fitted its services and products to meet the needs of the NMBCA's boards and auxiliaries as well as to serve churches, Sunday schools, the Baptist Young People's Union, and the annual Congress. There were several resource ministries: Leadership Development - discipline in the Sunday Church School, a workshop on nurturing, educating, instructing, regulating, and training; Leadership - workshop to guide Sunday Church School leaders to become more effective and efficient; Growth and Development - a workshop for the Baptist Training Union to develop new ideas and promote growth; and a comprehensive Growth and Development Workshop. The NBPB also offered Convention Resource Ministries in "Developing Church Training Curriculum," "Audio-Visual Aids and Teaching Techniques," and "Vacation Bible School." The publishing board's workshops used the latest technology and equipment to improve religious education and instruction in the church school.

The publishing board organized the Sunday School Congress like a University, with schools and academic deans. The schools included School of Methods, School of Missionary Education, School of Program Units, School of Practical Studies, and the Mini Congress. Each school had a dean and an assistant dean. To help equip the churches with trained workers, the publishing board began to offer a College Credit Program through its Sunday Church School Congress. Students could earn college credits through several Christian colleges and seminaries. Through attendance at the congress, the messengers could receive college credits and further their education. The students could earn two credits per course up to a total of fourteen credits.

The black Baptist denomination had returned full circle to the days of the 1880s, a century ago, when the black Baptists had several national

Citizens Bank's New Building, 1985 (NBPBLA)

New Citizens Bank Building, Opening Celebration,
September 22, 1985 (NBPBLA)

organizations before consolidating their organizations and efforts into one association, the National Baptist Convention, 1895. The National Baptist Convention split in 1897 when the Lott Carey Baptist Foreign Mission Convention (LCBFMC) was formed by factions from Virginia, Maryland, and other eastern states. Another split took place when the National Baptist Convention of the United States of America, Incorporated (NBCI), was created in 1915 when some leaders incorporated the organization. The unincorporated National Baptist Convention of America (NBCA) reorganized itself in support of the National Baptist Publishing Board. Then the National Baptist Convention, U.S.A., Incorporated, split in 1961 when the Progressive National Baptist Convention of the United States of America (PNBC) was formed because of differences about the civil rights movement and Martin Luther, King, Jr.'s tactics. Now, 1988, America had four major black Baptist associations: NBCA, NBCI, PNBC, and NMBCA.

The black Christians represented a "Frustrated Fellowship." The petty disputes about congresses, conventions, and publishing boards divided the black Baptists and even the black Methodists in America. If ever the black Christians, particularly the black Baptists, united their forces, black America would never be the same again.

During the late 1980s, an attempt was made to heal the wounds between the black conventions and forge them into a cooperative body. Bishop John Hurst Adams founded the Congress of National Black Churches, Incorporated, a voluntary, non-profit Christian organization designed to promote unity, charity, and fellowship among a coalition of seven historic black denominations. In December 1991, America's black church leaders met in Detroit for the Consultation of the Congress of National Black Churches, Incorporated. The Congress' theme read "Health, Wholeness and Healing in the African-American Community: The Role of the Church - Part II." The churchmen in attendance included ones from the National Missionary Baptist Convention of America, the African Methodist Episcopal Church, Christian Methodist Episcopal Church, Church of God in Christ, National Baptist Convention of America, National Baptist Convention, U. S. A., Inc., and the Progressive National Baptist Convention. Charles W. Butler directed the Congress of National Black Churches, Inc.[82]

The NBPB and the NMBCA energetically supported the Congress of National Black Churches. The NBPB's officers felt comfortable moving among different denominations. The publishing board had affiliated with national and international church and Sunday school organizations since the turn of the century. The NBPB wanted no part of religious politics. Simply, it wanted to serve the churches and the Baptist denomination.

Since 1896 the NBPB had viewed itself as a company to serve all Baptist denominational churches. By 1979 the National Baptist Publishing Board had a 95 page color-catalog, featuring thousands of products and various work-shops and services for sale. The publishing board provided services and printing for the National Missionary Baptist Convention and other black Baptist conventions. But during the 1990s, the NBPB paid special attention to its cooperative programs with the National Missionary Baptist Convention of America.[83]

The 1991 Annual Winter Board Meeting of the National Missionary Baptist Convention of America convened on February 24 in Phoenix, Arizona. The three-day meeting included discussion of the convention's business and that of the NBPB and the National Baptist Sunday Church School and Baptist Training Union Congress. Dr. T. B. Boyd, III presented reports on the latter two organizations. He announced that the Sunday School Congress would be held in June 1992 in Atlanta. The NMBCA's Foreign Mission Board also held its Foreign Mission Conference in Phoenix during the week of February 24, 1991.[84]

By 1991, the attendance at the Sunday School Congress and the NBPB's business had bounced back from the effects of the 1988 denomina-tional split. The NBPB continued to thrive in spite of the terrible economic recession of 1990-92. Dr. T. B. Boyd, III said:

> Our customers have stood by us despite the worsening condition of the nation's economy.... We have been bountifully blessed.... When we are competitive in our prices and offer a superior product - as has traditionally been the policy of the Publishing Board - our customers have always shown an element of pure loyalty. We are most apprecia-tive of this fact.... We pledge at the Publishing Board as we begin a new year that we will give 110 percent of ourselves to meet your needs, to maintain your confidence, and to continue to earn your respect.... We are doing every possible thing in our power to equip churches for the decade of the '90s as well as for the new 21st Century which will be upon us in a matter of eight short years . . . . [85]

In the meantime, the Citizens Bank continued to progress under the leadership of T. B. Boyd, III, chairman of the board of directors. His father, T. B. Boyd, Jr., had won election to the position of chairman of the board of directors of Citizens Savings Bank, the first of his family to hold that position. The Reverends R. H. Boyd and H. A. Boyd had held the position of president of the bank; however, things changed after the bank's holdings grew to a million dollars. Unlike days of old, the president, not the cashier (manager), directed the daily operations of the bank. The presidency became a full-time job. Meredith Gillespie Ferguson succeeded president Henry Allen Boyd as the third president of Citizens Savings Bank and Trust Company, 1959. Ferguson began working at the bank in 1924 as a bookkeeper. Under Ferguson's leadership, the bank moved, in 1974, to the Morris Memorial Building at Charlotte and Fourth Avenue North. The bank's president had to be an experienced, full-time banker. T. B. Boyd, III became chairman of the bank's board in March, 1982. The bank's assets grew to over $30,000,000 by 1984, and a branch bank was opened on Jefferson Street. The Citizens Bank moved into a new high-rise building, the Citizens Plaza, on August 19, 1985.

In 1992, the NMBCA met in Tulsa, Oklahoma during September 8-13 at the Doubletree Hotel and Tulsa Convention Center. The theme of the Convention was "The Gospel of Faith and the Power of God in a World Without Walls." It was one of the best conventions spiritually, numerically, and financially. A 500 voice choir and drill teams filled the convention center with song and the taps of children feet. President Lockridge said: "I know very well why our horizon continues to widen year by year. And so do you. It's because we are a Christian community working fearlessly in the Lord's vineyard. We have no fear, only faith that says if the Lord is with us, nothing or no one can defeat us," according to the Nashville *Pride*, October 2, 1992.

The National Congress underwent tremendous growth due to new ideas and concepts involving College Credits and new Course Topics. Attendance at the 1992 Atlanta Congress exceeded 31,000 messengers from across the nation.

Conclusion

When the National Baptist Publishing Board approached its 96th year, its publications had reached worldwide distribution, and the company had adapted to a technological age. The side enterprises of furniture manufacture, retail sales in colored dolls, and lesser activities had been dropped so that the NBPB could focus on its speciality—publishing religious literature. Its highly educated leaders readily accepted and installed the latest technology in the NBPB's facilities. Now, the National Baptist Publishing Board focused on providing printed materials, training, and services to churches, conventions, Baptist organizations, and the Baptist denomination.

Yet, the NBPB continued tradition and some old practices. The 9:30 morning religious services in the spacious chapel continued. Guest ministers and the board's many staff members who were ministers helped to direct the daily services of prayer, hymns, announcements, and the weekly (Friday) Sunday school lesson. Employees continued to form an in-house choir and participate in the Christmas pageant. And, many visitors continued to take a guided tour of the NBPB's facilities when visiting Nashville.

Few American companies had weathered the storms of time and the battles with opposing human forces like the NBPB did. Few companies had to endure the political and religious battles that the publishing board fought for nearly ten decades. The history of few African-American companies has survived for this period of time.

The National Baptist Publishing Board is indeed a rare and unique entity in our American society, it reflects what faith and dedication can accomplish. Through Richard Henry Boyd and his descendants, the publishing board has served as a source of pride and admiration for **THE FIRST ONE HUNDRED YEARS.**

NBPB's Sunday School Congress

Dr. S. M. Lockridge, President, MNBCA, 1992

One of the largest departments of the National Baptist Publishing Board is the Bindery, where all printed matter is folded, sewed, and made into the finished books or periodicals for use in Baptist Sunday Schools,

The Epilogue

The Epilogue

The life of Richard H. Boyd and the story of the National Baptist Publishing Board are amazing chapters of American black history. Born a slave in 1843, Richard H. Boyd survived human bondage, endured impressment in the Confederate army, and lived through the worst part of Reconstruction in Texas. By the 1870s, he had become well known in parts of Texas where he had engaged widely in church work, helping to organize Baptist associations and church congregations.

Not until 1888 did Richard Henry receive any formal education. He studied at Bishop College for only two years. Boyd left because of lack of funds, and he became disgusted with the white faculty who caused a black student strike in which Boyd became a leading defender of black rights. The student rebellion at Bishop College represented Boyd's first encounter with the northern white missionaries, who, he felt, acted too paternalistic toward black people.

A few years later, 1891, Boyd became an educational secretary for the Negro Baptist Convention in Texas. In the same year, he became involved in a controversy that split the Texas convention and created the General Missionary Baptist Convention. This controversy related to the northern white Baptists, the American Baptist Publication Society and the American Baptist Home Mission Society. Now, 1894, an officer in the "new convention" or General Missionary Baptist Convention of Texas, Boyd became convinced that the northern white Baptists, especially the American Baptist Publication Society, opposed black religious independence and black self-help. Particularly Boyd felt that blacks had to have control over the supply of literature to black churches and Sunday schools.

Really Boyd's conception of a publishing house began in Texas and grew out of his experiences dating to the 1870s. Boyd and others began ordering and distributing Sunday school materials from Nashville's Southern Baptist Convention's Sunday School Board by 1895. By this time, Boyd had become thoroughly convinced that blacks had the ability to publish and distribute their own Sunday school literature without relying on the American Baptist Publication Society, which, heretofore, had monopolized the distribution of Sunday school literature to black Baptist churches throughout America.

Drawing on his past experiences as a slave hand, a servant in the Confederate army, a foreman of a plantation, a cowboy, a lumber mill worker, a preacher, and a state missionary, Boyd boldly planned a publishing house for black Baptists. After gaining the support of his fellow preachers in the Texas and the Palestine Baptist associations, in July 1896, Boyd approached the National Baptist Convention's president, E. C. Morris, and the Southern Baptist Convention's Sunday School Board's head, James M. Frost.

Dr. F. Benjamin Davis, Chairman,
National Baptist Publishing Board

NBPB's Modern Bindery, Nashville

National Baptist Publishing Board
Nashville, Tennessee

With an unbelievably well-planned strategy, the Reverend Boyd secured his own financing and implemented his plans within the short time of five months, September, 1896 to January, 1897. Boyd moved with such deliberate speed that his critics had no time to counter his moves. The National Baptist Publishing Board began solicitation of orders in November 1896 and started its first quarter of sales in January, 1897.

Under Richard Henry Boyd, the publishing board became a reality in 1897, distributing 1,746,500 pieces of Sunday school literature, and spending a mere $5,664.29 for operations. From the beginning, the publishing board and Boyd suffered attacks by persons who opposed the black Baptists publishing their own church literature instead of continuing to rely on the white American Baptist Publication Society. The following year, 1898, Boyd increased the number of letters sent to potential customers (the black Baptist churches), and he and the publishing board realized $19,426.64 in revenues, nearly a fourfold increase over 1897.

Wisely, Boyd and the principal leaders of the publishing board obtained a charter for the National Baptist Publishing Board in 1898. This move made the publishing board permanent. And this charter protected the publishing venture from the factionalism and the politics within the National Baptist Convention.

The Reverend Richard H. Boyd built the early business by combining the work of the publishing board and the Home Mission Board. Also during the company's developmental years, the Reverend Richard H. Boyd affiliated several other businesses with the publishing board. These included church furniture manufacturing, Negro dolls, and book publishing. And the Reverend Boyd conceived the brilliant idea of an annual Sunday School Congress in 1905 to bring the black Sunday school representatives together and to promote the NBPB's publications, materials, and educational services.

The years 1904 to 1909 represented banner years for the National Baptist Publishing Board. The nation's economic depressions had less effect on the publishing board's business during these years. The publishing board increased significantly its number of periodicals and the revenues and expenditures. In 1904 the publishing board printed 7,273,700 periodicals and books and spent $87,769.95 compared to $167,741.19 and 11,717,876 publications for 1909. The next year, however, problems began for the publishing board.

Anti-NBPB factions within the black Baptist convention began a movement to separate the Home Mission Board from Boyd's leadership and thereby separate the Home Mission Board from the publishing board's operations. In 1912, this faction began a more serious movement to incorporate the national convention and force the boards, especially the NBPB, to change their charters to be subordinate to the national convention.

Even during the critical years, 1910-1915, the National Baptist Publishing Board thrived, doing business in the hundreds of thousands of dollars.

Comparatively, the African Methodist Episcopal Church's Sunday School Union publishing house in Nashville did much less in business for 1912.

The publishing board distributed 11,717,876 pieces of literature and books in 1911 but only 8,220,679 pieces of literature in 1914. The amount of money spent by the board increased from $167,741.19 in 1909 to $204,632.40 by 1914. Because of the bitter controversy about whether the National Baptist Convention would control the National Baptist Publishing Board, the publishing board's number of literature pieces dropped to 6,768,063 by 1915 when money spent also dropped to $160,798.33.

Perhaps because the NBPB company became so successful and maintained influence among black Baptists, a large group of black Baptists sided with the publishing board over the 1915 split of the black Baptist denomination. The unincorporated National Baptist Convention of America remained affiliated with the National Baptist Publishing Board. The anti-NBPB faction and others incorporated the National Baptist Convention of the United States of America and organized their own Baptist Sunday School Board to publish literature in Nashville.

NBPB Reports, 1915-1917

Year	Letters	Number Periodicals	Expenses
1915	311,173	6,768,063	$160,798.33
1916	278,214	8,212,131	$152,987.79
1917	275,472	7,266,270	$154,366.46

By allying itself with the National Baptist Convention of America (Unincorporated) in September 1915, the National Baptist Publishing Board preserved its autonomy and rebuilt its business. Money spent and revenues began climbing in 1917.

Richard Henry Boyd conceived and founded the National Baptist Publishing Board in 1896 when few large black businesses existed in America. Under his leadership, the company survived and prospered in spite of turbulent economic times, recurring American economic depressions, and denominational politics. The publishing board weathered the storm of 1915.

No doubt an important factor in the survival and growth of the National Baptist Publishing Board was its continuity and stability of leadership. For nearly one hundred years, the company's board of directors selected the chief executive from the Boyd family. And each of the Boyds, only four during this one hundred year period, received careful training and education by his predecessor, keeping in mind the possibility of taking charge of the business. Additionally the board chairmen and directors served long years and had great experience dealing with the publishing board's business and the religious politics that surrounded it.

Richard H. Boyd spent his energy trying to sustain and rebuild the publishing board during the Reconstruction Years, 1916-1922. His efforts proved to be highly successful.

The NBPB continued to prosper and expand after Boyd's death in 1922. Secretary-Treasurer Henry Allen Boyd brought the publishing board into focus during his administration, 1922-1959, thereby expanding the board's market among black Baptist churches in the United States and abroad. His successor and nephew, Theophilus B. Boyd, Jr., built a new modern facility and added high speed, color machines to make the National Baptist Publishing Board's materials more attractive and competitive. T. B. Boyd, Jr.'s son, the succeeding President and Chief Executive Officer of the National Baptist Publishing Board, Theophilus B. Boyd, III, modernized the company's business strategies, expanded its product line, and marketed aggressively the board's products in America and abroad.

After Henry Allen Boyd became secretary-treasurer of the National Baptist Publishing Board in 1922, by 1930, the National Baptist Publishing Board printed some 12,705,359 pieces of literature and books, an amount of literature that surpassed the peak year of 1911, and the budget for the publishing board totaled $314,387.72, one-third more than for the budget of 1914. The board continued its work in Panama. The board of directors divided itself into two subcommittees (executive and lessons) to direct efficiently the work. The plant now had seven buildings at Second and Locust Streets. The publishing board continued to sponsor the Sunday School Congress, the Camp Fire Girls (replaced the Doll Clubs), a band, and the Boy Cadets. The *Union Review* continued to lose money, but the National Baptist Publishing Board believed that this Baptist newspaper was an instrument of incalculable worth to the Baptist denomination.

Between 1959 and 1979, the Reverend Richard H. Boyd's grandson, T. B. Boyd, Jr. ably led the NBPB toward greater heights. The company built a modern plant in 1974. The Sunday School Congress expanded into a huge national event. The products and processes of the NBPB became modern and sophisticated.

Boyd, Jr.'s son, T. B. Boyd, III took the company's reins in 1979. He modernized the company's business practices and updated its products, expanding the NBPB's business into several services. He improved the board's Christian education classes and packaged them to include college credits and on-site workshops. The Congress grew even larger.

The National Baptist Publishing Board continued to grow and prosper, and the corporation enjoyed stable, experienced leadership that successfully adapted the NBPB's products and services to current market and political (religious) conditions. Few corporations in America thrived nearly one hundred years.

When the American economy shifted from manufacturing to services and technology in America, the National Baptist Publishing Board's leadership wisely diversified the NBPB's products into printing, publishing, and religious educational services. Particularly, T. B. Boyd, III trained the focus of the company more on services, expanding the product line into several training workshops using high technology including video tapes and computers.

After enduring the struggles of nearly a century, the National Baptist Publishing Board continued to grow. The $5,664 operation of 1897 became a multi-million dollar company by 1992.

Reference Index

Quotations

Because the Negro by unjust legislation and political discrimination is robbed of every vestige of self-government, his religious and benevolent institutions are his most important agencies for uplifting the race.—Richard H. Boyd

The Negro must furnish his Sunday school with religious knowledge, his choirs with music, and his firesides and parlors with wholesome literature, written and manufactured by his own energy. The literature that is best for the Caucasian of today is not always best for our children, under the present [Jim Crow] crisis.—Richard H. Boyd

Whatever is taught in the Sunday schools of this generation will be the doctrine of the church in the next generation.—Richard H. Boyd

Prayer is the grace that seasoneth all. Prayer moves the hand that moves the universe; it knocks till the door opens; and like Jonathan's bow returns not empty.—Richard H. Boyd

Since 1896, when the National Baptist Convention ordered its Home Mission Board to begin the publication of a series of Sunday school literature, there has been the 'battle royal' waged in the Negro Baptist camp, as to the wisdom of the Convention passing such an order and the propriety of the [National Baptist Publishing] Board attempting to execute it.—Richard H. Boyd

The white publishing societies have been the 'lazzaroni' or poor houses for Negroes so long that their [blacks] intellect has become impoverished. For want of mental exercise, we have produced only a few acceptable authors; we must produce more. We must make books and write literature in order to furnish this mental exercise and stimulate its corresponding mental activity.—Richard H. Boyd

The race that desires to make a place in the economy of men and things to stand forth amid the activities of other progressive peoples, and have its name and its deeds fully and accurately recorded in history, must make a literature that is *distinctively* and *peculiarly* its own.—Richard H. Boyd

Banking is the highest, most honorable and painstaking business of higher civilization.—Richard H. Boyd

Because the National Baptist Publishing Board is operating for the sole purpose of giving service to race and denomination, every phase of religious life has been considered. The interest of the institution is naturally centered on the things pertaining to religion and spirituality, and that interest is deep and abiding. 'Service' is the keynote of the institution.—Henry Allen Boyd

. . . It is in the nature of a labor of love, because we are all committed to the task of carrying on every phase of this activity so that it will reflect credit upon the denomination, because the institution known as the National Baptist Publishing Board's plant, is a part of our great denominational structure. I am conscious of the fact that it is, so to speak, the apple of the eye of millions of religious workers who make up the constituency of this body of Missionary Baptists. It is also the pride of people who are not Baptists, because they look upon it as a race institution. Its founder and builder, the late Richard H. Boyd, saw it in this way, because he too had but one aim in view, and that was to do something worthwhile, something that would stand, something that would be monumental not only in its effort to do good, but that would be lasting, so that this as well as unborn generations might look upon it as an institution, a business concern, a religious plant as an expression of what we can do in our day and generations as constructive builders, organizers and operators of a plant that is known throughout the world today. . . .—Henry Allen Boyd

. . . if we would be emancipated, Christian education is the process, basically, by which it is done.—T. B. Boyd, Jr.

It is a day of peace, a day of tranquility, a day of progress, and a day of recommitment to the very principles that our forefathers laid down before us. Although the mantle has fallen on my shoulders I will not let it hit the ground.—Theophilus B. Boyd, III

The life of Richard Henry Boyd and the story of the National Baptist Publishing Board represent amazing chapters in America's black social, business, and religious history. We are fortunate that the publishing board preserved its history to serve as a lesson for present generations and a foundation for the future.—Bobby L. Lovett

History does not repeat itself. But those who fail to learn the valuable lessons of history are condemned to repeat that history.—Bobby L. Lovett

Reference Index

Preface

1. Ina S. Lambin and L. L. Owens, *The Faith They Kept* (Nashville, 1954), 59; James M. Frost, *Sunday School Board, History and Work* (Nashville, 1914), 10-11.

2. Frost, *Sunday School Board, History and Work*, 10-11.

3. Ibid.

4. Ibid., 11-13.

5. Ibid., 11-14

6. *Encyclopedia of Southern Baptists* (Nashville, 1958), vol. 1, 512-513.

7. Donald F. Joyce, *Gatekeepers of Black Culture: Black Owned Book Publishing in the United States, 1817-1981* (Westport, Ct., 1983), 75, 96, 101, 105, 138, 200-01; Carter G. Woodson, *The History of the Negro Church*, 3rd ed. (Washington, 1921, 1945, 1951), 178, 231-35, 238, 273. Note: Woodson, the father of modern African-American history, called Boyd "the efficient Dr. R. H. Boyd" (238); R. H. Boyd and the National Baptist Publishing Board are called the "most successful black enterprises in the South" by Loren Schweninger, *Black Property Owners in the South, 1790-1915* (Urbana, Ill., 1990), 219.

8. Ibid., Woodson, *The History of the Negro Church*

9. *Ninth Annual Report, American Baptist Missionary Convention, 1849, Philadelphia* (New York, 1849), 1-21; Washington, *Frustrated Fellowship*, 39-40.

10. James M. Washington, *Frustrated Fellowship: The Black Baptist Quest for Social Power* (Macon, Ga., 1986), 55, 80, 84.

11. *Report of the Third Annual Meeting of the Consolidated American Baptist Missionary Convention, 1869, Paducah, Kentucky* (New York, 1869), 10, 20; Washington, *Frustrated Fellowship*, 80, 84.

12. *Thirty-First Annual Meeting of the American Baptist Missionary Convention, 1871, Brooklyn, New York* (New York, 1872), 31; Washington,
Frustrated Fellowship, 117, 125, 126-131.

13. Samuel W. Bacote, ed., *Who's Who Among the Colored Baptists of the United States* (New York, 1980) 185-189.

14. *Journal of the American National Baptist Convention, 1890, 1891* (Louisville, 1891), 6, 7, 27, 35-36; Washington, *Frustrated Fellowship*, 77-76, 145-146.

15. *Journal of the American National Baptist Convention, 1890, 1891*, 6, 7, 27, 35-36.

16. Sixth Anniversary of the American National Baptist Convention *Dallas, September 19-23, 1891* (Louisville, 1891), 42; *Journal of the First Annual Meeting of the National Baptist Educational Convention, Savannah, Georgia September 20-21, 1892* (Savannah, 1892), 1-10; Davidson County, Tennessee, Will Book No. 4, 1922-1924, R. H. Boyd, Last Will and Testament, August 20, 1922, 98.

17. William H. Brackney, *The Baptists* (Westport, Ct., 1988), 139-140; see also Miles M. Fisher, "Lott Carey, The Colonizing Missionary," *Journal of Negro History*, 7 (1922), 389; Leroy Fitts, *Lott Carey: First Black Missionary of Africa* (Valley Forge, 1978); William A. Poe, "Lott Carey: Man of Purchased Freedom," *Church History*, 39 (1970), 49-61; Benjamin Brawley, *A Social History of the American Negro* (New York, 1921), 68, 180, 181, 185; David W. Wills and R. Newman, eds., *Black Apostles At Home and*

Abroad: Afro-Americans and the Christian Mission from the Revolution to Reconstruction (Boston, 1982).

Reference Index

Chapter 1

Richard Henry Boyd, Founder: The Years of Struggle, 1843-1896

1. R. H. Boyd, *The Story of the National Baptist Publishing Board* (Nashville, 1915), 1-50.

2. Ibid., *National Baptist Union-Review,* Nashville, April 10, 1915.

3. James C. Ballagh, *A History of Slavery in Virginia* (Baltimore, 1902), 168, 169, 170.

4. Dunbar Rowland, edited, *Encyclopedia of Mississippi History,* 2 vols. (Madison, Wis., 1907, vol. I, 134-37; also see Jane T. Censer, "Southwestern Migration Among North Carolina Planter Families: The Disposition to Emigrate," *Journal of Southern History,* 62 (1991), 407-426, and Barnes F. Lanthrop, "Migration in East Texas, 1835-1860: A Study From the United States Census," Texas State Library (Austin, 1949), for additional background on the migration of slave owners.

5. John R. Skates, *Mississippi History* (Washington, 1979), 76, 94; Clement Eaton, *A History of the Old South: The Emergence of a Reluctant Nation,* 3rd ed. (New York, 1975), 209, 211, 213, 214, 235; see also Elizabeth Silverthorne, *Plantation Life in Texas* (College Station, 1986); *National Baptist Union-Review,* April 10, 1915.

6. W.E.B. Dubois, *Black Reconstruction in America, 1860-1880* (New York, 1933, 1962, 1977), 552-562.

7. See Frederic Bancroft, *Slave Trading in the Old South* (Baltimore, 1931); Charles Sellers, *A Synopsis of American History*, 3rd ed. (Chicago, 1974).

8. See Frederick L. Olmstead, *The Slave States*, Harvey Wish, ed. (New York, 1959); Randolph B. Campbell, *An Empire for Slavery: The Peculiar Institution in Texas* (Baton Rouge, 1989), 306.

9. Paul D. Escott, *Slavery Remembered: A Record of Twentieth Century Slave Narratives* (Chapel Hill, 1979), 26.

10. Ibid., 29.

11. Nashville *Globe*, May 22, 1908; see also Bromfield L. Ridley, *Battles and Sketches of the Army of Tennessee* (Mexico, Mo., 1906), 236, 245.

12. DuBois, *Black Reconstruction in America*, 533, 558; *Globe*, May 22, 1908.

13. DuBois, *Black Reconstruction in America*, 533, 558.

14. Escott, *Slavery Remembered*, 135, 163; see also Alwys Bass, *Black Texans: A History of Negroes in Texas, 1528-1971* (Austin, 1973); and Charles W. Ramsdell, *Reconstruction in Texas* (Austin, 1970).

15. Larry Elkins, "Richard Henry Boyd: A Portrait, 1843-1922," M. S. thesis, Tennessee State University, 1972, 1-21; see also J. M. Carroll, *A History of Texas Baptists* (Dallas, 1923); Nashville *Globe*, April 12, 1940.

16. See biographical sketch of R. H. Boyd in E. C. Morris, *Sermons, Addresses and Reminiscences and Important Correspondence* (Nashville, 1901), 1-16, 177, 278-279; also see *Texas: An Informal Biography* (New York, 1945).

17. Morris, *Sermons, Addresses and Reminiscences and Important Correspondence*, 278-279; Elkins, "Richard Henry Boyd: A Portrait, 1843-1922," 1-4.

18. Ibid., Clement Richardson, ed., *The National Cyclopedia of the Colored Race* (Montgomery, Ala., 1919), 44, 366, 410, 415, 416, 575, "R. H. Boyd," 414-415. See also A. S. Crabb, *Leadership in Nashville* (Nashville, 1961), 6; R. H. Boyd was among 116 men who were selected out of 154 persons for this book, a who's who in Nashville, blacks and whites. See also William Waller, *Nashville, 1900 to 1910* (Nashville, 1972), 24, 273, 312; *Union-Review*, March 20, 1937.

19. *The Story of the National Baptist Publishing Board*, 15, 16-17, 19, 20; Boyd biographical sketch in Morris, *Sermons, Addresses and Reminiscences and Important Correspondence*, 1-16, 177; see Boyd to T. P. Bell, Nashville, May 3, 1915, Boyd to J. M. Frost, Nashville, May 3, 1915, and Frost to Boyd, Nashville, May 7, 1915, NBPBLA.

20. *Globe*, February 12, 1909.

21. RHB to T. P. Bell, San Antonio, March 15, 1895, National Baptist Publishing Board Library and Archives, Nashville (NBPBLA).

22. Ibid., *The Story of the National Baptist Publishing Board*, 15-17, 18, 19, 20.

23. Ibid., JMF to RHB, Nashville, September 26, 1895, NBPBLA.

24. TPB to RHB, Nashville, May 2, 1895, NBPBLA.

25. Ibid., see *Index to Annuals, Southern Baptist Convention, 1845-1953*, Southern Baptist Historical Library and Archives, Historical Commission, Southern Baptist Convention, Nashville;

Proceedings of the Southern Baptist Convention, Fortieth Annual Session, Fiftieth Year, May 10-14, 1895, Washington, D. C. (Atlanta, 1895), 42-43.

26. RHB to Palestine Association, San Antonio, April 25, 1895, NBPBLA.

27. RHB to TPB, San Antonio, November 23, 1895, NBPBLA; Washington, *Frustrated Fellowship: The Black Baptist Quest for Social Power,* 173-176, 185.

28. RHB to TPB, San Antonio, November 23, 1895, NBPBLA.

29. Ibid.

30. RHB to JMF, San Antonio, April 26, 1896, NBPBLA; *The Story of the National Baptist Publishing Board,* 15-17, 18, 19, 20-21, 25.

31. Bacote, ed., *Who's Who Among the Colored Baptists of the United States,* 14-17; Milton C. Sernett, ed., *Afro-American Religious History: A Documentary Witness* (Durham, N. C., 1985), 272-284; Morris, *Sermons, Addresses and Reminiscences and Important Correspondence,* 176-179 .

32. *The Story of the National Baptist Publishing Board,* 1-50; *Journal of the Fifth Session of the National Baptist Convention, St. Louis, Missouri, September 1896* (St. Louis, 1896), 1-25; see *Journal of the Sixth Annual Session of the National Baptist Convention, Boston, September, 15- 20, 1897* (Louisville, 1898), 7, 29, 31.

33. Bacote, *Who's Who Among the Colored Baptists of the United States,* 235-237.

34. Ibid., *Journal of the Fifth Session of the National Baptist Convention, St. Louis, Missouri, September 1896,* 1-25.

35. *Journal of the Sixth Annual Session of the National Baptist Convention*, 1897, 15-20; *Cyclopedia of the Negro Race*, 575-76.

36. *Cyclopedia of the Negro Race*, 475-76.

37. *The Story of the National Baptist Publishing Board*, 1-50.

Reference Index

Chapter 2

The Creation and the Success of the NBPB, 1896-1905

1. *The Story*, 43-49; see also Sammie S. Caruthers, "A History of the Two Outstanding Negro Baptist Publishing Houses of the Nation Located in Nashville Tennessee," M. S. thesis, Tennessee A and I State College, 1944.

2. *The Story*, 43-49.

3. Ibid., Bacote, *Who's Who Among the Colored Baptists in the United States*, 229-233.

4. Ibid.

5. Ibid.

6. *The Story*, 42-43.

7. Ibid., 49-50.

8. Ibid., 50-51.

9. Ibid., 53-56; RHB to JMF, San Antonio, October 31, 1896, NBPBLA.

10. *The Story,* 59.

11. Ibid., 61.

12. Ibid., 64-65.

13. Ibid.

14. Ibid., 69.

15. *The Story,* 71.

16. Ibid.

17. Ibid., 74.

18. Ibid., 70-71.

19. Ibid., 77.

20. Ibid., 79.

21. *The Story,* 80.

22. Ibid.

23. Ibid.

24. Ibid.

25. Ibid., 80-83.

26. Ibid., 83-85.

27. Ibid., 85, 88.

28. Ibid.

29. Ibid.

30. Ibid., 88-90.

31. *The Story,* 90.

32. Ibid.

33. Ibid., 90-92.

34. Ibid.

35. Ibid.

36. Ibid.

37. *The Story,* 90-93; Martin Luther King, Jr. headed the Dexter Avenue Baptist Church during the 1950s and the Montgomery bus boycott.

38. *The Story,* 96-97.

39. Ibid.

40. Ibid., 100.

41. AJR to JMF, Philadelphia, December 1, 1896, in Appendix C, "Sixth Annual Report of the Sunday School Board," *Proceedings of the Southern Baptist Convention, Forty-Second Annual Session, Fifty-Second Year, May 7- 10, 1897, Wilmington, North Carolina* (Atlanta, 1897).

42. JMF to AJR, Nashville, December 8, 1896, Ibid.

43. Ibid., *The Story,* 104.

44. Ibid., 106.

45. Ibid.

46. Ibid.

47. Ibid., 108.

48. Ibid., 110.

49. *Journal of the Eighth Session of the National Baptist Convention, Kansas City, Missouri, September 14-18, 1898* (Nashville, 1898), 1-55.

50. *Journal of the Ninth Annual Session of the National Baptist Convention, Nashville, Tennessee, September 13-19, 1899* (Nashville, 1899), 3, 12-13.

51. *Journal of the Tenth Annual Session of the National Baptist Convention, Richmond, Virginia, September 12-17, 1900* (Nashville, 1900), 76, 79; *National Baptist Union,* November 30, 1901.

52. *Journal of the Tenth Annual Session of the National Baptist Convention, Richmond, Virginia, September 12-17, 1900,* 76-79.

53. Ibid.

54. Ibid.

55. Ibid., 92-93.

56. Ibid., *Official Program, Tenth Annual Session, National Baptist Convention, Richmond, Virginia, September 12-17, 1900* (Nashville, 1900), 28- 29.

57. *Official Program, Tenth Annual Session, National Baptist Convention, Richmond, Virginia, September 12-17, 1900,* 31.

58. *The Story,* 119-123.

59. Ibid., 124-126; *Journal of the Eighth Session of the National Baptist Convention, Kansas City, Missouri, September 14-18, 1898,* 34.

60. Ibid.

61. *Journal of the Tenth Annual Session of the National Baptist Convention, Richmond, Virginia, September 12-17, 1900,* 108.

62. Ibid., 104-105, 115.

63. Ibid., 184.

64. Ibid.

65. *Journal of the Annual Session of the National Baptist Convention, Cincinnati, Ohio, September 11-16, 1901* (Nashville, 1901), 11-19; see also *Proceedings of the Southern Baptist Convention, Forty-First Annual Session, Fifty-First Year, May 8-12,* 1896, *Chattanooga, Tennessee* (Atlanta, 1896), 33.

66. *Journal of the Woman's Convention, Auxiliary of the National Baptist Convention, Cincinnati, Ohio, September 11-16, 1901* (Nashville, 1901), 17-19, 36.

67. *Journal of the Annual Session of the National Baptist Convention, Cincinnati, Ohio, September 11-16, 1901* (Nashville, 1901), 11-19, 76; *Journal of the Twenty-Second Session of the National Baptist Convention, Birmingham, Alabama, September 17-22, 1902* (Nashville, 1902), 26.

68. *Journal of the Twenty-Second Session of the National Baptist Convention, Birmingham, Alabama; September 17-22, 1902* (Nashville, 1902), 26.

69. Ibid., 58-59.

70. Ibid., 64.

71. *Journal of the Fifth Annual Assembly of the Woman's Convention, Austin, Texas, September 14-19, 1904* (Nashville, 1904), Austin's 2nd Baptist Church, 304, 322, 327, 384.

72. *Journal of the Third Annual Assembly of the Woman's Convention, Birmingham, Alabama, September 17-22, 1902* (Nashville, 1902), 17, 19; Nashville *Globe,* May 24, June 21, 1902.

73. *The Story,* 40-61.

74. Ibid.

75. Ibid; *Journal of the Twenty-Fourth Annual Session of the National Baptist Convention, Austin, Texas, September 14-19, 1904* (Nashville, 1905), 113.

76. Ibid.

77. *Journal of the Third Annual Assembly of the Woman's Convention, Birmingham, Alabama, September 17-22, 1902,* 17, 19; *National Baptist Union,* July 19, September 27, 1902.

78. *National Baptist Union,* September 27, 1902.

79. Ibid., December 13, 1902.

80. Ibid.

81. *National Baptist Union,* September 12, 1903.

82. Ibid., March 14, 1903.

83. Ibid., February 21, 1903.

84. *Journal of the Third Annual Assembly of the Woman's Convention, Birmingham, Alabama, September 17-22, 1902,* 17, 19, 21, 29.

85. Ibid.

86. See the *Journal of the Third Annual Assembly of the Woman's Convention, Birmingham, Alabama, September 17-22, 1902; Journal of the Twenty-Third Annual Session of the National*

Baptist Convention, Philadelphia, Pennsylvania, September 16-21, 1903 (Nashville, 1903), 24, 100.

87. *National Baptist Union,* December 6, 1902, February 21, 1903.

88. Ibid., December 20, 1902.

89. See the *Journal of the Twenty-Fourth Annual Session of the National Baptist Convention, Austin, Texas, September 14-19, 1904; Journal of the Twenty-Third Annual Session of the National Baptist Convention, Philadelphia, Pennsylvania, September 16-21, 1903,* 87.

90. *Journal of the Twenty-Third Annual Session of the National Baptist Convention, Philadelphia, Pennsylvania, September 16-21, 1903,* 87, 88-89, 91.

91. Ibid.

92. *The Story,* 111, 112, 117, 127-128, 131, 133; *Journal of the Twenty-Third Annual Session of the National Baptist Convention, Philadelphia, Pennsylvania, September 16-21, 1903,* 87, 91.

93. *Journal of the Twenty-Third Annual Session of the National Baptist Convention, Philadelphia, Pennsylvania, September 16-21, 1903,* 87, 91.

94. *Journal of the Twenty-Fourth Annual Session of the National Baptist Convention, Austin, Texas, September 14-19, 1904,* 113.

95. Ibid.

96. Ibid., 94.

97. Ibid., 113.

98. Ibid., 100, 112, 149, 157-158.

99. Ibid.

100. *National Baptist Union,* October 7, 1904.

101. *Journal of the Twenty-Fifth Annual Session of the National Baptist Convention, Chicago, Illinois, October 25-30, 1905* (Nashville, 1905), 29, 78-79, 96-99, 155.

102. Ibid., 162.

103. Ibid., 162-163.

Reference Index

Chapter 3

The NBPB and the National Baptist Convention, 1906-1915

1. *National Baptist Union,* August 6, 1902; *Globe,* January 1, 1907.

2. *Globe,* December 6, 1907.

3. *Journal of the National Baptist Convention, 27th Annual Session, Washington, D. C., September 11-16, 1907* (Nashville, 1908), 98-100, 123, 150.

4. Ibid., 37; *Journal of Eighth Annual Session of the Assembly of the Woman's Convention, Washington, D. C., September 19-23, 1907* (Nashville, 1908), 159, 178-179, 184, 209.

5. *Journal of the National Baptist Convention, 27th Annual Session, Washington, D. C., September 11-16, 1907,* 98-100, 123, 150; *Journal of Eighth Annual Session of the Assembly of the Woman's Convention, Washington, D. C., September 19-23, 1907,* 159, 178-179, 184, 209; *The Story,* 102-105.

6. *Journal of the National Baptist Convention, 27th Annual Session, Washington, D. C., September 11-16, 1907*, 123.

7. Ibid.

8. *Globe*, January 3, 1908.

9. *The Story*, 102-105; see also *Journal of the National Baptist Convention, 28th Annual Session, Lexington, Kentucky, September 16-21, 1908* (Nashville, 1909), 45.

10. Ibid., 27-29.

11. Ibid., 27-29, 130-139.

12. *Globe*, January 9, 1909.

13. *Journal of the National Baptist Convention, 29th Annual Session, Columbus, Ohio, September 15-20, 1909* (Nashville, 1910), 106-120, 123; *Journal of the National Baptist Convention, 30th Annual Session, New Orleans, Louisiana, September 14-19, 1910* (Nashville, 1911), 109, 110, 113, 151-187. Inventory of the NBPB, August 31, 1909, and 14th Annual Report of the NBPB, September 11, 1909-August 31, 1910, NBPBLA.

14. Ibid.

15. Ibid.

16. Ibid.

17. *Journal of the National Baptist Convention, 29th Annual Session, Columbus, Ohio, September 15-20, 1909*, 123.

18. Ibid., 110, 161, 169.

19. Ibid., *Globe,* January 9, October 15, 1909.

20. *Globe,* January 7, 1910.

21. *Globe,* February 4, 11, 25, March 18, 1910.

22. Ibid.

23. *Globe,* March 18, 1910.

24. *Journal of the National Baptist Convention, 30th Annual Session, New Orleans, Louisiana, September 14-19, 1910,* 110, 113, 115, 124, 151-187; *Globe,* May 26, 1911.

25. *Globe,* January 12, September 8, 1911.

26. *Journal of the National Baptist Convention, 31st Annual Session, Pittsburgh, Pennsylvania, September 13-18, 1911* (Nashville, 1912), 36, 38; *Journal of the National Baptist Convention, 32nd Annual Session, Houston, Texas, September 11-16, 1912* (Nashville, 1913), 51-53.

27. *Journal of the National Baptist Convention, 31st Annual Session, Pittsburgh, Pennsylvania, September 13-18, 1911,* 38.

28. *Globe,* July 14, 1911.

29. *The Story,* 102-105.

30. *Journal of the National Baptist Convention, 32nd Annual Session, Houston, Texas, September 11-16, 1912,* 101, 103; *Annual of the Northern Baptist Convention, 1912, 5th Meeting, Des Moines, Iowa, May 22-29, 1912* (Philadelphia, 1912), 22, 58.

31. *Journal of the National Baptist Convention, 32nd Annual Session, Houston, Texas, September 11-16, 1912,* 101, 103.

32. *Journal of the National Baptist Convention, 32nd Annual Session, Houston, Texas, September 11-16, 1912,* 101, 103, 107-108.

33. *Globe,* October 15, 1909; *Journal of the National Baptist Convention, 27th Annual Session, Washington, September 11-16, 1907,* 112.

34. Ibid., 112-113; *Journal of the National Baptist Convention, 32nd Annual Session, Houston, Texas, September 11-16, 1912,* 101, 103; *Journal of the 34th Annual Session of the National Baptist Convention, Philadelphia, Pennsylvania, September 9-14, 1914,* (Nashville, 1914), 47, 54-55.

35. *Globe,* June 9, 1911.

36. Seventh Annual Session of *the Sunday School Congress, Birmingham, Alabama, June 9-14, 1912* (Nashville, 1912), 17, 19-20.

37. Ibid.

38. *Globe,* February 16, September 6, 1912.

39. *Globe,* September 6, 1912.

40. *Journal of the National Baptist Convention, 32nd Annual Session, Houston, Texas, September 11-16, 1912,* 101, 103.

41. *Journal of the National Baptist Convention, 32nd Annual Session, Houston, Texas, September 11-16, 1912,* 101, 103; *Globe,* May 31, 1912.

42. *Journal of the National Baptist Convention, 32nd Annual Session, Houston, Texas, September 11-16, 1912,* 53, 101, 103.

43. Bacote, *Who's Who Among the Colored Baptists of the United States,* 181, 233-234.

44. See *Journal of the National Baptist Convention, 32nd Annual Session, Houston, Texas, September 11-16, 1912,* 101-113.

45. Ibid., *Journal of the 34th Annual Session of the National Baptist Convention, Philadelphia, Pennsylvania, September 9-14, 1914,* 47, 54-55.

46. Ibid., 63-64.

47. *Annual of the Northern Baptist Convention, 1912, 5th Meeting, Des Moines, Iowa, May 22-29, 1912,* 174.

48. Ibid.

49. *Journal of the 34th Annual Session of the National Baptist Convention, Philadelphia, Pennsylvania, September 9-14, 1914,* 47, 54-55.

50. *Journal of the 34th Annual Session of the National Baptist Convention, Philadelphia, Pennsylvania, September 9-14, 1914,* 47, 54-55; *Annual of the Northern Baptist Convention, 1912, 5th Meeting, Des Moines, Iowa, May 22-29, 1912,* 174-175.

51. *Journal of the National Baptist Convention, 32nd Annual Session, Houston, Texas, September 11-16, 1912,* 53, 101, 103.

52. Ibid., *16th Annual Report of the National Baptist Publishing Board, September 1, 1911 - August 31, 1912* (Nashville, 1912), 91-106, NBPBLA.

53. *Globe,* January 3, 17, February 7, March 14, 21, May 2, July 25, 1913.

54. *Globe,* July 25, August 15, September 12, 1913; see also *Journal of the National Baptist Convention, 33rd Annual Session, Nashville, September 17-22, 1913* (Nashville, 1914); *Report of the Committee Upon the Propriety of the Incorporation of the National Baptist Convention, Nashville, Tennessee, September 17-22, 1913* (Nashville, 1913), 22.

55. *Globe,* July 25, September 26, 1913.

56. *Journal of the 34th Annual Session of the National Baptist Convention, Philadelphia, Pennsylvania, September 9-14,*

1914, 39-41; *Journal of the National Baptist Convention, 30th Annual Session, New Orleans, Louisiana, September 14-19, 1910*, 46.

57. *Journal of the 34th Annual Session of the National Baptist Convention, Philadelphia, Pennsylvania, September 9-14, 1914*, 39-41.

58. Ibid.

59. Ibid.

60. Ibid., 96.

61. Ibid., 96-98; *National Baptist Union-Review*, October 10, 1914.

62. *National Baptist Union-Review*, October 10, 1914.

63. Ibid., 1, 16.

64. Ibid.

65. Ibid.

66. Ibid.

67. Ibid.

68. Ibid.

69. National *Baptist Union-Review*, October 17, 1914, 8, and October 24, 1914.

70. Ibid., October 24, and October 31, 1914, 1-10.

71. Ibid., November 7, 1914, 12, 13.

72. Ibid.

73. Ibid.

74. *National Baptist Union-Review,* November 28, 1914, 1.

75. Ibid., 1, 14.

76. Ibid., November 14, 1914, 1.

77. Ibid., October 31, and November 7, 1914, 1-10.

78. Ibid., and December 5, 1914.

79. *National Baptist Union-Review,* December 26, January 9, 1915, 1-10.

80. Ibid.

81. Owen D. Pelt and Ralph L. Smith, *The Story of the National Baptists* (New York, 1961), 108, 111-113; Washington, *Frustrated Fellowship: The Black Baptist Quest for Social Power,* 143.

82. *Globe,* January 16, 1915.

83. *Minutes of the National Baptist Convention (Unincorporated), Atlanta, Georgia, September 5-11, 1917* (Nashville, 1917), 68.

84. Ibid., *Journal of the National Baptist Convention, 35th Annual Session, Chicago, Illinois, September 8-3, 1915* (Philadelphia, 1916), 21.

85. *National Baptist Union-Review,* Nashville, January 16, 30, February 6, 20, 1915.

86. *National Baptist Union-Review,* February 6, 1915.

87. Ibid., June 26, 1915.

88. *National Baptist Union-Review,* February 13, 1915.

89. Ibid., February 27, 1915.

90. Ibid.

91. Ibid., May 13, 1915.

92. *National Baptist Union-Review,* March 27, 1915.

93. *Union-Review,* April 24, 1915.

94. Ibid., April 29, 1915.

95. Ibid., April 24, 1915.

96. Ibid., May 15, 1915.

97. Ibid., 5.

98. Ibid.

99. *Annual of the Northern Baptist Convention, May 19-26, 1915, Los Angeles, California* (Philadelphia, 1915), 317, 1015, 1019; *Annual of the Northern Baptist Convention, May 6-13, 1910; Chicago, Illinois* (Philadelphia, 1910), "Eighty-Sixth Annual Report of the American Baptist Publication Society," 1-51.

100. *Annual of the Northern Baptist Convention, May 19-26, 1915, Los Angeles, California,* 317; *Annual of the Northern Baptist Convention, May 21-27, 1908, Oklahoma City, Oklahoma* (St. Louis, 1908), "Abstract of the Eighty-Fourth Annual Report of the Board of Managers of the American Baptist Publication Society," by A. J. Rowland, Corresponding Secretary, 63-74; *Annual of the Northern Baptist Convention, June 25-July 2, 1909, Portland, Oregon* (Philadelphia, 1909), "Eighty-Fifth Annual Report of the American Baptist Publication Society," 1-49; *Annual of the*

Northern Baptist Convention, May 17-23, 1916, Minneapolis, Minnesota (Philadelphia, 1916), 324.

101. *National Baptist Union-Review,* July 10, 1915.

102. Ibid., August 14, 1915.

103. Ibid., July 31, 1915.

104. Ibid.

105. *Union-Review,* August 28, 1915.

106. Ibid.

107. Ibid., February 2, 20, 1915.

108. Ibid., *Journal of the National Baptist Convention, 35th Annual Session, Chicago, Illinois, September 8-3,* 1915, 21, 31, 51-79.

109. *Journal of the National Baptist Convention (Unincorporated), Kansas City, Missouri, September 6-11, 1916* (Nashville, 1917), 3-7, 59-61.

110. Lewis G. Jordan, *Negro Baptist History* (Nashville, 1930), 12, 49.

111. *National Baptist Union-Review,* Nashville, October 5, August 10, 1918.

112. *National Baptist Union-Review,* July 15, 1916.

Reference Index

Chapter 4

Struggle for Survival: National Baptist Publishing Board,
1916-1922

1. *Baptist Voice,* January 22, June 4, 1921; *Journal of the National Baptist Convention of America (Unincorporated), Atlanta, Georgia, September 5-11, 1917,* 41, 48.

2. *Journal of the National Baptist Convention, 35th Annual Session, Chicago, Illinois, September 3-8, 1915*, 1-10.

3. Pelt and Smith, *The Story of the National Baptists*, 108, 111-113.

4. *Annual of the Southern Baptist Convention, 1919, Atlanta, Georgia, May 14-18, 1919* (Nashville, 1919), 433; see also *Annual of the Northern Baptist Convention, 1916, Ninth Meeting, Minneapolis,Minnesota, May 17-23, 1916* (Philadelphia, 1916), 859-996; *Annual of the Northern Baptist Convention, 1910, Third Meeting, Chicago, Illinois, May 6-13, 1910* (Philadelphia, 1910); *Annual of the Northern Baptist Convention, 1912, Fifth Meeting, Des Moines, Iowa, May 22-29, 1912* (Philadelphia, 1912), 60-61, and ABPS's report, 1-4.

5. *Journal of the National Baptist Convention (Unincorporated), Kansas City, Missouri, September 6-11, 1916* (Nashville, 1917), 3-7; see also *Sixteenth Annual Session of the Woman's Auxiliary Convention, National Baptist Convention (Unincorporated), Kansas City, Missouri, September 6-11, 1916* (Nashville, 1917).

6. *Journal of the National Baptist Convention (Unincorporated), Kansas City, Missouri, September 6-11, 1916*, 20-22, 35-37, 41, 193.

7. Ibid., 57.

8. Ibid.

9. Ibid.

10. *National Baptist Union-Review,* June 15, 1918; *National Baptist Voice*, May 21, 1921.

11. Ibid., 63-64, 73-74, 75.

12. Ibid., 80-81, 99-101.

13. Ibid.

14. *National Baptist Union-Review,* January 6, 1917.

15. Ibid.

16. *Journal of the National Baptist Convention (Unincorporated), Atlanta, Georgia, September 5-11, 1917,* 60, 64, 68, 73; *National Baptist Union-Review,* June 16, September 22, October 6, 1917.

17. *National Baptist Union-Review,* June 30, September 15, 1917.

18. *Journal of the National Baptist Convention (Unincorporated), Atlanta, Georgia, September 5-11, 1917,* 60, 64, 68, 73; *Journal of the National Baptist Convention (Unincorporated), Kansas City, Missouri, September 6-11, 1916,* 22.

19. Ibid.

20. Ibid., 35, 84-87.

21. Ibid., 7.

22. *Proceedings of the Woman's Auxiliary to the National Baptist Convention (Unincorporated), Atlanta, Georgia, September 5-11, 1917* (Nashville, 1918), 1-21, 68, 73.

23. Ibid., *Nineteenth Annual Report of the National Baptist Publishing Board, September 1915* (Nashville, 1915), 7, 9-11, 25.

24. Journal of the National Baptist Convention (Unincorporated), Atlanta; Georgia, September 5-11, 1917, 68, 73.

25. *National Baptist Union-Review,* January 6, April 7, 1917; *Journal of the National Baptist Convention (Unincorporated), Atlanta, Georgia, September 5-11, 1917,* 60, 64, 68, 73; *Nineteenth Annual Report of the National Baptist Publishing*

Board, September 1914 (Nashville, 1914), 69; *Seven Reasons Why the National Baptist Convention Should Elect a New President* by W. H. Moses, pastor of the First Baptist Church of Knoxville, Tennessee (Nashville, 1915).

26. *National Baptist Union-Review,* May 19, June 16, 1917.

27. Ibid., September 22, 1917.

28. *National Baptist Union-Review,* June 16, 30, September 15, 22, ·27, October 6, 1917; *Journal of the National Baptist Convention (Unincorporated), 37th Annual Session, Atlanta, September 5-11, 1917,* 11, 42; *Globe,* January 4, 15, May 3, 24, December 27, 1918.

29. *National Baptist Union-Review,* November 8, 1917.

30. *National Baptist Union-Review,* September 14, 1918.

31. *National Baptist Union-Review,* June 16, 30, September 15, 22, 27, October 6, 1917; *National Baptist Union-Review,* January 13, 20, February 3, 10, 24, 1917; *Journal of the National Baptist Convention (Unincorporated), Fortieth Annual Session, Columbus, Ohio, 1920* (Nashville, 1921), 28, 29, 43.

32. *National Baptist Union-Review,* January 18, April 26, 1919.

33. Ibid., May 10, 1919.

34. Ibid., January 18, April 26, May 10, 1919; Ruth M. Powell, *Ventures in Education with Black Baptists in Tennessee* (New York, 1978), 75-83.

35. *Journal of the National Baptist Convention (Unincorporated), Fortieth Annual Session, Columbus, Ohio, 1920,* 1-10.

36. Ibid., 17-21.

37. Ibid., 43-45.

38. Ibid., 71.

39. *Report of the Board of Trustees of the National Baptist Theological and Training Seminary, 1919-1920*, 239-248.

40. *Journal of the National Baptist Convention, Fortieth Annual Session, Columbus, Ohio, 1920,* 71, 72.

41. Ibid., 140, 150.

42. *Twenty-fourth Annual Report of the National Baptist Publishing Board for the Fiscal Year Ending August 31, 1920* (Nashville, 1920), 169.

43. Ibid., 169.

44. Ibid., 175.

45. Ibid., 169.

46. *Journal of the National Baptist Convention, Fortieth Annual Session, Columbus, Ohio, 1920,* 71, 72, 181, 183.

47. Ibid., 184.

48. Ibid., 186.

49. Ibid., 189, 203.

50. Ibid., 189, 203; *Journal of the National Baptist Convention, Unincorporated, Forty-First Session, New Orleans, Louisiana, 1921* (Nashville, 1922), 60-61, 93.

51. *National Baptist Voice,* January 1, 1921.

52. Ibid.

53. Ibid.

54. *National Baptist Voice,* January 22, 1921.

55. Ibid., December 31, 1921.

56. Ibid.

57. *Journal of the National Baptist Convention, Fortieth Annual Session, Columbus, Ohio, 1920,* 71, 72, 73, 181, 183.

58. *Twenty-Fifth Annual Report of the National Baptist Publishing Board for the Fiscal Year Ending August 31, 1921* (Nashville, 1922), 1-10, 23.

59. *Journal of the National Baptist Convention, Unincorporated, Forty- First Session, New Orleans, Louisiana, 1921,* 48-49.

60. Ibid., 150.

61. Ibid., 163, 164.

62. *Twenty-Fifth Annual Report of the National Baptist Publishing Board for the Fiscal Year Ending August 31, 1921,* 1-10, 23, 36.

63. *National Baptist Voice,* May 26, 1921.

64. "R. H. Boyd, Will," in Davidson County, Will Book No. 41, Tennessee State Library and Archives, Archives Division, Nashville.

65. *National Baptist Union-Review,* April 17, 1937.

66. *Journal of the 42nd Annual Session of the National Baptist Convention (Unincorporated), Nashville, September 6-11,*

1922 (Nashville, 1923), 59; *National Baptist Voice,* September 23, 1922.

67. Morris, *Sermons, Addresses and Reminiscences and Important Correspondence,* 15.

68. Ibid.

69. Davidson County, Tennessee, Will Book No. 4, 1922-1924, RHB, 98, Tennessee State Library and Archives (TSLA), Nashville.

70. Davidson County, Tennessee, Index to Warranty Deeds, 1899, 1905, 1911, 1912-1913, Boyd, TSLA.

71. Davidson County, Tennessee, Trustee Office, Tax Books, 1923, 133-134, TSLA.

72. Davidson County, Tennessee, Trustee Office, Tax Books, 1928, A-D, 154-155, TSLA.

73. Davidson County, Tennessee, Trust Deeds, vol. 245; 1899-1900, 367 Davidson County, Tennessee, Register's Office, Deed Books, 1930, 417, 205, 213, TSLA; *Golden Jubilee and 50th Anniversary Celebration and 34th Annual Report of the Secretary of the National Baptist Publishing Board, July 31, 1930* (Nashville, 1930), 39.

Reference Index

Chapter 5

R. H. Boyd: Preacher, Entrepreneur, and Leader

1. Nashville *Globe,* November 26, 1909. Note: Booker T. Washington was no stranger in black Nashville. In 1892, he married a Fisk University graduate, Margaret Murray, a friend to Nettie Langston Napier, wife of James C. Napier, who became

Boyd's close friend, attorney, and business associate. Washington's son attended Fisk University. Washington served on that university's board of trustees. And Margaret and Booker T. visited Nashville on an annual basis. For relations between Booker T. Washington and J. C. Napier, as well as some insight into the connection between the two men and R. H. Boyd, see also: Louis R. Harlan, *The Booker T. Washington Papers,* 8 vols. (Urbana, 1972-1980); James Carroll Napier Papers, 1854-1940, Special Collections, Fisk University Library, Nashville; *Ridgely Torrence, Story of John Hope* (New York, 1948); Jacqueline A. Rouse, *Lugenia Burns Hope, Black Southern Reformer* (Athens, Ga., 1989); *The Tennessee Centennial and International Exposition Held in Nashville, Tennessee, May 1 to October 31, 1897* (Nashville, 1898).

2. See October 1914 issues of *National Baptist Union-Review* and *Globe.*

3. *Globe,* November 2, 1910; see Raymond G. Lloyd, *Tennessee Agricultural and Industrial State University* (Nashville, 1962); Lester C. Lamon, "Tennessee Agricultural and Industrial State Normal School: Public Education for Black Tennesseans," *Tennessee Historical Quarterly,* 32 (1973), 42-58.

4. Lester C. Lamon, *Blacks in Tennessee, 1791-1970* (Knoxville, 1981), 61-62, 67, 68, 70, 72, 73. For other information on Tennessee State University, see also: Lois C. McDougald, ed., *A Time-Line Chronology of the Tennessee A & I State College Campus, 1909-1951* (Nashville, 1988); Samuel H. Shannon, "Slow Birth in White and Black: Tennessee State's Colleges in the Formative Years," *Border States,* 4 (1983), 28-39; Samuel H. Shannon, "LandGrant College Legislation and Black Tennesseans: A Case Study in the Politics of Education," *History of Education Quarterly,* (1982), 139-157; W. J. Hale, "Tennessee Agricultural and Industrial State Normal School for Negroes," a report in *The Appendix to the Senate and House Journals, Tennessee General Assembly, 1915* (Nashville, 1915), 225-263; Herman H. Long, "The Negro Public

College in Tennessee," *Journal of Negro Education,* 31 (1962), 341-348.

5. *Globe,* December 15, 1916.

6. *Journal of the National Baptist Convention, 32nd Annual Session, Houston, Texas, September 11-16, 1912,* and *Journal of the 34th Annual Session of the National Baptist Convention, Philadelphia, Pennsylvania, September 9-14, 1914,* 1-50; *National Baptist Union-Review,* October 10, 24, 1914.

7. Powell, *Ventures in Education with Black Baptists in Tennessee,* 1-50.

8. *Journal of the National Baptist Convention Unincorporated, Atlanta, Georgia, September 5-11, 1917,* 7, 11, 68, 73.

9. Ibid., *Annual of the Southern Baptist Convention, 1919, Atlanta, Georgia, May 14-18* (Nashville,1919), 49-51.

10. R. H. Boyd to Pastors in Tennessee Baptist Churches, March 10, 1900, NBPBLA.

11. Ibid.

12. *Globe,* May 22, 1907.

13. *Globe,* May 22, 1907.

14. See Bobby L. Lovett, "Nashville's Fort Negley: A Symbol of Blacks' Involvement with the Union Army," *Tennessee Historical Quarterly,* 51 (1982), 3-22.

15. *Globe,* May 4, 1908.

16. Ibid., *National Baptist Union-Review,* March 13, 1915.

17. *Globe,* May 22, 1907.

18. *Globe,* May 27, 1910, March 3, 1911.

19. *Globe,* March 3, May 17, October 3, 1911.

Note: for additional information on blacks and politics in Nashville and the South during this time, see: F. Wayne Binnings, "The Tennessee Republicans in Decline, 1869-1879," *Tennessee Historical Quarterly,* 39 (1980), 471-484; Joel Williamson, *A Rage for Order: Black/White Relations in the American South Since Emancipation* (New York, 1986); David D. Lee, *Tennessee in Turmoil: Politics in the Volunteer State, 1920-1932* (Memphis, 1979); Paul D. Casdorph, *Republicans, Negroes and Progressives in the South, 1912-1916* (University, Alabama, 1981).

20. See *Globe* issues, November 1911.

21. *National Baptist Union,* August 6, 1902.

22. *Citizen Bank* (Nashville, 1986), 1-10.

Note: For additional sources that have some information on local black businesses, see: Donald F. Joyce, *Gatekeepers of Black Culture: Black Owned Publishing in the United States 1877-1981* (Westport, Ct., 1983); Don E. Doyle, *Nashville Since the 1920s* (Knoxville, 1985).

23. See Carl N. Ostaus, *Freedmen, Philanthropy: A History of the Freedman's Savings and Trust Company Bank* (Urbana, 1979), 190, 196, 230, 231; U.S., Registers of Signatures of Depositors, Freedman's Savings and Trust Company, Nashville Accounts, National Archives and Record Service, Washington, D. C.; *Nashville Union and American,* March 13, 1874.

24. J. C. Napier to charter members, Nashville, November 30, 1903, Special Collections, Tennessee State University Library.

25. One-Cent Savings Bank, Minutes of the charter meeting, November 3, 1903, Special Collections, Tennessee State University.

26. See 1931 issues of the *Globe* and Taylor's obituary.

27. See 1940 issues of the *Globe* and Napier's obituary.

28. *Globe*, December 3, 1907.

29. *Globe*, January 18, November 8, 1907.

30. Ibid., January 3, 17, 1908.

31. Ibid., January 6, 1908.

32. Ibid., January 18, 1908.

33. *Globe,* December 3, 1909.

34. Ibid.

35. *Globe,* January 14, 28, 1910.

36. Ibid.

37. Ibid.

38. *Globe*, January 14, 1910, January 12, 1912.

39. Ibid.

40. *Globe,* January 14, 1910; December 15, 1911.

41. *Globe,* March 22, 1912.

42. See *Globe* issues, 1914.

43. *National Baptist Union-Review,* January 23, 1915.

44. Ibid.

45. *Globe,* January 18, 1911.

46. *Globe*, January 7, 1910.

47. *Globe*, October 25, 1907.

Note: Microfilm copies of the *Globe* are available in most major libraries. However, the copies for 1920-1930 are missing. Only a few pages of the *Globe* exist at the National Baptist Publishing Board for the years 1920-1930. However, the NBPB has laminated and bound original copies of the *Globe.*

48. *Globe*, January 14, 18, February 8, 1907.

49. *Globe,* November 4, 1909.

50. *Globe*, March 26, 1908; May 2, July 25, December 5, 1913.

51. Lamon, *Black Tennesseans: 1900-1930 (Knoxville, 1977)*, 123,125, 127.

52. *Globe*, September 21, 1917.

53. See issues of the *Globe,* 1917.

54. *Globe*, November 24, 1917.

55. *Globe*, September 26, 1917, December 27, 1918.

56. *Globe*, August 2, 30, October 11, 25, December 27, 1918.

57. *Proceedings of the National Baptist Convention, Unincorporated, Atlanta, Georgia, September 5-11, 1917, Woman's Convention,* 1-21.

58. Ibid., December 3, 1909.

59. Ibid., August 28, September 4, 1908.

60. Ibid., December 3, 1909.

61. Napier to Washington, Nashville, July 21, October 28, 1902, in Louis C. Harlan, *The Booker T. Washington Papers, 1903-1904* (Urbana, 1977), 199-200, 216-217.

62. Ibid.

63. "Nashville's Revolt Against Jimcrowism," *Voice of the Negro*, 2 (1905), 827-830; Tennessee, *House Journal, 54th General Assembly, 1905* (Nashville, 1905), 896; *Indianapolis Freeman*, October 7, 1905; Lester C. Lamon, *Black Tennesseans: 1900-1930*, 25-27. See also Robert Hawes, *The Age of Segregation: Race Relations in the South, 1890-1945* (Jackson, Miss., 1979), 1-10, and NAACP, *Thirty Years of Lynching in the United States, 1889-1918* (New York, 1921).

64. *Nashville Clarion* quoted in Kansas City *American Citizen*

(March 3, 1905).

65. See Don H. Doyle, "Nashville As a Historical Laboratory for Teaching Undergraduates," unpublished manuscript, Nashville Room, Nashville Public Library, 1975, 452, 467, 476, 487-488.

66. *Globe*, April 12, 1907; Lamon, *Black Tennesseans, 1900-1930*, 27.

67. Lena Marbury, "The 1905 Streetcar Boycott in Nashville," M. S. thesis, Tennessee State University, 1985, 11, 21, 34, 56.

68. Lamon, *Black Tennesseans, 1900-1930*, 33-35.

69. Ibid., *Globe*, September 4, 1908.

70. Richard H. Boyd, *The Separate or "Jim Crow" Car Laws, or, Legislative Enactments of Fourteen Southern States* (Nashville, 1909), 1-6.

71. Ibid.

72. Ibid.

Reference Index

Chapter 6

After R. H. Boyd: The NBPB, 1922-1992

1. John B. Keeble to H. A. Boyd, Nashville, 1922, NBPBLA.

2. Henry A. Boyd, Obituary, NBPBLA.

3. Pittsburgh *Courier*, October 25, 1930.

4. Nashville *Globe*, October 2, 1931.

5. See January issues of the *Globe*, 1934-1940.

6. *Globe*, April 26, 1940; also see James Carroll Napier, 1845-1940, Papers, 1848-1939, Special Collections, Fisk University Library, Nashville; National Baptist *Union-Review*, February 9, 16, 23, April 26, 1940.

7. *Globe*, September 15, November 3, December 4, 1944.

8. Ibid., October 2, 1931.

9. *National Baptist Union-Review,* January 25, 1930.

10. *National Baptist Union-Review,* February 22, 1930

11. Ibid.

12. *National Baptist Union-Review,* October 18, 1930.

13. *Globe,* March 16, 19, 1934; *National Baptist Union-Review,* June 14, 1930.

14. Leroy Fitts, *A History of Black Baptists* (Nashville, 1985), 95-96.

15. *National Baptist Voice,* October 7, 1922.

16. *National Baptist Union-Review,* June 19, 1937.

17. Ibid.

18. *National Baptist Union-Review,* January 2, 1937.

19. *Globe,* March 30, May 1, 1934.

20. *Globe,* March 4, 1960.

21. See *National Baptist Publishing Board Annual Report, July 31, 1946* (Nashville, 1946); *National Baptist Union-Review,* September 7, 1946.

22. *National Baptist Union-Review,* September 7, 1946.

23. *National Baptist Union-Review,* August 21, 1946.

24. *Official Journal of the Seventy-Third Annual Session of the National Baptist Convention of America, September 9-13, 1953, Denver, Colorado* (Nashville, 1954), 44.

25. Ibid., 39.

26. Ibid.

27. Ibid., 23-24, 33.

28. Ibid.

29. *1954-55 National Baptist Publishing Board, Annual Report, July 30, 1955,* 39.

30. Ibid., 41, 53; *Official Journal of the 7th Annual Session of the National Baptist Convention of America and Auxiliaries, Chicago, Illinois, September 7-11, 1955* (Nashville, 1955) 47-49, 101-109.

31. *Official Journal of the 75th Annual Session of the National Baptist Convention of America and Auxiliaries, Chicago, Illinois, September 7-11, 1955,* 47-49, 101-109; *Story of the 54th Annual Session of the Sunday School Congress, June 11-15, 1958, Fort Worth, Texas* (Nashville, 1958), 112.

32. *Official Journal of the National Baptist Convention of America and Auxiliaries, Seventy-Eighth Annual Session, September 10-14, 1958, Detroit, Michigan* (Nashville, 1959), 37, 38.

33. Ibid., 24; see also President G. L. Prince's speech at the 1956 NBCA session.

34. *Official Journal of the National Baptist Convention of America and Auxiliaries, Seventy-Ninth Annual Session, September 9-13, 1959, Kansas City, Missouri* (Nashville, 1960), 28, 29, 49-50, 80-83; also see Highlander Folk School Papers, Library of Congress, Washington, D.C.; James B. Jones, "Myles Horton, Tennessee's 'Radical Hillbilly', the Highlander Folk School," *The Courier,* Nashville, 29, No. 1 (October, 1990), 3-5; David Lewis, *King: A Critical Biography* (Baltimore, 1970); August Meier, *Negro Protest Thought in Twentieth Century America* (Indianapolis, 1965).

35. *Annual of the Southern Baptist Convention, One-Hundred and Ninth Annual Session, One-Hundred and Fourteen Years, May 19-22, 1959, Louisville, Kentucky* (Nashville, 1959), 78, 88; *Official Journal of the National Baptist Convention of America and Auxiliaries, Seventy-Ninth Annual Session, September 9-13, 1959, Kansas City, Missouri,* 28, 29, 49-50, 80-83; see also the SBC's Annuals for 1956 and 1958, 103, 79.

36. *Official Journal of the National Baptist Convention of America, New Orleans, Louisiana, September 7-11, 1960* (Nashville, 1960), 87, 145; *Official Journal of the National Baptist Convention of America and Auxiliaries, Oklahoma City, Oklahoma, September 6-10, 1962* (Nashville, 1962), 66, 127-130; *Official Journal of the National Baptist Convention of America and Auxiliaries, Dallas, Texas, September 4-8, 1963* (Nashville, 1963), 190-193.

37. *Globe,* May 27, 1960.

38. *Official Journal of the National Baptist Convention of America and Auxiliaries, Seventy-Ninth Annual Session, September 9-13, 1959, Kansas City, Missouri,* 28, 29, 49-50, 80-83, 115.

39. *Official Journal of the National Baptist Convention of America and Auxiliaries, Eightieth Session, September 7-11, 1960, New Orleans, Louisiana* (Nashville, 1961), 1-21.

40. *Official Journal of the National Baptist Convention of America and Auxiliaries Seventy-Ninth Annual Session, September 9-13, 1959, Kansas City, Missouri,* 118.

41. Ibid., 1-16, 20; *The 1959-1960 Report of the Secretary-Treasurer of the National Baptist Publishing Board for Fiscal Year Ending June 30, 1960* (Nashville, 1960), 87, 88-89, 145.

42. *Official Journal of the National Baptist Convention of America and Auxiliaries, Eighty-First Annual Session, September 6-10, 1961, San Francisco, California* (Nashville, 1962), 1-21, 73; *The 1960-1961 Report of the Secretary-Treasurer of the National Baptist Publishing Board for the Fiscal Year Ending June 30, 1961* (Nashville, 1961), 73, 74-75.

43. The 1960-1961 Report of the Secretary-Treasurer of the National Baptist Publishing Board for the Fiscal Year Ending June 30, 1961, 74-75.

44. Ibid.

45. Ibid.

46. Ibid.

47. Ibid.

48. *Official Journal of the National Baptist Convention of America and Auxiliaries, September 4-8, 1963, Dallas, Texas* (Nashville, 1963), 1-10, 43; see also *The 1962-63 Report of the Secretary-Treasurer of the National Baptist Publishing Board of the National Baptist Convention of America* (Nashville, 1963); *Official Journal of the National Baptist Convention of America and Auxiliaries, September 9-13, 1964, Los Angeles, California* (Nashville, 1965), 21.

49. *The 1968-1969 Report of the Secretary-Treasurer of the National Baptist Publishing Board for the Fiscal Year Ending June 30, 1969* (Nashville, 1969), 111-114.

50. See Joseph H. Jackson, *A Story of Activism: The History of the National Baptist Convention, U.S.A., Inc.* (Nashville, 1980), 227, 237, 283, 285, 360, 431-35, 440, 448, 491; Fitts, *A History of Black Baptists,* 100-106.

51. National Baptist *Union-Review,* March 9, September 14, 1968.

52. *Official Journal of the Ninety-Third Annual Session of the National Baptist Convention of America and Auxiliaries, September 4-9, 1973, Chicago, Illinois* (Nashville, 1974), 1-13; *The 1972-1973 Report of the Secretary-Treasurer of the National Baptist Publishing Board for Fiscal Year Ending June 30, 1973* (Nashville, 1973), 1-9.

53. *Official Journal of the Ninety-Fifth Annual Session of the National Baptist Convention of America, September 10-14, 1975, Philadelphia, Pennsylvania* (Nashville, 1976), 25, 105; *National Baptist Union-Review, April 27, 1975.*

54. Ibid.

Index

Index

A

Adams, Hurst A.   191
Abner, D.   23, 24, 26, 140
Abner, E. M.   46
Adkins, E. W.   25
African Methodist Episcopal Church   5, 30, 33, 36, 51, 85, 96, 194
Alcorn A. & M. College   129
Allen, M. C.   175
Alpine, W. H.   7-8
American Baptist Home Mission Society   1-5, 7, 23, 25, 28, 37, 68, 136-137
American Baptist Publication Society   1-5, 23, 24, 25, 28, 29, 37, 45, 92
American Baptist Missionary Convention   6
American National Baptist Convention   8, 31, 45
Armstrong, Anne   63
Ashburn, G. B. Debaptiste   120, 121

B

Baker, Lula   175
Baker, W. R.   39
Ball, W. B.   27
Bartlett, A. L.   111
Baskin, D.   189
Battle, A. T. 153
Battle, J. O.   51, 145, 153
Beckham, William   27, 62, 70, 85, 102, 147
Bell, T. P.   2, 24, 25
Binkley, W.A.   8
Bishop College   20, 22, 23, 136
Bolton, E. B.   131
Booker, J. A.   45, 97, 98-100
Booth, C. O.   46
Borden, E. H.   175
Boscobel College   140-141
Bosley, J. B.   146
Bostic, J. W.   147
Boy Cadets 87-89, 93
Boyd, Annie E. (Hall)   22, 96, 170

D

E